HOLD ON

HOLD ON
The Life, Science, and Art of Waiting

PETER TOOHEY

OXFORD
UNIVERSITY PRESS

Oxford University Press is a department of the University of Oxford. It furthers the University's objective of excellence in research, scholarship, and education by publishing worldwide. Oxford is a registered trade mark of Oxford University Press in the UK and certain other countries.

Published in the United States of America by Oxford University Press
198 Madison Avenue, New York, NY 10016, United States of America.

© Oxford University Press 2020

All rights reserved. No part of this publication may be reproduced, stored in a retrieval system, or transmitted, in any form or by any means, without the prior permission in writing of Oxford University Press, or as expressly permitted by law, by license, or under terms agreed with the appropriate reproduction rights organization. Inquiries concerning reproduction outside the scope of the above should be sent to the Rights Department, Oxford University Press, at the address above.

You must not circulate this work in any other form
and you must impose this same condition on any acquirer.

Library of Congress Control Number: 2020932760
ISBN 978-0-19-008361-8

CONTENTS

List of Illustrations   vii
Prologue: *"Go on Taking My Tablets"*   xi

A PORTRAIT

1. "Everyone Is Just Waiting": Three Versions of the Experience of Waiting   3
2. Alan Rabinowitz and the Jaguar: Are Some Brains Better at Waiting than Others?   29

PAIRS

3. Hall Porter Senf's Wife Is in Labor: Childbirth, Friendship, Marriage, and Waiting   59

4. Happiness—Is It Just a Matter of Waiting to Meet Your Double? A Chapter on the Life and the Lore of Waiting and Fulfillment   87

THE PAUSE

5. Miles Davis Breaks for a Smoke: The Power and the Pleasure in Pausing   119
6. Dithering: A Chapter on the Strategic Advantages of Indecisive Waiting   148

DEATH, RELIGION, AND DREAD

7. Heaven Can Wait: That Empty Chair, Waiting, and the Beyond   179
8. "The Littler Waiting Room": Can You Make the Best of Dread—and of Waiting for Approaching Death?   207

Epilogue: One-Two-Three: A Better Description for Waiting?   235

Acknowledgments   257
Notes   259
Index   291

ILLUSTRATIONS

1.1. Evelyn Dunbar (1906–1960), *The Queue at the Fish Shop*, 1944, The Imperial War Museum, London. © Imperial War Museum (Art.IWM ART LD 3987). 8
1.2. Hilaire-Germaine-Edgar Degas (1834–1917), *Waiting (L'Attente)*, c. 1882. Pastel. 26 × 31¼ × 2 in. The J. Paul Getty Museum, Los Angeles, with the Norton Simon Art Foundation, Pasadena. 17
1.3. Kōshirō Onchi (1891–1951), *Diving*, 1932. Japanese, Shōwa era, about 1933 (Shōwa 8). 47.8 × 30.8 cm. Museum of Fine Arts, Boston, Asiatic Curator's Fund 56.489. Photograph © 2000 Museum of Fine Arts, Boston. 20
1.4. Vilhelm Hammershøi (1864–1916), *Woman in an Interior, Strandgade 30,* 1901. Private Collection. Photo: © Christie's Images/ Bridgeman Images. 24
2.1. Cats Waiting for Fishermen to Return. 32

2.2. Winslow Homer (1836–1910), *Waiting for Dad*, 1873. Transparent and opaque watercolor. 24.13 cm × 34.29 cm. Mills College Art Museum, Gift of Jane C. Tolman. 33

3.1. Greta Garbo (Greta Garbo as Madame Grusinskaya in the movie *Grand Hotel*, 1932). Suedeutsche Zeitung Photo / Alamy Stock Photo. 61

3.2. Pieter de Hooch (1629–1684), *A Mother Delousing Her Child's Hair*, known as "A Mother's Duty," around 1658–1660. Oil on canvas, w 610 mm × h 525 mm. Rijksmuseum, Amsterdam. On loan from the City of Amsterdam (A. van der Hoop Bequest). Photograph courtesy of the Rijksmuseum. 67

4.1. *The Cholmondeley Ladies*, c. 1600–1610. Unknown artist. Oil paint on wood. 886 mm × 1723 mm. Presented anonymously in 1955. Tate Gallery, London. Photo Credit © Tate, London 2019. 99

4.2. René Magritte (1898–1967), *La reproduction interdite (Not to Be Reproduced)*, 1937. Museum Boijmans van Beuningen, Rotterdam, Netherlands. © Estate of René Magritte / SOCAN (2019). Image: Peter Horre / Alamy Stock Photos. 113

5.1. Trumpet player Miles Davis and pianist and arranger Gil Evans in 1957 / © Bridgeman Images. 121

5.2. Hilaire-Germaine-Edgar Degas (1834–1917), *Singer with the Glove*, about 1878. Pastel on canvas. 53.2 cm × 41 cm. Harvard Art Museums/ Fogg Museum, Bequest from the Collection of

ILLUSTRATIONS | ix

	Maurice Wertheim, Class of 1906. Photo: © President and Fellows of Harvard College.	132
5.3.	Barbara Hepworth (1903–1975), *Family of Man*, sculpture created in 1970. Snape Maltings, Suffolk, England. Geophotos / Alamy Stock Photos.	146
6.1.	Hilaire-Germaine-Edgar Degas (1834–1917), *Monsieur and Madame Edouard Manet*, 1868–1869. Oil on canvas. Municipal Museum of Art, Kitakyushu, Japan. Asar Studios / Alamy Stock Photo.	159
6.2.	The skeleton of Death with the antiquarian hoarder in a bedroom filled with musical instruments, books, manuscripts, armor, a globe, a bust, rats, etc. Hand colored copperplate drawn and engraved by Thomas Rowlandson from *The English Dance of Death*, Ackermann, London, 1816. © Florilegibus/Bridgeman Images.	173
7.1.	Lucio Fontana (1899–1968), *Spatial Concept "Waiting,"* 1960, Tate Gallery, London. Photo Credit: © Tate, London 2019.	180
7.2.	Harriet Andersson in Ingmar Bergman's *Sasom i En Spegel/ Through a Glass Darkly*, 1961. Photo 12 / Alamy Stock Photo.	186
7.3.	Silk Cut cigarettes magazine advertisement, UK. © The Advertising Archives/Bridgman Images.	203
8.1.	Pierre Bonnard (1867–1947), *Early Spring. Little Fauns*, 1909. Oil on canvas. 102.5 cm × 125 cm. The State Hermitage Museum, St. Petersburg. Photograph © The State Hermitage Museum / photo by Vladimir Terebenin.	208

8.2. Pierre Bonnard (1867–1947), *Autoportrait dans la glace du cabinet de toilette/Self-Portrait in The Bathroom Mirror*, 1939–1945. Oil on canvas. 73 cm × 52 cm. AM1984-698. Photo: Jacques Faujour. Musée Nationale d'Art Moderne. © CNAC/MNAM/Dist. RMN-Grand Palais / Art Resource NY.   232

E.1. Edward Le Bas (1904–1966), *Saloon Bar*, 1940. Canvas. 34 3/4 × 43 1/4 in (88 × 110 cm). Tate Gallery. Photo Credit: © Tate, London, 2019.   237

E.2. François Barraud (1899–1934), *Le malcontent*, 1930. The Picture Art Collection / Alamy Stock Photo.   242

E.3. Manuel Álvarez Bravo (1902–2002), *Figuras en el Castillo (Figures in the Castle)*, 1920s. © Archivo Manuel Álvarez Bravo, S.C.   244

E.4. Vanessa Bell (1879–1961), *A Conversation*, 1913–1916. Oil on canvas. Samuel Courtauld Trust, The Courtauld Gallery, London, UK / Bridgeman Images.   248

E.5. László Mednyánszky (1852–1919), *The Absinthe Drinker*, 1898. Oil on wood. 45 cm × 34.5 cm. Hungarian National Gallery, Budapest.   254

PROLOGUE

"Go on Taking My Tablets"

"Never, ever again, stop eating or drinking. Don't smoke. Avoid alcohol and too much physical or mental exertion, get lots of fresh air, rest, and sleep. And, above all, go on taking my tablets." Jenny was offered this recommendation when she was just about to be released from her psychiatric clinic. She had been admitted for anxiety attacks, depression, dissociation, aphasia, and attempted suicide.

Jenny's silent reaction to Dr. Vlemingck's advice was "in short, don't go on living." This was not a sensible reaction and it did not bode well for her recovery. I'm not sure why on earth Jenny could have thought that stopping eating and drinking was not living. Jenny was Swedish. Didier was the name of her French husband. She ended up waiting tensely for the next assault from her quintet. Her life was put on hold. But she survived and she appears in a very good book about a life of holding on.

I haven't been in a psychiatric clinic yet as either a visitor or as a patient. The Johns Hopkins psychiatrist and popular author Kay Redfield Jamison has, often. She says, in her biography of the American poet Robert Lowell, "Like all patients in a mental hospital, he waited. He waited for the doctor; he waited for medication; he waited for sanity; he waited for his wife to return."[1] Robert Lowell, like Professor Redfield Jamison, was bipolar. Mental illness is something that always seems just around the corner in many of our lives and it seems to entail lots of waiting, whether you are in a clinic, whether you've been released, or whether you're just holding on. Remember being 21? I've read that this age was when Dick Cavett had his first bad bout of depression too. He was an undergraduate student at Yale.[2] It was, it is a terrible age for depression and for anxiety. I wonder if it really goes away? Some years ago, I went to a psychiatric conference. It was the only one I've ever attended. One of the speakers, a distinguished Greek psychiatrist with an attitude so confident that it would have made Philip II of ancient Macedon gasp, stated boldly in his talk, "show me a person who has had a strong depressive incident who has not had a repeat—or several." The comment was an assertion, not a question. The man's name should have been Dr. Vlemingck. Go on taking my tablets. Why? Why not just shrug and wait? But the medical audience calmly nodded. So much for being cured, Jenny might have thought. I've read since that the rate of recidivism for victims of depression can be greater than 46%.[3]

There are lots of other people—maybe you?—in this slow boat. David Bowie came from a family that, at least on his mother's side, had a strong streak of mental instability. One recent article suggests that this mental instability "was viewed as a curse and an accepted part of his family folklore."

Bowie's "Aunt Vivienne [a sister of his mother, Peggy] was diagnosed with schizophrenia; Aunt Una died in her early thirties after extended stays in mental hospitals, and Aunt Nora's 'bad nerves' were treated with a lobotomy." This article also claims that David Bowie's brother Terry was a victim of schizophrenia.[4] Terry "was institutionalized and later committed suicide by stepping in front of a train." David Bowie may have feared he'd inherit the gene too. Dylan Jones, a Bowie biographer, quotes the musician on his dread of mental illness and his long life of waiting: "One puts oneself through such psychological damage trying to avoid the threat of insanity, you start to approach the very thing that you're scared of. Because of the tragedy inflicted, especially on my mother's side of the family, there were too many suicides for my liking—that was something I was terribly fearful of."[5] It would be easy to speculate that the waiting and the dread pushed David Bowie's musical creativity.

To want to write about people's lives being somehow "holding on," as being shaped by slow waiting, appears almost to offer an insult to all of the sensible and busy people in the world by whom you and I are surrounded. To that all I can say is, wait, as there is a lot more to waiting and to holding on than meets the eye. I am not going to write about mental illness. Jenny Didier dramatizes that waiting in the most vivid of manners. But there's more to it than Dr. Vlemingck. For every Jenny there is a David Bowie getting by and trying to turn waiting to their nervous advantage. Just as you can be lonely in the midst of a crowd, or you can be perched in the quiet eye of a tornado, so you can be, in the very midst of the mundane maelstrom of family life, somehow feeling frozen or holding on or waiting—Jenny Didier had a husband and children and a family. Lots of people feel this way, but are mostly too embarrassed to own up. I'd like to go a little further than just Jenny's feelings of holding on and to try to understand waiting more broadly, in such places as literature, art, daily life, music, psychology, and science. I'd also like to show how being on slow hold can very often be a very good thing. That will be a harder sell.

We're all just waiting, that's what I believe. Here are some figures. About one-third of the life of humans is spent working. Maybe this sum is reckoned from the estimate that most people, in the United States at least, work for about 30 to 35 years of their 78-odd-year life span. Their work can occupy about 40 hours per week. If 30% of your life is passed working then it's probably reasonable to speculate that for most people, who are not too thrilled at the prospect of work, 30% of their life more or less is spent waiting, waiting to go home, waiting for the weekend, or waiting for retirement. There are other sorts of waiting than waiting at work. You have to get to work, and this means holding on hold in traffic. And then you have to get home again. You might stop at the supermarket for some rations before you arrive there. If you do, you'll probably have to wait at the checkout. And when you get home you and your children will be waiting for those supermarket peas to steam. There's more. A few years ago Adam Hadhazy wrote on bbc.com, "Reach your 78th birthday and according to some back-of-the-envelope calculations, you will have spent nine of those years watching television, four years driving a car, 92 days on the toilet, and 48 days having sex."[6] Then, when it's all done, you'll finally go to bed. Hadhazy says, "when it comes to time-consuming activities, there's one that sits head and shoulders above them all. Live to 78, and you may have spent around 25 years asleep." That's unless you have insomnia. Then my guess is that you'll have spent about 5 years waiting for that 25 years to come true. Tell me that it's not true. Tell Jenny that it's not true.

Here is a very interesting set of observations that say even more about waiting. They're as heartening as they're depressing. I came across these in Claudia Hammond's book called *Time Warped*.[7] This psychologist and BBC broadcaster makes a fascinating observation: "Research . . . reveals a staggering finding: contemplating the future could be the brain's *default* mode of operation. But this is not wasteful daydreaming or, as the phrase goes, a case of 'wishing our lives away.' Mental time-travel into the future matters. . . . It affects our judgments, our emotional states and the decisions we make." It would be very good to have some figures on this default mode of waiting. Claudia Hammond provides them: "on average people think about the future 59 times a day or once every 16 minutes during waking hours." If you have a deep worry, these statistics suggest, an awful lot of it is going to play out in those 59 times. The same would apply to something very pleasant that you are waiting for—like getting home from work or eventually quitting work. Imagine that half of the 59 future imaginings you have per day are devoted to just one worry, or one thing that you are really looking forward to. That's a minimum of 8 minutes of every day of your life devoted to mental waiting. That's 2,920 minutes of every year in the waiting freezer. Claudia Hammond's statistics make throat-catching reading. You can probably see where I am heading. If you are a worried individual like Jenny Didier or David Bowie, that means your mental default mode is "what could be coming maybe isn't good." But let's be fair. If you are a happy individual, you might be looking forward to something very attractive. Life is not all dread. Life is not absurd. Life is not meaningless. If you feel that's the case for you, then you'll have 2,920 minutes of holding on, 2,920 minutes of waiting pleasure every year.

One last example. On the Saturday morning of April 15, 2017, a 15-year-old giraffe, named April, gave birth to a calf.[8] April's famous gestation proves a very simple point, that all waiting is not gloomy. April's pregnancy went near to the usual term for a giraffe's pregnancy, an astounding 400 to 450 days. That's about 15 months for April, a very long wait by human standards, before the baby can see the world. The giraffe baby (weighing about 129 lbs and standing 5.9 feet tall at birth) was born at the Animal Adventure Park in Harpursville, New York. At least 1.2 million people tuned into the zoo's Facebook Live and YouTube stream, anticipating Tajiri's much publicized delivery. (The calf's name in Swahili means hope, another version of waiting.) The giraffe-cam had been going since February 10, 2017, and its waiting viewers were initially said to be in the thousands, but they soon swelled to the millions. The only glitch in this very public pregnancy happened later in February 2017 when YouTube briefly shut down the 24-hour April-stream. There had been protests concerning the broadcast's "nudity and sexual content." Public protest against the public protest had the giraffe-cam restored quickly.

The slow wait for the birth of the giraffe was not, I suppose, unalloyed pleasure for all of the 1.2 million people who watched. The birth was pleasure fraught with anxiety for some viewers. It's been reported by Global News in Canada that a "Farmington, New Hampshire, songwriter even posted a music video on YouTube called, "I'm Going Crazy Waiting (For a Giraffe)."[9] The response to Tajiri's coming on Twitter was less troubled. This is what Global reproduced: "We did it, internet! We had a giraffe baby together"; "Everybody sticking their neck out for this baby giraffe"; and "On a day where 'mother of all bombs' is a trending phrase, I love how the world unites over the birth of a baby giraffe." Anxiety or no, the wait for Tajiri's birth was a pretty happy occasion and it makes, for me, the simple point that waiting is often—really, I'd say, mostly—associated with pleasure.

When I first mentioned Jenny Didier I didn't say who she was. That's an old trick. I wanted to keep you reading on to see who she might be. I wanted to keep you *waiting*. If that worked and if you are still waiting (and I hope that you are), then let me tell you the answer. Jenny is a facsimile of the sister of the famous Swedish film and theatre director, Ingmar Bergman. She's the narrator of Margareta Bergman's novel, *Mirror, Mirror . . .* Margareta was Ingmar's real-life sister, the model for Fanny in Ingmar's 1982 movie *Fanny and Alexander*. Jenny is Margareta and she is Fanny. Jenny, in *Mirror, Mirror . . .* , waits and waits, not always with success, "to reclaim the neglected parts of her life, especially her art." It's mental illness that makes the reclamation such a wait. Margareta's own life mirrored Jenny. And Fanny, a great, though not always happy waiter, shows the origins of the grief suffered by Jenny and Margareta. We'll meet them again. Now let's go on taking *my* tablets.

A PORTRAIT

1

"EVERYONE IS JUST WAITING"

Three Versions of the Experience of Waiting

Waiting for the fish to bite
or waiting for wind to fly a kite
or waiting around for Friday night
or waiting, perhaps, for their Uncle Jake
or a pot to boil, or a Better Break
or a string of pearls, or a pair of pants
or a wig of curls, or Another Chance.
Everyone is just waiting.

"The Waiting Place" is the name of the popular poem from which these lines are taken. It's probably something I don't need to tell you about. "The Waiting Place," if you've had children or grandchildren, or nieces or nephews, or just about any sort of a young relative, is a poem that they'll have read or have had read to them, at least if they live in the United States. The verse comes from Dr. Seuss and it can be found in his last children's book, *Oh, The Places You'll Go*. It was published in 1990. Too bad that Dr. Seuss was slowly waiting for the outcome of oral cancer as he wrote *Oh, The Places You'll Go*.[1] But Dr. Seuss proves that enduring the prospect of death doesn't always diminish creativity and optimism.

"The Waiting Place" appears across two pages of *Oh, The Places You'll Go*, and it's accompanied by a lavish and funny illustration of some of the waiting situations described in the poem. There are people stuck on a broken down bus, a man is fishing in a sewer-hole, a vast queue of people is waiting to get into a single toilet, a soldier is waiting for a disconnected phone to ring, a boy is waiting for a breeze to fly a kite, a woman waits for snow on a barren ski slope, and another woman is waiting for a kettle to boil. "The Waiting Place" is part of a children's book, but, because the book, *Oh, The Places You'll Go*, is so widely read and so enjoyed by so many adults, it's probably the most perused and the most influential characterization of waiting in English. In the United States it's one of the top selling presents for graduating students, from high school or college. By May 2016 the book had sold 12.5 million copies. *Oh, The Places You'll Go* is held in such high esteem that in September 2017 Melania Trump, the US first lady, donated a collection of titles by Dr. Seuss, that included this book, to award-winning education programs around the country. Melania Trump's generous gift was a success nearly everywhere. Everyone is just waiting. The gift was only turned down, as far as I know, by the Cambridgeport Elementary School Library, in Cambridge, Massachusetts. The school librarian maintained the book is "clichéd" and "racist."[2] Maybe that shows just how popular Dr. Seuss and this book really are if they've become a target for those activists concerned with social diversity and inclusivity. They're definitely waiting too. Cambridgeport Elementary School Library or no, *Oh, The Places You'll Go* leaves Samuel Beckett's *Waiting for Godot*, the other great waiting book, situated in the slow but politically proper shadows.

Despite all of my affection and all of my admiration for Dr. Seuss, I believe that he does waiting something of an ill service. Dr. Seuss' waiting is a dour, hopeless, and boring affair. You could even call it existential, something that aims to tell us about the very nature of human existence. It's the sort of portrait of waiting that, though at times funny enough, wants to make a very serious comment on the gloomy nature of what it is to breathe. Fair enough, maybe. But waiting, much more often than not, entails many other characteristics than gloominess, the dour, the hopeless, and the boring. Waiting can quite often be OK. Waiting can even be fun. Waiting can sometimes be something to look forward to. Waiting, when you come to think of it, can be a very sympathetic characteristic in another person that you know well. It can show their capacity for kindness and for thoughtfulness and it can even demonstrate their affection. Here is just such a version of waiting (the descriptor occurs as the last word in the quotation). I've taken it from *Moshi Moshi*, a recent novel by the gifted and sometimes underrepresented Japanese novelist, Banana Yoshimoto. *Moshi Moshi*, which is apparently the Japanese greeting equivalent to "hello" on the telephone, is a story about a mother and daughter learning to cope with the death of Imo, their straying musician husband and father. He died with his death-wishing, psychopathic, and extremely persuasive girlfriend. In the passage to follow, the musician's daughter is speaking to Imo's drummer, Yamazaki-san, and she is asking about her father's death. Yamazaki-san really knows how to wait:

> I slammed my palms down on the table and started wailing. I wrung more tears out of that bottomless well, which never

> seemed to dry up no matter how much I cried. Yamazaki-san didn't put his arm around my shoulders, or stroke my head.... When I raised my swollen eyes and my snot-stained face, there was Yamazaki-san, with his kind face and tears in the corners of his eyes, waiting.

Yoshie doesn't get the answer that she needs concerning her father's suicide pact death with the woman she'd never met, with the woman who'd become her loved father's new and fatal and last companion. But she does receive an awful lot of sympathy and of comfort from the very kind and waiting Yamazaki-san. This is not the sort of experience that Dr. Seuss is speaking of, is it. But it's a kind of waiting that can be just as common as toilet queues or phones that won't ring or kites that won't fly. It's also just as important. I'm not sure that all of this quite gets that grumpy librarian at the Cambridgeport Elementary School off the hook. My book will be about a little more than just "The Waiting Place" and *Oh, The Places You'll Go*.

You're always waiting for something. Dr. Seuss was right about that. But it doesn't have to mean that you're always stuck in some awful location like "The Waiting Place." Nor does it mean that you're stuck in a long queue at the self-checkout in Safeway. You could be at a table with a man like Yamazaki-san or we could be in a delivery room waiting for the birth of a child. Most of us are holding on, or pausing, staying ("but stay still, I beg of you," says Pozzo), biding our time, staying put, staying in holding pattern, liming (Trinidadian slang, Stefan Vranka tells me), anticipating (something good or bad), aroused, watchful, posted up, cooling our heels or cooling our jets, experiencing homoeostasis, or broody, brooding, sitting tight, compounding the interest (who'd be so lucky), clogged up, counting on it, expecting, figuring on, holding our horses, marinating (yes, really), dithering, afloat or even floating, frozen, hibernating, hanging, hanging about, standstill, lollygagging, postponing, procrastinating, wavering, yearning, longing, restricted, holding our horses, holding on, idling, hanging about, deferring ("nothing to be done," as Vladimir and Estragon would say), putting it off, not leaving ("I won't leave, I won't ever leave you"), abiding, showing endurance, being patient (Patrick Leigh Fermor cooks up "impavid patience"), hoping, hanging on, hanging around, hanging fire, remaining, tarrying, meandering, dreading, or stopping (Stop!).[3] That is just how it is. All of them. And we don't always mind it. The waiting can be as often as good as it can be bad. I think it's more often good than bad, but that may just be me.[4] Though I can tell you now that I'm no optimist. That's just how it is. What we'll be looking at in particular are some of the good waiting situations.[5] That's because they are often ignored. But you can't ignore the bad ones, "the dusk . . . the strain . . . the waiting," as Pozzo warns, and the grieving, the slow dying, and the dead children. And dread is such a part of the nature of waiting that it can't be passed over either. I'll also talk a lot about how there seem to be coping devices that people use to transform an emotional situation like waiting, when it is intolerable or just bad, into something not just good, but even useful. That of course is when it's possible to do this. Your chances for transformation mightn't be good if you're waiting in front of a firing squad like Maximilian I of Mexico.

You're more likely to be queuing than facing the gun. Just like that endless line of people waiting to get into the toilet

8 | A PORTRAIT

FIGURE 1.1. Queuing can be as good as it can be bad. Evelyn Dunbar, *The Queue at the Fish Shop*, 1944. The Imperial War Museum, London. © Imperial War Museum (Art.IWM ART LD 3987).

in Dr. Seuss' illustration for "The Waiting Place," we're often in a long line of some form or another. Queuing is a big part of city life. This little list to follow offers a compilation of the amount of time that the English are said to spend waiting in line each week for the following select activities.[6]

Queuing for Toilet	17 minutes
Queuing for food and drinks on a night out	19 minutes
Queuing in the supermarket	29 minutes
Queuing in traffic	60 minutes
TOTAL	125 minutes

FIGURE 1.1. Continued.

That's not much time for traffic, is it? I spend a lot more time than this stuck in my car on 14th Street every day and I'm sure you do too. The list makes its point all the same, even if contemplation of all this wasted time can make you pretty irritable, and especially if your list is much longer than the English one. But, then, the level of irritability all depends, doesn't it, on who's in the car with you and on what occasion the queuing happens. It might be with someone you like very much and then the waiting may be very enjoyable. The waiting offers a chance to wait together and to chitchat. That's why I don't think that lists like this really tell you very much at all. This is because the experience of queuing, not the waiting itself, can be good and it can be bad as well. It rests so much on the circumstances of the waiting and how you feel about it. The painting by Evelyn Dunbar (Figure 1.1) might help you to understand the circumstances of waiting a little better. The image offers a real-life example of how people may be queuing for food during the day in a time of food shortages. It shows how waiting for a long time in a queue can be good and how it can be bad.

What's going on in the line-up of Evelyn Dunbar's fish shop canvas? The 1944 painting, which took the English artist Evelyn Dunbar two years to complete, shows a queue of people aiming to buy fish. They are waiting their turn in Rochester, Kent, Evelyn Dunbar's home town. Why the fuss about fish? There were food rationing and food shortages in England during World War II when this portrait was completed. (Produce was being siphoned off for the troops fighting in North Africa and Europe.) Meat especially was rationed but fish, because it was perishable, was never rationed and it became a staple protein source for the home population. My mother-in-law used to tell us how hard the war years were in England if you were feeding the very young or old—or yourself for that matter. That didn't dampen Dunbar's humor. The Imperial War Museum, where her painting now hangs, explains: "Dunbar's gentle sense of humor is evident in the sign reading 'Large supplies of fresh fish from the coast daily,' since normal fishing was restricted both by the Royal Navy's requisitioning of boats, and by German naval operations." That's Dunbar's husband in uniform on the bike and her sister crossing the road with the basket.

A painting like *The Queue at the Fish Shop* shows that there may be two ways of contemplating waiting. You can focus on the *situation* or you can focus on the *experience*. The situation is mostly about "how long?" It's something that comes down to mathematics. And it is based on the assumption that queues irritate and bore people. Jason Farman in his *Delayed Response* reckons that "we hate waiting in all its forms" and that this emotion has found its way into "smaller moments of waiting, such as standing in line." The assumption is that all people in queues really want to know is how long they'll be clogged up in this situation and that they all want to get out of it as quickly as possible. The *experience* of waiting in the queue may be quite different. Maybe you like being in that queue. Who knows? Your daily job might be so busy that a bit of idle time in a queue may feel like a blessing. Or maybe you like the opportunity to chat with friends from Rochester.

Let's ponder the *situation*. How long will it take you to wait through the fish shop queue? That really would be good to know, because it might allow you to decide to quit the queue and come back later or even to go someplace else. You could join the shorter queue around the corner in the green grocers, for example. The longer the time, the more logic there is in the idea of giving up on N. Hill & Son Fishmongers and Poulterers and of going around the block to P. Toohey's Family Fruiterama. You can work out how long it will take to wait at N. Hill's with a clock and a calculator and this will enable you dispassionately to make that choice about waiting. Whether you should go around the corner to P. Toohey's depends, for example, on how long it takes the fishmonger to locate and pack up the produce and how many people are there to help. It depends as well on how much food each person is able to order. It depends on how efficiently the orders are given and taken and how quickly the lucky people inside will move on. There are about 27 people in that queue, and they look to me like they've been waiting for a while. Maybe there are about four people inside buying. If each person inside only orders two pieces of fish, and if the

Hill's counter staff can manage to wrap the fish fast, collect the cash quickly, and if they don't gossip too much about life in Rochester, then the queue might be dealt with reasonably quickly. That sounds sensible, but who knows for sure? The people serving might be drones. Most of the energetic Hills could be on the front line in uniform. It actually looks that way, doesn't it, because the queue in the painting appears to be pretty static.

Quite a few books and university courses look at this situational version of waiting—waiting to get somewhere and to get something from the climax of a queue. The well-subscribed university courses sometimes have the alarming descriptor of "queuing theory" or even probability theory.[7] These sorts of courses and this sort of literature can help you with the math as you stand in the winter outside N. Hill & Son of Rochester, Kent, wondering, "how long will I have to wait?" Situation is what concerns such punters and such probability theorists whose concern is to decipher the amount of time that will be entailed in the situation of waiting. The feelings of the waiters, for such theorists, are assumed to be all the same, or at least weaker or stronger versions of the same. Here is an example of how queuing theory can work. It was described by Ian Sample, the science writer from the *Guardian*, and was published to coincide with the Boxing Day sales of 2017.[8] The story concerned the unpublished work of Dr. Ryan Buell who is an associate professor in "service management" at the Harvard Business School. In one of his experiments Buell has found, "about one in five people grew impatient at the back of the queue and switched to the other line in the hope of speeding things up," explains Ian Sample. "But on average, those who switched waited 10% longer than if they had stayed put. Those who switched twice fared even worse and ended up waiting 67% longer than if they had never moved." Shoppers feel most impatient when they are at the very end of a queue. Dr. Buell avers that we should not swap queues: "strike up conversation with the person in front which, if nothing else, passes the time until someone else joins behind you. Failing that, he said, simply don't look back."

What about the *experience* of waiting? It embodies a second way of understanding what's going on with the waiting in the Kent fish shop queue. This way of looking at waiting focuses on how it feels to be waiting and it isn't interested at all in the mathematics of the situation. Just imagine, therefore, that you are in that Rochester queue. How do you feel about it? The gray-haired woman at the front of the queue is peering toward the shop entrance and she looks ready to move and happy enough. The pair to follow is chitchatting and look pleased—is the second woman in the line relaxedly leaning back on the window frame? The couple to follow, a man and a woman, aren't talking. They look bored to me. Or maybe they are just reserved because they don't know one another well (they have separate shopping baskets.) Take a look at the two adults to follow, flanking the child. Now they are really talking. Time seems to go quickly in a queue when you can gossip with your friends. Queuing with your friends is often enjoyable when it's like this. I read in another survey of waiting among the English that when they are stuck in a queue a talkative 68% of them will usually embark on a yack with those standing in front or behind them, just to pass the time pleasurably. That seems to be how it is with this pair in the queue. You could work your way through the remainder of the people in the Rochester queue and I think you'd agree with me that they all seem to project different experiences—some are happy and talking, some seem calm and relaxed, others seem bored and even hating their waiting, others are even less pleased and project the death stare. They'd like the queue to get moving and to let them wrap their hands around a slice of haddock. And maybe some people don't like each other very much. Who'd know? Queuing with people you don't like isn't amusing at all. Time can go very slowly when you feel like that. You could conclude, after contemplating the first eight people in the queue, that the experience of waiting for these individuals may be quite a different thing. Their experience of the queue hinges a lot on whom they are with. Claudia Hammond, in *Time Warped*, has an even stranger formulation for the experience of queuing. She explains "people at the back of a queue are more likely to see time as moving towards them, while people at the front see themselves as moving through time."[9] Hammond points out elsewhere that the experience of waiting in a queue can also vary from culture to culture. She tells us, "Having spent her young adult life in communist Poland, the writer Eva Hoffman [who wrote a good book on boredom] says that because there was nothing to hurry for, queues did not present a problem. But after living in the United States and returning to Eastern Europe after the fall of communism in 1989, she found the queues intolerable."[10] What does all this show to us? Queuing theory can factor in the raw calculation for how long something may take according to a clock, but it doesn't have much to say about the experience of time's passing when you wait and how this *experience* differs dramatically for different people and even for different cultures.

Thanks to queues and to mathematics and to Kent, there is a description of waiting. But, before going any further we should formulate a definition of waiting, just to keep things in perspective. This is what I suggest (with a little thanks to the *Oxford English Dictionary* online): "waiting entails the emotional experience of a situation that involves staying where you are until a particular time or event or until the arrival of a particular person—or both." This definition places as much stress on how it feels to be waiting as it does on the situation. The emotional experience of waiting is what I'll concentrate on. I'll neglect the math of the waiting situation, unless it leads directly to an understanding of the experience of waiting. I'm going to try to show you three versions of the experience of waiting. Although it'd be an exaggeration to say that they capture the totality of the experience, I've found them very helpful. I believe that these three versions snag the diverse spirit of the waiting experience better than any others I can think of. They've helped me more or less—it's always more or less because we're always waiting to get it right—to understand how to simplify and to tie together the varied waiting that we've just seen in the fish shop.

And what are these three versions of waiting? Pairs represent my first version. There is such an unexpectedly large amount of waiting where pairing is involved. Companionship, friendship, love, sexual desire, and happiness all seem to start from and even to continue from waiting. If you were to try to envisage waiting and to imagine how you would paint or photograph a portrait of waiting it would most commonly entail two people. Pausing captures the flavor of my second version of waiting. Imagine someone paused up and waiting to launch themselves from a high diving tower. How do they feel? In this moment there's liable to be excitement and arousal (it takes nerves to do it) but also dread and fear (what if something goes wrong?). The passage of time, strangely, seems to slow for the diver and for their viewer. Loss is the third version. What makes loss so hard to tolerate is the impossibility of waiting when your partner or your friend dies. I can't speak too readily for you, but I find myself waiting for them to come back. So did Joan Didion for her husband John Gregory Dunne after his fatal heart attack. She tells about this in her book *The Year of Magical Thinking*. I know that the dead can't come back. So does Joan Didion, but the grief and anger is all built on the impossibility of the waiting. Now you might not have much confidence in my wild claims about the importance of these three ways of understanding the waiting experience. They may seem vague and very speculative and even arbitrary. Why not, for example, some more about queues? I think that I've said enough about queues. (There is only so much that you can say about queues and Vladimir Sorokin's and Basma Abdel Aziz's novels, both called *The Queue*, prove it.) Be patient, therefore, and wait. You might be convinced. I hope that's the case. You see, waiting always gets you off the hook.

It's the 1880s and we're in Paris. We're backstage at the ballet. It's a bird's eye view that we enjoy. Somehow, we've managed to fly behind the scenes, and, from our vantage, we spot a pair of women (Figure 1.2). The winged eye view is of a ballerina and her chaperone. The ballerina is waiting to go on stage to perform, or perhaps is she waiting for an audition for a ballet corps, or is she just waiting for a rehearsal? The chaperone is in the very center of the stool on which they're seated. She is waiting for the very same events. Is she there just to protect the young dancer or is she waiting to egg her on?[11]

There's an emotional story in Degas' pastel, entitled *Waiting*, and it concerns the experience of waiting. In

"EVERYONE IS JUST WAITING" | **17**

FIGURE 1.2. "Everyone is just waiting." Edgar Degas, *Waiting*, c. 1882. Pastel. 26 × 31¼ × 2 in. The J. Paul Getty Museum, Los Angeles with the Norton Simon Art Foundation, Pasadena.

Waiting, it's the pairing that makes the picture unmistakably all about waiting and about the future and the past of the two players in this scene. It's the pairing that hints at the story behind the picture. If either of the characters were seated on their own, but in the same posture, you really wouldn't know what was going on. The chaperone, seated solo, might as well be angrily depressed or impatient. The ballerina, seated on her own, might just be rubbing her sore ankles and hoping for some relief from their pain. Degas has other drawings of that very situation. But because the women here are paired so closely the viewer tries to figure out what's in store for each of Degas' actors, what they're waiting for, and what each woman tells us about the other.

How does Edgar Degas' pastel, *Waiting*, become such a study in waiting? The chaperone is the key. This is a point made by Richard Thomson in his 1995 monograph on just this picture. Degas' preparatory sketches for the painting, Thomson explains, showed only the young ballerina waiting to perform. In the final version Degas has added the older, but not too old, chaperone and placed her, not the young ballerina, dead center. When Edgar Degas pairs the two women together he aims to highlight the future and the past for both characters. When we look at the two women in the pastel it's hard not to think, "ah, the life of the chaperone—that's what the young ballerina is really waiting for!" She doesn't know or feel that yet. Her innocence toward aging and to the passing of time makes the chaperone's victimhood—is that the right word for getting beyond it?—all the more evident. But one day the young woman will probably be a chaperone too, the painting is saying, and she'll be looking back at those sore ankles and wishing that she could have them too. How long will she have to wait for this to happen? In ten years maybe, if the young ballerina is unlucky, she will be a chaperone too. That's the waiting the painting's title refers to.

And the chaperone? What is she waiting for now that she's past her dancing prime? Perhaps this will be the second-hand pleasure of the young woman's success. Or perhaps it's just the end of her assignment with the young dancer. The pairing might also offer another answer to this question and it's one that relates to time. You could almost say that the chaperone and the ballerina wait in different ways and that this relates to their experience of time. Time must drag for the older woman. Her dancing days are past. She's not so old. But it's all about the triumphs of someone else now. That's what the passing of time brings with it. Time must race for the younger woman as she waits tensely and with arousal waiting to perform. Her glory days are all, she must hope, to come. She must be nervous but at the same time excited. The comparison with the chaperone makes this all the clearer. Time changes the way the experience of waiting is felt, as Marc Wittmann would say, but in this pastel, it needs the pairing for it to make its point clearly and for Degas' story to be told. Time varies from person to person and from situation to situation for sure. But you understand this variation and this "complex response," this experience of waiting, most easily when there are pairs involved.

I've not mentioned the most obvious aspect of pairing in this picture. This is companionship. You can't have companionship without pairs and the ballerina and the chaperone exhibit, in their closeness, some degree of companionate interaction. We'll never know how strong this is. But there's an indifferent ease between the pair that makes it feel as if this is so. Perhaps it's also the case for pairs that waiting together really does seem to encourage companionate bonding. If you were to try to envisage waiting and to imagine how you would paint or photograph waiting, it would usually entail two people.

Whoosh goes the diver in Japan in the 1930s. The diver shows that there are other ways of envisaging waiting. Our diver has no pair, but her dive captures the spirit of waiting. It's very exciting to imagine diving in this way, paused in the air, no matter how many times that you've seen it depicted. Figure 1.3 may appear to be the sort of image that once might have been shown on a Carnival or on a P&O cruise travel poster.

Japanese artist Kōshirō Onchi (1891–1955) dramatizes this moment of waiting, this moment of almost invisible

FIGURE 1.3. A pause, a milli-moment of waiting in Kōshirō Onchi's *Diving* (1932). Japanese, Shōwa era, about 1933 (Shōwa 8). 47.8 cm × 30.8 cm. Museum of Fine Arts, Boston, Asiatic Curator's Fund 56.489. Photograph © 2000 Museum of Fine Arts, Boston.

pause sometimes to be glimpsed, or almost glimpsed, in vigorous action.[12] This is in his woodblock print called, what else, *Diving*. Kōshirō Onchi knows how to show what we might just be able to see or wish we could see. It seems as if he perceives, in his milli-moment of waiting and of pausing, the very essence of an action. Is that what he's trying to show in his *Diving*? I think that's the case and that Onchi catches a split second in the fall of the diver and renders it as if it were something we could all see. For a fraction of a moment the diver hangs in space and seems to be frozen. And we wait. Then it's over with a whoosh and a splash. Kōshirō Onchi's *Diving* is as beautiful as it is exciting. One of his earlier but more famous pictures also seems to focus on this same moment of waiting and pause. It's a woodblock print from 1914, and it's called *Things Suspended in the Sky*. It appears to represent the lower portion of a huge dark wave getting ready to break. We're offered a chance to participate in that split second as the wave hangs, waiting to crash. The woodblock print is as beautiful and exciting as his *Diving*, but the dread is more obvious. Kōshirō Onchi's *Diving* is also concerned with things suspended in the sky and it shows waiting in the just the same startling manner.

How did Kōshirō Onchi's diver feel as she fell? Time decelerates when you fall from a height, especially if there is fear mixed in with it. I suspect that fear or some version of fear-like arousal, something close to dread, is present in most high diving. Claudia Hammond speaks about the diving of the neuroscientist, David Eagleman, who now works apparently as an adjunct professor at Stanford University's Department of Psychiatry and Behavioral Sciences. He is, Hammond explains, the same scientist who wrote the best-selling imagined stories of the waiting in the afterlife, *Sum: Forty Tales from the Afterlives*. Eagleman is given to the dramatic, but his experiment was a fascinating one. He performed a test that gives a sense of how it can feel to dive from a height and whether time slows and, with it, whether your capacity to wait is heightened. Eagleman carried out a scientific test with volunteers (himself included) on a version of diving, free-fall. The idea was to check whether people's sense of time warped when they undergo a terrifying version of diving. Eagleman's plan was to drop harnessed research subjects, facing backwards, 150 feet from the top of a building. They were in a 33-foot-high metal cage mounted on the roof of the building. At the peak speed of their dive in the cage their top velocity reached 70 miles an hour. They were caught safely at the bottom and, because you're reading this, they lived to tell their story to the professor. The steady-nerved David Eagleman was able to tell the story too. He acted as the first research subject for the cage dive. He tried it out three times.

David Eagleman wanted to know whether dread and terror, produced in this case by the free-fall dive, would speed up his volunteers' ability to process information. Would time slow sufficiently for the volunteers in their dive to enable them to see things that, in their lay life, they might have missed? Would their perceptions slow down almost to a pause? To this end he placed a line of giant wristwatches inside the cage. These clocks alternated very quickly between two screens that displayed random numbers. To the unterrified eye they were just a blur. Would the terrifying dive slow time and, rendering the divers frozen and Onchi-like, would it allow the subjects to see the numbers? No, it didn't work. The volunteers couldn't read the clocks. But everyone in the experiment claimed that it felt as if time had decelerated, just as it seems to do for Onchi's diver. It decelerated enough for them to experience a sense of waiting. There was for the cage divers what Hammond calls "subjective time dilation." Did David Eagleman prove anything else with this dramatic experiment? Claudia Hammond suggests that Eagleman shows that "time itself doesn't actually slow down when we're afraid, and nor does the brain's sensory processing speed up.

What changes is our perception of time." This is again Marc Wittmann's "felt time." Does Kōshirō Onchi capture all of this? I like to think that he does. I'd add that that fear and dread, captured in the image of diving, lets us wait with remarkable acuity.

The pause, the expectation, and excitement produced by this freeze-frame experience and the representation of diving is a second version of waiting. It has a number of other reflections. The almost invisible pause is there in most music. It is called *ma* in Japanese music.[13] The pause is also present in such frowned upon states as dithering and procrastination where the pause, at least some people argue, is a version of waiting. There are number of other types of waiting that seem to catch the emotional sense of the dive: stalking and hunting, waiting for good or potentially bad news, or waiting, I am not fooling you, for divine intercession. The stillness of the subjects in this sort of situation implies that we're on the brink of something exciting happening.

It's not present in my next illustration (Figure 1.4). Who is the woman waiting in the shadows thirty years before Kōshirō Onchi imagined *Diving*? Has this woman just risen from that empty chair behind the open door? Why is she waiting near the door to the third room with the window that looks out at Copenhagen in the 1900s? There's a story about waiting here, if only we could wait to hear it. Vilhelm Hammershøi tells it again and again and it's one that stays as perplexing as ever.

The empty chair has a long association with death. The chair is my third version of waiting. In Scandinavia an empty chair is sometimes part of the "furniture" of the mourning process. It is sometimes kept in the room with the corpse on display as a symbol of the deceased's departure from the

24 | A PORTRAIT

FIGURE 1.4. "The Year of Magical Thinking." Vilhelm Hammershøi, *Woman in an Interior, Strandgade 30,* 1901. Private Collection.
Photo: © Christie's Images/Bridgeman Images.

family. The chair belonged to the dead person. I believe that this is the strongest visual association to be drawn from the representation of the empty chair. It is in art a common enough symbol for loss, and then for mourning and for grief. There might be even more significance to this image of the empty chair than just the irrevocable loss of a loved one. For the very closest mourners there's often a feeling that the chair, if it's left unused, might somehow encourage the return of the person who's died. Joan Didion speaks a lot about the fear of denying the return to the realm of the living of her recently dead husband, John Gregory Dunne. That's if she were to get rid of his possessions. She calls this "magical thinking" in her memoir *The Year of Magical Thinking*. The empty chair, left alone and waiting for the return of the departed, could also play a part in the "magical thinking" of mourning and of loss and grief. Keep it closer, in other words, and you might bring the lost loved one back to use it. That's if you can wait long enough.

Three doors are open in *Interior Strandgade 30* and they seem to lead towards a window placed, spatially, at the back of the painting. Vilhelm Hammershøi's wife, Ida, stands bolt still in the central room, paused, and waiting, expectant, watchful, and hesitant, in the shadows of the inner room. Why is she waiting? The empty chair may offer one clue. Hammershøi has imagined Ida as if she were mourning the lost individual whose presence might be signified by that empty chair. She's waiting for her grief to pass, perhaps wondering will it ever pass? She could also be waiting, like Joan Didion, for the magical return of the deceased. Who is the person she's waiting for? There's a hint at this provided in the paired pictures hung on the wall immediately above the empty chair. Are they of Ida and her beloved? Ida, well really the fictionalized Ida, has lost the other part of her pair. Her partner maybe? Ida's story, her waiting, seems to be all about that mourning, loss, and grief.

Ida occasionally makes it onto one of those empty chairs in that bleached apartment in early 20th century Copenhagen. In the last week of November 2017 Ida sat down and Vilhelm Hammershøi's appeal to modern audiences was made clear again. *Interior with a Woman at the Piano, Strandgade 30* (same address and same rooms as in the painting in Figure 1.4) painted in 1901 (same year as the painting in Figure 1.4) was sold for about US$6.3 million in an auction at Sotheby's in New York. This is the largest sum ever paid in a public sale for a piece of Danish art.[14] I don't think it's fair to say that Vilhelm and Ida have been waiting 100 years for recognition, although it often feels that way. But Ida and Vilhelm have certainly been waiting 100 years to really come into their own.[15] Vilhelm Hammershøi, dead in 1916 aged 51, has become very popular these days. His draftsman-like modesty, his sense of profound order (it's almost like Bach for some viewers), his almost mathematical canvases, and his sense of the "magical thinking" of waiting and loss have a strong but strange appeal for the modern audiences.

These three versions of waiting seem to me to capture much of the essence of the experience of waiting. Together they offer a portrait of the nuance required for seeing waiting. These three highlights of the waiting experience will shape this book to a large extent, two by two by two. I've chosen to try to illustrate these in a more comprehensible and attractive way by linking them to a visual image. You may not necessarily find this convincing, but I find it very helpful to be able to see what I'm talking about. There remains one version of waiting that I haven't yet given much consideration to and it is one that is very hard to see. This is patience. I'd like to finish with that virtue, and I'll try to say to you that patience has much less to do with waiting than you might have expected.

Harold Wilson, the British prime minister, was very concerned with patience. He is going to be my exemplar for patience. Wilson claimed that he'd settled on becoming a British member of parliament and a prime minister before he had turned 12 years of age. He succeeded in that childish ambition and went on to be elected as an MP in 1945, aged 29, then as a prime minister of Britain for two terms, from 1964 to 1970 and from 1974 to 1976. Harold Wilson was born in 1916. He had to wait nearly 36 years until he achieved his greatest life ambition. He must have been very patient or else he was very good at waiting. He claims of his childhood insight concerning high office: "after that it was a question of waiting and waiting."[16] I wonder if patience, which is related to waiting, is sometimes an emotion of the will? I wonder if patience wills achievement and hopes for achievement, while waiting, an almost passive condition, is something that is thrust on us—though we can willingly (and patiently) accept the condition. Waiting and waiting it might have been, but Harold Wilson seems to me to be talking more about patience, about his will and his hopes. If you are patient long enough, if you exercise will and keep on hoping, Wilson seems to me to suggest, and if this shows up in your capacity to hang on, then you may just get your heart's desire.

Now, finally, here is a little test. When you are a bit of a drunk, not too big of a drunk though still a practicing alcoholic enthusiast, anticipating drink is a very enjoyable thing. Soon after lunch your mind will turn to the promise of a gulp at the end of the working day. Or just the end of the day. I stress just day, for the anticipation of that gulp is not spoiled by unemployment or retirement or sabbatical. The prospect produces a slight catch in the throat, when this thought first emerges and, if you are sufficient of a devotee, the catch will repeat, benignly, as the afternoon goes on. The first few drinks, when they finally arrive, are balm for that throat-catch. The rest, it's been my experience, is an attempt to hold and to repeat that initial pleasure of the first shoulder sloping drink. But the waiting has gone now and with it that initial pleasure. Time for this boozer is no arrow. It moves in a circle that is driven by expectant and frequently pleasurable passing of sober time. It moves in a strange circle, from enforced and sober time to pleasure and then to the slow extinction of anticipation as the hooch does its best. What is going on here? Is the boozer during the dry afternoon showing patience or waiting? What do you think? Patience or waiting? Are they the same thing? For the answer to this question you will have to turn to the illustration by Laszlo Mednyasnszky at the very end of this book. But wait. Don't be turning just yet.

ALAN RABINOWITZ AND THE JAGUAR

Are Some Brains Better at Waiting than Others?

> I was in the jungles of Belize, following the largest jaguar tracks that I had ever encountered. There was a new animal in my study area, and I wanted to know where it was headed.... But hours later, after all tracks and sign had long since disappeared and darkness was closing in over the jungle, I turned to go back to camp. As soon as I turned, I froze. There he was. The jaguar ... had circled around long ago and had been tracking me.

ALAN RABINOWITZ TELLS THIS STORY in his book *An Indomitable Beast: The Remarkable Journey of the Jaguar*, a tale of how this scientist and author grew up to work to save big cats, especially jaguars. Alan Rabinowitz (once dubbed by *Time Magazine* "the Indiana Jones of wildlife preservation") was one of the world's best known and admired big cat experts. His was a very generous life, especially if you're a big cat, and Rabinowitz explains that one of his proudest achievements was the Jaguar Corridor—"a series of biological and genetic corridors for jaguars [to roam safely] across their entire range from Mexico to Argentina."[1] It took him a long time to achieve the corridor. Rabinowitz really knew how to wait. Until his death aged 64 on August 5, 2018, of lymphatic cancer, he was the CEO of Panthera in New York City, a nonprofit organization that aims to conserve and protect the world's 37 wildcat species. Before Panthera, Rabinowitz worked for 30 years as the executive director of the Science and Exploration Division for the Wildlife Conservation Society.

But what did happen after Dr. Rabinowitz met the giant jaguar that was waiting and watching? "Not entirely sure what to do next," he recounts, "other than not to run away, I squatted down and wrapped my arms around my knees to make myself small and non-threatening."

What is it in a human brain that allows individuals like Alan Rabinowitz to achieve such a remarkable capacity to wait when placed in a situation where most people, consumed by fear, would bolt? Rabinowitz's response goes beyond simple self-control. Patience seems irrelevant in a situation that ought better to be defined by fear. And courage seems an excessively pious term to invoke. There are two brain chemicals that appear to enable an individual's capacity to wait and that could have assisted Alan Rabinowitz. Both seem to do this by "modulating" the value of waiting for a reward to come. (Modulating is a synonym for enabling.) There are two great enablers of waiting, the neuromodulators dopamine and serotonin. The one primes you for a future reward by offering you a reward right now—this is dopamine. The other primes you for a future reward without offering a reward right now—this is serotonin. You may now be wondering from which of the two did Alan Rabinowitz benefit.

What then is dopamine? It's a brain chemical produced, notably but not only, in the regions of the brain called the substantia nigra (a small tissue on either side of the base of the brain) and by the ventral tegmental area (located close to the middle of the brain, at its base). Dopamine plays a role in the reward and pleasure centers of the brain. As well as helping to adjust movement (it can aid in the battle against Parkinson's Disease) it also helps to adjust human emotional responses. It allows us creatures to perceive future rewards and to act in such a way as to achieve them. Research has suggested that while you are waiting for something usually stimulating or sometimes enjoyable to happen—before it happens, I mean—there can be a dopamine release. This dopamine release is pleasurable and seems to act as a little gift to the brain for the waiting. Expectation, you could say, is followed by a reward.[2] I suppose that if this process of expectation and reward is repeated, then learning will follow. Dopamine can assist a creature to acquire valuable knowledge, through this repeated process of expectation, reward, and learning.[3] But the levels of dopamine have to be just right. Lowered levels of dopamine have been linked with risk-taking behavior, linked with the behavior of individuals who will have no truck with waiting.[4] That would be of no help in the jungles of Belize. Of equal importance for researchers like Rabinowitz is that too much, rather than too little dopamine is also harmful for waiting. Dread and fear are associated with an excess of dopamine.[5] That's something that would have been no help at all to our scientist. It seems that you have to get the dopamine levels just right. Did Alan Rabinowitz?

Look at these domestic cats (Figure 2.1). No stalking here. They are all sitting on the dockside in a row waiting. For what? This is for the fishermen's boats to return. That's when they'll get their cut of the catch, their little reward. That's what they expect. But why don't they wander away? They look well fed and fish is not the only food that cats enjoy. There might be some tasty mice in the quayside buildings to their rear. The felines I've shared a house with all possessed the attention spans of peanuts. I'd have expected any cat of

FIGURE 2.1. Cats Waiting for Fishermen to Return. The photographer is unknown. Source: http://www.thisiscolossal.com/2013/10/cats-waiting-for-fishermen-to-return/.

mine to wander away and to look for some mice or even rats. Cats get very bored very easily.

But not these moggies. There doesn't seem to be a boat or a sailor in sight to keep them at the ready. You'd really expect them to begin to drift off. I'm quite sure I would if I were in their situation. But they don't. They are relaxed, but intent, aroused, and, it seems to me, they are excited. Look at the tensed and extended neck of that cat to the front of this photograph. It means business. Do the felines enjoy this waiting? It really appears as if enjoyment's what keeps them there.

Winslow Homer's *Waiting for Dad* (Figure 2.2) offers another version of the same sort of situation, but this time, there's a human in the picture, rather than a cat. The little boy in this painting is just about as tensed as the cat in the

FIGURE 2.2. Winslow Homer, *Waiting for Dad*, 1873. Transparent and opaque watercolor. 24.13 cm × 34.29 cm. Mills College Art Museum, Gift of Jane C. Tolman.

right foreground of my last picture. The boy is waiting with excitement for his fisherman father to return with the catch. Which does he look forward to most, the flopping fish or his father? I'd say both of them, but Winslow Homer goes for the father. The excitement is dopamine driven, no doubt about it, and the boy, upright like a cat on a quay, seems to be tense with expectation. The watercolor is a sentimental one unless you come at it with the cats and with their neuromodulator in mind. If you can get the sentimentality out of your mind, then the picture has something real enough to convey.

Can you remember how it felt to be like Winslow Homer's child?[6] It's dopamine that holds the boy and those cats in position. When there's a reward involved, such as the fish for the cats and maybe for the boy as well, then the prospect of the reward generates a pleasurable dopamine release within the brain. Can you remember? This release takes place during the period of waiting or expectation. It's well before the feline gluttony's enacted or the father returns with fish and friendship. It makes the waiting, the expectation, a pleasurable event. The repetition is what fixes the link of pleasure with expectation. Arif Hamid, the lead author of a study on the role of dopamine and learning, explains that the "mesolimbic dopamine signals the value of work." He continues to explain that "abrupt dopamine increases, when a person perceives stimuli that predict rewards, is a dominant mechanism of reward learning within the brain—a concept similar to Russian physiologist Ivan Pavlov's dog hearing the bell and salivating at a response to stimuli." This is what Hamid and his team argued in their 2015 paper in *Nature Neuroscience*. They achieved these results by measuring the "dopamine levels in rats while they performed a decision-making task," and then by comparing "it with how motivated the rats were and how much they learned. They also increased dopamine levels to artificially motivate the rats and repeatedly made them learn to perform actions that did not produce rewards."[7]

It doesn't look like this is the first time the felines have been found waiting for fish on the dock, nor the boy. It appears as if the cats have learned to wait for their fish on the quay by repeating the experiencing many times.[8] This learning, produced by the reinforcement of the dopamine reward, is another of the benefits of this beneficent neuromodulator.[9] Not only does dopamine increase a creature's sense of pleasure, but, as Carolyn Declerck and Christophe Boone explain, it also "increases attention to and exploration of distant space."[10] Now that is precisely what the cats, or the fisherman's son, need if they're to spot the boats returning. Dopamine offers another advantage. It "facilitates remembering past rewards associated with a particular stimulus." The dopamine surge that the cats experience at the docks helps them to remember their fish of the past and the roiling opioids and endocannabinoids that accompanied their consumption. This dopamine-induced recollection also assists them to stay put and to wait. As Declerck and Boone sum it up: dopamine "enhances the motivation to earn the reward." That is another way of saying that dopamine assists the cats and the boy to learn.

In our pictures the cats and the boy stay put and look so happily alert, therefore, because of the dopamine release produced by the learned expectation of what the boats will bring in. It's the dopamine that keeps them waiting in learned anticipation of the fishy feast and their father. Thus the process of expectation, reward, and learning keeps cats and boy waiting for the boats. The cats will receive another dopamine boost as well when they're about to sink their sharp little fangs into the flapping fish. But when the waiting finishes for the cats and when they finally do eat their fish, the reward will be from a different medium in the brain. This will be derived from the brain's natural production of opioids and endocannabinoids. These substances seem to act in just the very manner that their names seem to suggest—almost as blends of opium and cannabis. That sounds against the law, but it's how things work, and, anyhow, civic laws do not really apply to quayside cats.

Let's look at some more of the science relating to dopamine levels. If you suppress the level of dopamine in the brain you will reduce "wanting." This is what Declerck and Boone stress. Although the pharmacological suppression of dopamine, they go on to say, will reduce "wanting" (that is to say it will reduce your cravings for a substance such as fresh dockside fish), it will not reduce "liking" (dockside fish will still taste good if you are a cat). This is because the "liking" is the result of a preference within the brain that is unrelated to dopamine. It requires no waiting at all and is generated by those opioids and endocannabinoids that surged as the cats and perhaps the little boy ate the fish. Does this mean, for the cat situation, that if you could suppress the dopamine levels within the brains of these maritime cats, then they would wander off and miss their fish? Would they go in search of mice or rats or just sleep? Would the same would be true for the fisherman's son? Would the lowered dopamine level within their brains dampen their wanting or their craving? The answer seems to be, it all depends. Arif Hamid explains, "aside from affecting immediate mood and behavior, dopamine also produces changes in the brain that are persistent, sometimes lasting a life time."[11] The process of expectation, reward, and learning needs to be repeated sufficiently for the message to stick. If the cats and the boy have experienced the dopamine rise sufficiently, then the brain would have changed sufficiently to keep them at their posts, waiting and concentrating. Is that how it worked for Alan Rabinowitz?

To follow is a very intriguing story that illustrates how dopamine may work—and how can benefit human lives in the most unexpected of ways—but stay where you are, I'll get back to Alan Rabinowitz. It concerns a Mr. Lawrence John Ripple, then 70, from Kansas City. In 2017 he entered the Bank of Labor, which is just down the road from the Kansas City police headquarters. He was furnished with a hand-written note announcing that he wanted money and, "I have a gun." Mr. Ripple had composed the threat at home and, though this is hard to fathom, he had composed it right in front of his wife. He told her he would "rather be in jail than at home." That was reported by the *Kansas City Star*.[12] As far as I can tell his wife did nothing to stop him. Perhaps she was sick of Mr. Ripple. Lawrence managed to get $2,924 from a Bank of Labor teller. Instead of then hotfooting it off to celebrate with his loot at the nearest fish shop, he went and, just like Winslow Homer's boy, he waited in the bank lobby, alert and concentrated. He was waiting for officers from the nearby police headquarters to arrive and to arrest him. They did. It seems to me that Mr. Ripple must have enjoyed waiting to be saved from his home life, as he waited to be arrested and even waited to be sentenced, despite the fact that normally in the state of Kansas he could have been looking at up to 20 years in jail. Can it have been dopamine that kept Mr. Ripple waiting there in such a satisfied and cat-on-the-quayside, boy-on-the-boat state? It certainly seems so.

The *Kansas City Star* states that before the robbery, Mr. Ripple lived a normal, "law-abiding life as a husband

and stepfather to four children." But recently, in 2015, Mr. Ripple had undergone quadruple bypass heart surgery and he was also a victim to undiagnosed depression. His lawyers described the robbery not as a typical act of villainy, but rather as a "cry for help." I think they meant that Mr. Ripple wanted the police to arrest him and that instinctively he hoped this might lead to some treatment for his depression. That he chose to rob a bank just near to the Kansas City police headquarters shows just how deliberately he had planned his crime, his arrest, and his plea. According to the *Kansas City Star* it all worked: "at the sentencing trial Mr. Ripple said he had sought medical help for his mental health and said he felt 'like his old self.' " Somewhere along the line Mr. Ripple seems to have convinced himself, or better to have learned, that if you can provoke people to help you, then they will. I wonder if Mr. Ripple had practiced his crime, or at least the sitting-in-the-bank-lobby part? Perhaps he had taught his brain about the exciting reward to be associated with his arrest. With that happy expectation dopamine, rather than just simple foolishness, may have kept Mr. Ripple seated in the Bank of Labor lobby and, like Winslow Homer's boy on the boat, kept him alert and waiting for his reward—prison, escape from home, and treatment for his depression.

There's a happy ending to this story and I believe we can put it down to the benign action of dopamine. "Though Lawrence John Ripple pleaded guilty to bank robbery in January and could have spent up to 37 months in prison," the *Kansas City Star* reports, "his attorney and federal prosecutors asked a U.S. District Court judge for leniency. That request was supported by the vice president of the bank and the teller whom Ripple frightened, said Assistant U.S. Attorney Sheri Catania." The Kansas City court determined that Lawrence would "serve three years of supervised probation and must do 50 hours of community service." There would be no jail time. "[Mr. Ripple] was ordered to pay $227.27 to the bank he robbed—the amount representing the billable hours for bank employees who were sent home on the day of robbery—and $100 to a crime victims fund." And his wife wasn't sick of Mr. Ripple after all. She attended court with him.

Before we leave dopamine there is one more thing to be said: in the last chapter I highlighted three varieties of waiting. One of these was the pause. I attempted to dramatize this version of waiting through the time-frozen image of the diver created by the Japanese artist Kōshirō Onchi. We've learned enough about the workings of dopamine now to link the affects and the characteristics of the pause with what we've seen happen when raised dopamine levels are present within the brain. It would be easy to connect the arousal, the intentness, and the excitement of the quayside cats or even the fisherman's son with Onchi's diver. It would be easy enough to connect, as well, the vision of Mr. Ripple, seated expectantly in the foyer to the Bank of Labor in Kansas City just like a cat or a fisherman's son. Onchi's diver must have learned, just like the cats, that what she is doing can be safe. The dopamine paradoxically may keep it that way by altering brain structures. The pause and the dive offer vivid ways to understand the operation of dopamine and how it feels to be a quayside cat, a seaside son, or a Mr. Ripple in the lobby.

But what about Alan Rabinowitz? We seem to be drifting away from his predicament in Belize with the giant jaguar that early jungle evening. Was it dopamine that held him firmly waiting in the presence of that mighty cat? It doesn't look very much like that's the case, does it. I can't see "the Indiana Jones of wildlife preservation" as a double of Lawrence Ripple. There can't have been much excitement or pleasure to be derived from squatting in front of a very large jaguar at dinnertime. Research has connected another neuromodulator, serotonin, with waiting as well.[13] Waiting generated by serotonin is a rather different experience to that generated by dopamine. It's a chemical released by a small set of cells in an area of the brain called the nuclei raphe, located at the bottom of the brain, near the brain stem at the top of the spine. The serotonin released from the nuclei raphe has as its function, explains the Japanese neurological team from Okinawa compromising K. Miyazaki, K. W. Miyazaki, and K. Doya, "to modulate [or enable] the value of waiting for a future reward."[14] They maintain, "increased serotonergic neuronal firing facilitates waiting behavior when there is the prospect of a forthcoming reward and that serotonergic activation contributes to the patience that allows rats [their experimental animal] to wait longer." Such a description would work well for the experience that Alan Rabinowitz describes as waiting, staying still, and successfully facing and finally addressing his jaguar stalker. Rabinowitz's future reward was, he hoped, not to be eaten for dinner. His modulation or enablement was waiting. The neuroeconomists Carolyn Declerck and Christophe Boone offer some insights into situations that require serotonin-based waiting. They explain that serotonin, when its levels are low, is associated with an "impaired ability to learn and relearn stimulus-reinforcement associations." Rabinowitz, in other words, might never have learned to stay and to wait if his neuromodulator, serotonin, was habitually low. This is because depleted levels of serotonin are associated, alarmingly so if you are in the jungles of Central America, with a "compromised capacity to delay gratification." The diminution of serotonin, it appears, predisposes an individual to be "selfishly tempted by short-term impulses . . . [and it will] increase the impulsive but socially inappropriate response that is usually suppressed." The impulse for Rabinowitz to scamper could have been overpowering.[15]

In a brain that is adequately endowed with serotonin, what goes on? To try to purchase an image on the link between serotonin and waiting, Madalena Fonseca and a team of researchers in Lisbon at the Champalimaud Neuroscience Programme (specifically at the wonderfully named Champalimaud Centre for the Unknown) carried out a trial with mice and blue light.[16] Pretend here that Rabinowitz is the mouse—though I'll admit that a more unlikely mouse could not be imagined. To process their experiment the team from the Champalimaud Centre for the Unknown "made serotonin neurons sensitive to light, so when [they] illuminated them, they were activated and released serotonin in the brain." This technique of the behavioral control of cells within the brain and of making neurons light sensitive is called optogenetics. It's breathtaking in its simplicity, as well as in its complexity. Optogenetics uses light, the light a creature can see with its own eyes, to control the operation of cells in living tissue. The light is usually blue. For Fonseca and her team, the cells destined for treatment are the neurons that control behavior such as that of Alan Rabinowitz in the jungles of Belize. The Champalimaud Centre for the Unknown team genetically modified these neurons "to express light-sensitive ion channels." This enabled the team to switch on or switch off the neuronal and ultimately behavioral activity. This technique can even be used with free-moving animals such as mice. Once the research team had switched on or off the mice's serotonin neurons, they provided the little rodents with a task that offered them a reward, but a reward that arrived at a variety of unpredictable times. When serotonin neurons were activated with blue light, Fonsesca's team discovered that the mice became better at waiting for their reward. Masayoshi Murakami, also part of the Champalimaud Centre for the Unknown team, explained, "we tested how different levels of activation influence waiting and saw that stronger activation resulted in longer waiting durations—the more serotonin neurons were activated, the longer the mice would wait."[17] Could this have been the situation in Alan Rabinowitz's brain, and perhaps even in the jaguar's as well?

Alan Rabinowitz's endowment with abundant serotonin becomes even more likely if we look at other aspect of the working of the neurochemical. One unexpected feature of the presence of a heightened level of serotonin is that it offers no specific recompense. Zachary Mainen, who founded the Champalimaud Neuroscience Programme in Lisbon, points out emphatically in *Cell Biology* (2015) that having heightened serotonin confers no immediate reward.[18] To demonstrate this, long-suffering laboratory mice were brought into play again. "If the sensation of serotonin was pleasant or rewarding for the mice, this could have explained why they waited longer," said Mainen's colleague, our serotonin expert, Madalena Fonseca. To test this hypothesis her team came up with a process and with experiments that were quite simple. The researchers aimed to see "whether mice preferred to perform actions associated with serotonin stimulation." They did not. It appears that an increased capacity to wait was not a consequence of reward. Or, at least, it was not the consequence of an immediate reward. The pay-off, if there is one at all, is long term. How would this relate to

Alan Rabinowitz? If it were serotonin that was helping him, then he wouldn't have felt good about making himself small and non-threatening and waiting. But he would have felt good about not being eaten. This seems to have been just how it was. Squatting down, wrapping his arms around his knees to make himself small and non-threatening, was liable to have worked, but it can't have been especially pleasurable. Try it for yourself in front of a mirror. It really does look like this is the answer to the question, from which of the two neuromodulators did Alan Rabinowitz benefit? Alan Rabinowitz was protected not by dopamine, but by serotonin.

Let's stay in Belize. When Alan Rabinowitz confronted the great jaguar in the dense forests of Belize, he says that he did what he had done "so often by the cage at the zoo." What was he getting at by this reference to the Brooklyn Zoo and how did it give him the brain endowment to wait? Here is Rabinowitz describing a very important and character forming part of his young life. It occurs when he was a child and when he was in the Brooklyn Zoo:

> I could see before I reached him that the jaguar had stopped pacing and was waiting. . . . Reaching the cage, I leaned against the safety railing. . . . It was always the eyes that drew me in, eyes that seemed filled with perpetual pain. Ignoring any people standing nearby, I started whispering in a voice that no one else could hear, stepping inside a private world . . . that no one else in the world deserved to hear.

Alan Rabinowitz was five years old when he met the cat. It wasn't just profound kindness and empathy for the aging jaguar that caused him to whisper in this manner. The young Rabinowitz had such a severe stutter as a child and even as an adult that he was unable to finish a full sentence.

He had to wait painfully to make himself understood. It seems strange to say that, like many severe stutterers, he could talk without hindrance to animals. And so it was with the old jaguar in the Brooklyn Zoo. His story is as touching as it is instructive. Rabinowitz gained personal benefit from his realization that he could speak without stutter to the old cat. He learned to repeat the freedom that the old jaguar offered him at home as well. There he "would step into his bedroom closet and whisper to his pet turtles, snakes and hamsters."[19] Adversity, the enforced waiting of an isolated and semi-articulate child, seems to have driven the young Alan Rabinowitz to practice and to learn to wait and to whisper at the zoo and at home. He learned to copy the waiting of creatures like the old jaguar and through his own version of waiting he learned to communicate with them. He whispered in part because it seemed to work, in part because he wanted no one to hear him, but also because it offered him the freedom from his disability that was lacking him in his dealing with other children and adults. Animals, it seems, gave him a voice and gave him an understanding of the power of waiting. The animals seemed to teach Rabinowitz that he would eventually learn to gain his voice and to give them a voice, if he waited. But there was no reward yet. Someday, the young Rabinowitz vowed to his animals, "he would find his voice, and then he would speak for the creatures that couldn't."[20]

Is there something in this story that points, again, to certain brains having a greater capacity to wait than others? Was Alan Rabinowitz's brain better wired from birth for waiting? Or did Rabinowitz's disability and the circumstances of his upbringing teach him a greater capacity to wait than most other people? It really does seem that Alan Rabinowitz learned to wait, though perhaps this learning began at pretty much the same time he started to speak—well within his first year of life. He appears to have spent long periods of time as a child practicing waiting or being forced to practice waiting—waiting to be able to communicate, waiting to be heard, waiting for his animals to understand his repeated conversations. If high skills in waiting can be learned, Rabinowitz may show that the ability probably does not best come from school learning, from willpower, from neurochemical adjustment, from the exhortation of elders and betters, or from plenty of affiliative behaviors. That's not to say that these things do not help. It seems to be that the capacity to wait, to be a super-waiter like Alan Rabinowitz, and to have all of the serotonin that must course through his brain with it, are capacities that emerge through learning from prolonged adversarial circumstances that are experienced first at a very young age. It's probable, I believe, that Alan Rabinowitz was more in touch with waiting that many people. It's probable that the causation for this had something to do with the isolation that he experienced as a disabled child. It also feels as if to stutter is to wait: stutterers struggle and wait to get their language out and, when they do, they wait to see if they've been understood and they wait to see the reaction of their interlocutor. With animals Rabinowitz could speak without stuttering. It appears, and he implies, that he was able to bring his capacity to wait to bear on animals. It's his capacity to wait that enabled him to "whisper" in situations like the one described here. This is not happy reading for people like me, who are by nature serotonin poor. But it is perhaps good news for all those of you who feel their childhood resembled an inarticulate version of Oliver Twist's, or worse.

Some people may be born as super waiters, rather than having it forced on them as an infant like Alan Rabinowitz. Chris Kyle was perhaps the most famous sniper of all time and he may illustrate the super-waiter who is just born that way. In his four tours of duty for the Navy Seals during the Iraq War, Chris Kyle is claimed to have achieved the highest number of "kills" of any sniper in US Army history. This is sometimes said to have engrossed 160 deaths. He describes his waiting life as a life-taking sniper in his bestselling 2012 autobiography, *American Sniper: The Autobiography of the Most Lethal Sniper in U.S. Military History*. Clint Eastwood made a very popular movie with the same name. In fact, Clint Eastwood's *American Sniper* was so popular that it's sometimes claimed to be the highest grossing American war movie of all time. (That, I'm afraid, is no great recommendation for the value of any movie, but let's leave those strange statistics be.) As for Chris Kyle, you would think that being a really successful sniper would require serotonin or dopamine in bucketsful. If ever there were a vocation characterized by a remarkable capacity to wait for exactly the right moment, then being a sniper would be it.

Perhaps we should pause to emphasize how important is waiting for the work of the sniper. Chris Kyle may have been the most successful sniper, but he doesn't hold the record for long-range strikes. An unnamed Canadian sniper achieved this in June 2017 when he killed an ISIS fighter, maybe also a sniper, in combat near Mosul in Iraq. This was from a distance of 11,319 feet. According to one report, "the bullet was fired from a McMillan TAC-50 rifle set on a high-rise tower and took 10 seconds to travel the 2.14 miles towards the fighter, who was attacking Iraqi soldiers."[21] There was a very vivid description of the sniping process in this shoot by Deborah Haynes in *The Times*.[22] It's all about waiting. The process is so complex—and so fraught with waiting—that it deserves a description. The sniper sets up his rifle and scopes out his target (the scope is attached to his rifle). The shooter is accompanied by a spotter who assists with his laser rangefinder binoculars. These find the target and calculate the distance. The spotter will also have a Kestrel, a handheld computer that "calculates wind speed, humidity and any other environmental factors that could have an effect on the bullet." The sniper and the spotter, in constant contact with HQ, will wait for hours or even days to get their target right. And

> once set up to kill, they would have had to watch and wait.... When the target was identified and authority to strike given, the spotter ... would relay this information to the sniper along with the wind speed and humidity levels. This information is plugged into the sniper's rifle so he can adjust the crosshairs accordingly.

A sniper, you would imagine, must have more than just a good eye and a sure aim and a very competent spotter. Snipers must also have calm and stillness if they are to achieve their aim. Here is where the heightened levels of the neuromodulator would come in to play. In a sense, the sniper's life is a mirror of the life of the stalking animal. Stalking animals, like Alan Rabinowitz's jaguar, require plenty of waiting neuromodulator. If they didn't have it, they'd pounce too soon. Maybe the sniper is a little like the quayside cats. Might it be more logical to attribute their capacity to wait to a surge in dopamine ("and through [this surge] increased attention for distant cues") than to a raised level of serotonin?

But such raised levels of dopamine, if that is what it was, do not always work to the long-term advantage of the brain. The capacity to wait that is dopamine driven may have its downside. Carolyn Declerck and Christophe Boone suggest it's likely that the dopamine system contributes "to impulsive and selfish decisions, and it is unlikely to be related to insightful, long term prosocial decision making." Declerck and Boone conclude gloomily that "in the social domain . . . [this dopamine activity] translates only to selfish decisions." The sniper Chris Kyle maybe more resembles the cats on the quayside than Alan Rabinowitz being confronted with the jaguar. Maybe, in fact, Chris Kyle resembles the jaguar. The rewards are similar—the pleasure of the hunt and of the killing, the invigorating exercise of skill—and different—the recognition and the respect from peers. Kyle's was a dopamine-based version of waiting and of stalking and it seems to have been one that, long term, did much harm to his private life. Chris Kyle has periodically been accused of being subject to, if not to personality disorders, at least to selfish decision-making. It's been claimed that Kyle, who was murdered at a shooting range in 2013 by the mentally ill ex-marine, Eddie Ray Routh, had exaggerated the decorations he'd received from his service in the Iraq War. In his autobiography Kyle claimed that he received two silver stars and five bronze stars for valor. But the *Intercept* website, quoted in the *Guardian*, claims that Kyle "in fact received one silver star and three bronze stars for valor. The website obtained the information through a data request application."[23] Chris Kyle is claimed also to have made exaggerated comments, according to the same news article, by stating he had punched the former governor of Wisconsin and retired wrestler, Jesse Ventura. This was at a wake for Kyle's friend

Michael Monsoor, in Colorado. Ventura took Kyle to court and won.

Does this fit with Carolyn Declerck and Christophe Boone's summarizing statements that dopamine "can be linked to . . . emotional states, such as grandiosity, elation, and even euphoria . . . [but that it is] also associated with emotional detachment and social isolation"?[24] We will never know whether this was the case for Chris Kyle. The reports that I am citing, furthermore, come from a newspaper that is well known for its dislike of most things militaristic and one that has a periodical reserve relating to the tastes of Clint Eastwood. Chris Kyle therefore might just represent journalistic collateral damage. But if that's not the case, then you might want to say that in his instance it sounds like dopamine might have made him a good sniper, rather than serotonin, and that his raised dopamine levels came at an awful cost. Perhaps we should leave this matter and the effects on waiting of dopamine right here and see if there are other ways in which mature brains may become better at waiting, but without the pitfalls of the dopamine-driven sniper's life. Is it possible that there are chemicals or foods that might be taken to remedy some of the shortfalls that brains like mine experience? I don't think I'd like to become another Chris Kyle, but just a little of Alan Rabinowitz's steadiness would be a real help.

Can you redress a shortage of either dopamine or serotonin? Most of us are not nurtured or born like Alan Rabinowitz or Chris Kyle. How could you achieve helpful levels of dopamine or of serotonin in the brain without being born or acculturated into super-waiting status? Dopamine, it appears, can be increased by risk-taking activities. That doesn't seem to be much of a long-term solution. The dopamine levels will fall again, or you may be killed or injured from over-enthusiastic paragliding. You can boost dopamine-using chemicals, with, for example, L-Dopa or with anticholinergics or dopamine receptor agonists. But their side effects can be extreme, and physicians are normally as cautious with L-Dopa as they are with anticholinergics and dopamine receptor agonists. With L-Dopa you can lose not just your shirt like the day trader, but also your hair.[25]

Serotonin at raised levels may offer a much better chance for a stable long-term ability at waiting. But where does serotonin come from? Is it the result of luck, is it in-born, genetic that is to say, or can an attitude like that of Alan Rabinowitz encourage the maintenance of a health supply of this neuromodulator? Or can you eat it? The news is not good. One neuroscientist, Dr. Larry Siever, formerly of New York's Mount Sinai School of Medicine, explained cautiously: "Our serotonin systems are affected not only by what we ingest but by our genes, experiences and attitudes—and by the countless other chemicals racing through our brains. Scientists may someday learn how all these forces interact, but a good life will still take work." On the other hand, Siever states, "Your serotonin system doesn't rule you. . . . If you have vulnerabilities associated with low serotonin functioning—guilt, submissiveness, low self-esteem—you can learn to compensate for them."[26] It seems that affiliative behaviors (friendship, family, a supportive workplace) may have the same effect. Presumably patience and, with it, self-control also increase the release of serotonin and this in turn causes more serotonin to be released.

Could we take a "waiting pill?" Or could we eat our way to waiting? You can certainly take a pill. It might help. Serotonin levels can be artificially increased with drugs, the so-called serotonin re-uptake inhibitors (SSRIs) for example, that are used to treat depression. Their ability to encourage beneficial waiting, however, may be limited by some nasty side effects: drowsiness, nausea, dry mouth, insomnia, diarrhea, nervousness, agitation or restlessness, dizziness, or sexual problems (relating to desire and to completion). Side effects like these might make waiting come at too much of a cost. There's also tryptophan, an amino acid that can be produced artificially and that can help in the production of serotonin. It may be taken as a supplement and, unlike SSRIs, it can be purchased over the counter in the United States (though it was banned between 1989 and 2005) and in the United Kingdom as a dietary supplement for use against depression, anxiety, and insomnia. It's also sold as a prescription drug in portions of Europe for use against major depression. The neuroscientist Simon Young, from Montreal's McGill University, notes, "in healthy people with high trait irritability, tryptophan, relative to placebo, decreased quarrelsome behaviors, increased agreeable behaviors and improved mood."[27] But there are problems with tryptophan just as there are with SSRIs. The possible side effects are similar to those of SSRIs and may include nausea, diarrhea, drowsiness, light-headedness, headache, dry mouth, blurred vision, sedation, euphoria, and nystagmus (involuntary eye movements). Nor are its side effects and its interaction with other drugs well known yet. It really does appear that taking tablets may be an unpleasant or even risky way to encourage the satisfactory production of the waiting neurochemical, serotonin.

Are there more natural and less harmful ways to increase serotonin levels? Will behavioral adjustments help? Can you exercise or munch your way to waiting? Simon Young surveyed the evidence in an editorial in 2007 to the *Journal of Psychiatry and Neuroscience*. He makes four points about the "natural" ways that the brain chemical, and so waiting, may be increased and strengthened.

(1) Self-induced changes in mood through psychotherapy can influence serotonin synthesis. It's possible that "the interaction between serotonin synthesis and mood may be 2-way, with serotonin influencing mood and mood influencing serotonin," Young suggests.

(2) "A few studies also suggest that . . . [exposure to bright light] it is an effective treatment for non-seasonal depression and also reduces depressed mood in women with premenstrual dysphoric disorder and in pregnant women suffering from depression. . . . In human post-mortem brain, serotonin levels are higher in those who died in summer than in those who died in winter."

(3) "A comprehensive review of the relation between exercise and mood," writes Simon Young, "concluded that [exercise's] antidepressant and . . . [anxiety-decreasing] effects have been clearly demonstrated."

(4) "Can tryptophan ingested through food help? The blood-brain-barrier (BBB), a protective endothelial membrane, guards the brain against potential interlopers, both good and bad." Young speculates, "The possibility that the mental health of a population could be improved by increasing the dietary intake of tryptophan relative to the dietary intake of other amino acids remains an interesting idea that should be explored."

As you can see, there are a number of possibilities that would allow the natural increase of the waiting neuromodulator, serotonin. Such an increase may improve mood as well. A virtuous circle may then allow mood improvement to increase the levels of serotonin and with it the capacity to wait.

The variety of the experience of waiting is more limited than I'd have predicted when I set out to sketch this portrait. So far, I've been focusing mainly on the way that waiting may work within the brain. The really astounding thing about the experience of waiting is that, far from being a neutral, ineffable experience that's best dealt with by stopwatches and mathematics it has a science of brain and body behind it. Waiting is an experience that's firmly rooted within the animal body—it's not just rooted in the situations relating to time (like queuing, for example) in which the body is situated. Waiting, or a waiting that is effective, a waiting that doesn't spill over into the opposite extremes of dread and fear or of exuberance, is based on just the right measure within the brain of either serotonin or dopamine. In the case of dopamine, there's a certain degree of pleasure involved and subsequent learning (expectation, dopamine reward, learning). In the case of serotonin, waiting seems to show itself as something that's calm and neutral. When it's based on a suitable level of either dopamine or serotonin, the experience of waiting appears to function as a golden mean located between the two extremes I've mentioned, dread and fear or exuberance. I am not sure that anyone knows quite how to achieve or to measure this right level of dopamine or of serotonin. Not yet at any rate. But you can sure enough see when the right measure is doing its job. And you can also see when one of the two extremes is involved and the waiting experience spirals out of control. Perhaps the best we can say now—at least until more is known of the detailed brain chemistry of waiting—is that waiting may most easily be thought of as one of those "new emotions" such as interest or confusion or worrying or gratitude or pride or dignity.[28] All emotions seem to be harmful when taken to extremes.

Waiting has its own brain chemistry just like other emotions. It may have its own visible characteristics or visual phenotypes (pausing, hesitating, freezing still) just like other emotions. It may have its own psychology, again like other emotions. This gives the experience of waiting the status of almost a real emotion. It certainly has the status of a universal in the lives of humans and animals.[29] What's gained by this understanding? Waiting, like all other emotions, is advantageous for creatures from an evolutionary point of view. Waiting is an element within the human emotional complex that can be experienced and used for good or for ill, just like all other emotions. If we can allow waiting this constitution, then it may be possible to say of it some of the same things that have been said of other emotions such as boredom and jealousy. Emotions, you could say, exist to provide creatures with an evolutionary leg up. They exist to help creatures to prosper in their day-to-day lives. And so it may be for waiting. It has, or can have, a benign purpose if managed. But if mismanaged, just like any other emotion, it can harm. Like all other emotional states, waiting can be experienced for better and for worse. But it aims to assist, and it certainly did assist Alan Rabinowitz.

And speaking of Alan Rabinowitz, what did happen finally between him and that jaguar in Belize? Let's hear Rabinowitz's own words:

> The jaguar never took his eyes off me. . . . I remembered the feeling I had staring into the face of the jaguar so many years

earlier as a child at the Bronx Zoo . . . in the eyes of this jaguar there was only wildness and strength. I leaned forward a little, as I had so often by the cage at the zoo. "It's alright now," I whispered. It's going to be alright."

And it was. Waiting was something that Alan Rabinowitz learned through the hardship of his childhood. The lessons derived from the hardship hadn't left him as an adult. The childhood experiences offered Rabinowitz the ability to confront the jaguar. He didn't bolt, but he waited and then he whispered. The jaguar left this environmental Indiana Jones alone. They both went home to their separate dinners rather than sharing one. I wonder, if we were able to wait like Alan Rabinowitz, whether we'd enjoy comparable advantages? And from what? Not from jaguars, but in our daily lives. Maybe, as I've just been suggesting, waiting could help us because there's an evolutionary advantage to be had from this capacity for waiting—but just how waiting might be a good evolutionary idea in our daily lives is something we haven't looked at yet. I'll do this in the next chapter. The focus will be on pairs and on waiting, as they relate to the family, to children, and to friendship. As far as evolution goes you can't get more basic experiences than these. Families allow us to protect our young, and the young protect our species. Friends provide protective nets for both families and for children. I'll try to show you just how important waiting is for these sorts of relationships. We'll see once more how central serotonin is for waiting, and the possibilities it and waiting can offer for such pairing relationships. Vervet monkeys turn out to be at the heart of things. Monkeys?

PAIRS

3

HALL PORTER SENF'S WIFE

IS IN LABOR

Childbirth, Friendship, Marriage, and Waiting

The scene is in one of the metropolis' finest hotels. The exchange happened in 1929.

"What was it?" asked the operator of the switchboard, earphones over his head and red and green plugs between his fingers.

"They've suddenly taken my wife to the hospital. I don't know what that means. She says it's beginning. But, good heavens! It can't have got that far already."

The operator was only half listening. He had a call to put through. "Well, don't worry, Mr. Senf," he said. "You'll have a fine boy first thing in the morning—"

The young and blonde-haired Mr. Senf is the Hall Porter of Berlin's Grand Hotel. In those days there was no time off for being a good husband or for being a concerned parent, especially in an important hotel. Nor, if they managed to get there, were fathers allowed beyond hospital waiting rooms. You could even smoke cigarettes or celebratory cigars or a pipe with your coffee as you stayed in those waiting rooms.

"Just so. And when the baby's here I'll ring through," said the operator absentmindedly and carried on with his calls. The

> porter took off his cap and went off on tiptoe. He did this unconsciously because his wife had been taken to hospital and was about to have a child . . . he exhaled deeply and ran his hands through his hair. He was surprised to find them wet, but there was no time to wash his hands. After all, the routine of the hotel could not be upset because Hall Porter Senf's wife was having a baby.

Mr. Senf will be waiting for a very long time and no one seems very much to care. Friendship really does seem to be in short supply, if you work in the Grand Hotel. We meet Senf next at the end of his shift.

> Hall Porter Senf . . . was relieved by the night porter at about eleven, and went off half-dazed to the hospital, in such a state of anxiety that his teeth chattered. On arriving there he was sent home by an unfriendly night nurse, who told him that it would be twenty-four hours till the baby was born, but this, of course, was his own affair and did not concern the hotel.

It will be a long and worrying wait. Will the baby be well? Will the mother be well? Babies and marriage, they are perhaps the most waiting experiences that we, or Mr. Senf, can have. In his own anxious and modest manner Hall Porter Senf acts as a model for the well-intentioned parent and partner. His capacity to wait is surely tested, but not his desire to do the best, by waiting, for his wife and for Baby Senf.

Vicki Baum appears to have thought so too. We learn about Hall Porter Senf at the very beginning of her 1929 novel, *Grand Hotel*. It is a book all about waiting, good versions and bad versions. There is the famous Madame Grusinskaya, the aging ballerina who is waiting for her fame to return. Greta Garbo (Figure 3.1) plays her in the 1932 Oscar winning movie version of the book and Grusinskaya is not such a good waiter at all.[1] "I want to be alone," she impatiently proclaims in the movie. Greta Garbo looks for all the world like you'd imagine that chaperone from Degas' pastel *Waiting*, if she'd the chance to dress up again as a ballerina and to try to recreate her days of hope and expectation. Or could it be that Gru is the young dancer grown older? What can she be waiting for as she reclines on the floor in her amazing tutu?

I'll come back to the likable Mr. Senf, but not Madame Grusinskaya. For now, I'd like to shift well away from Berlin and go right back into the jungle, but this time not to Belize, but to those where vervets live. Just like Mr. Senf, vervets are very familiar with waiting. They can also tell us a great

FIGURE 3.1. Holding On. Greta Garbo as Madame Grusinskaya in the movie *Grand Hotel*, 1932. Suedeutsche Zeitung Photo/Alamy Stock Photo.

deal about the science of marriage and rearing babies, if not necessarily life in hotels during the Weimar Republic. This is because vervet monkeys, just like the Hall Porter, care very much for their families—and for their friends. They are virtuosos of affiliative interaction.

Monkeys, vervet monkeys, like Hall Porter Senf, are hard not to enjoy. They are not built like Senf, but are engagingly small, about 20 inches (for males) to about 16 inches (for females). They have appealing black faces, ears, hands, and feet. Even the tip of their tails is black. With their turquoise blue scrota, the males are riotously easy to spot.[2] Their body hair is grey, and these friendly little beasts are mostly vegans. The vervet monkey does no one any harm, even when they exercise their fondness for alcohol.[3] These boozy monkeys come mostly from southern Africa, but they've been introduced to the southerly states of the United States (which is where they learned to drink, I suspect), to much of the Caribbean, as well as Ascension Island and Cape Verde. Vervets look like they'd make amusing pets, but I am not so sure that this is very common. Just like humans, these monkeys live in social groups, but their groups are larger, ranging from 10 to 50 or so individuals. Vervets miss their families and their friends in captivity, and they tend to pine. They can become victims to hypertension and to anxiety, just like me. Within their bands they are said to communicate actively, calling to one another, I have read, by chirping and chittering. Vervets scream and squeal when they are in danger.

Where marriage, babies, and friendship, and vervets are concerned, the capacity to exploit the experience of waiting well turns out to be very important. That's the idea that I'll try to explain. It's a very simple one: for marriage, for looking to babies, and for friendship it appears to be the case that you won't bother staying with your partners, babies, and friends—*wait* for them I mean—unless you've had a lot of practice. Strangely enough in the case of the vervets, that practice doesn't seem to depend on the specific partner, baby, or friend. It's provided by the community in which the creature lives and by its expectations and habits. This is how it is for the loyal little vervet, especially with their young. They worry over their babies, these vervets, just like the Hall Porter. The females are a long time pregnant and they are a long time looking after their babies. In the southern hemisphere the vervets breed from April to June and their pregnancies last for five and a half months. These end with one pink-faced and black furred baby. The babies suckle for about four months.[4] Weaning can take up to a year—that is as long a wait as for humans. Vervet mothers can be just as clingy with their babies as humans. Some of them won't allow young females, or even other adult females, to hold or carry their children. But it's true that others, again like humans, are sharing of their baby's company. Vervets like their babies very much and their babies will form bonds with their troop that last throughout their short lives. These bonds seem to be linked closely to all of the waiting that they do as they wait for their children to mature.

The long pregnancies and the long rearing periods experienced by vervets require stable groups. Adult females, young females, and their children make up this primate family and the males seem to come and go. Female children stay for their lives within this feminist band. The group appears to center around an adult female. It sounds for all of the world like the Ekdahl family from Uppsala in Ingmar Bergan's 1982 movie *Fanny and Alexander* (remember Jenny Didier? She was Fanny). One of the most important ways by which stability in vervet troops is established is through what is termed affiliative grooming (soon to be affiliative interaction). And this is precisely how the community provides the monkeys with their impressive ability with babies and with friendship. It is afforded in the oddest of waiting manners—through the grooming of the fur of other vervets within their group.[5] Vervets are said to pass several hours each day waiting around and performing this strange version of hair combing. They remove muck and crawling things from one another's bodies—just about anything that might mess up their handsome fur. This endearing waiting practice appears to encourage both calm and loyalty. What is a little more unexpected is that this practice minimizes impulsivity in vervets, a habit that is as useful in Berlin as it is in Cape Verde or in Uppsala. Grooming also reflects status and hierarchy. What's more and what's very important is that grooming is linked to the production of the neurochemical serotonin. M. J. Raleigh and his research group demonstrated as far back as 1980 that stability among vervet groups was related to elevated serotonin levels, and that this stability could be diminished by artificially lowered serotonin.[6] Grooming then seemed less prevalent. All of this waiting around to be groomed seems to make the vervets happier and, paradoxically, all the more capable of the waiting that is needed for the maintenance of their long-term dependent babies and of the friendly communities that will look to them. It's that virtuous circle again.

The more grooming a monkey receives the more satisfactory is its level of serotonin. The grooming and the serotonin encourage impulse control and the capacity to display patience and to manage the experience of waiting in a manner that is beneficial both to individuals and to the group. The grooming works in two directions. This is genuinely surprising. While grooming may benefit the one groomed, it also benefits the groomer. A Japanese team comprising M. Ueno, K. Yamada, and M. Nakamichi, who worked with a different but similar primate group, the Japanese macaques, have found that anxiety levels decrease after giving grooming to affiliated partners *and* after receiving grooming.[7] Lower levels of anxiety are to be expected where higher than normal levels of serotonin become possible. Giving grooming to affiliated partners is a gift to both the groomer and to the groomed. This Japanese team links the decrease in anxiety firmly to beneficial levels of serotonin. It's easy to see how this capacity to wait, this minimizing of anxiety, benefits the group. The stability that affiliative grooming and its resulting serotonin enables seems to create a very safe world in which the little vervet can function.

Affiliative grooming does more than keep these monkeys calm, loyal, and cautious of impulsive behavior. It seems also to keep the vervets loyal to their groups and to their children during the long period of their gestation and nurture. It encourages the production of the neuromodulator serotonin and, with it, the capacity to exploit and manage waiting. Affiliative grooming helps the vervet with the skills required for the long haul of managing babyhood. The grooming and the resultant serotonin seem to be the grease in the moving mechanism of vervet society. It enables mating, family groups, and even a stable hierarchy. It appears to produce a very pacific world and one in which Mr. Senf might have enjoyed himself more than in Weimar Berlin at the Grand Hotel. It is a world that is very comfortable with waiting—or at least it is better at waiting than many others. How, we must ask next, is this world like that of humans and what does this say of marriage and friendship and of human babies?

And now a skerrick of an answer to that question. The seventeenth-century painting *A Mother Delousing Her Child's Hair* (Figure 3.2) gives a clear sense, within a human setting, of some of the elements of the grooming and the cooperative behavior that are displayed by the vervet monkeys. The painting is of a Dutch mother grooming her daughter. In this instance the mother is removing head lice from her little girl's hair in a manner that can't be too different from that which a vervet would employ.

The family pair in this seventeenth-century room needs to be able to wait. It's especially true for the little girl, whose almost affectionate waiting is mirrored in the calm of the small dog who looks like she's waiting to get out that half-open back door and into the relaxing sunlight. How does the child wait so calmly and, apparently, with such stillness? Perhaps she enjoys being so close to her mother. But the process of delousing cannot be much fun. It is tedious and can entail pinching and scratching. It can be painful, and it has to be repeated often. Nor can the experience be fun for the mother—it's her "duty" as the alternate title for the canvas tells. The long-term payoff for the pair for this sort of affiliative grooming is a strengthening of family ties. But there can't be any immediate reward for waiting through the delousing. To wait through an event like this with such equanimity would require the heightened serotonin levels we've been talking about with the vervets.

Affiliative grooming is common enough in all families, but, thanks to more effective methods for lice control, the version in de Hooch's painting mightn't be quite as common as it was in the seventeenth century. Where it does occur, I doubt that affiliative grooming ever occupies the same amount of time as it did in the seventeenth century either.

FIGURE 3.2. Affiliative grooming in humans. Pieter de Hooch (1629–1684), *A Mother Delousing Her Child's Hair*, known as "A Mother's Duty," around 1658–1660. Oil on canvas, w 610 mm × h 525 mm. Rijksmuseum, Amsterdam. On loan from the City of Amsterdam (A. van der Hoop Bequest). Photograph courtesy of the Rijksmuseum.

But affiliation, though without grooming, plays just as important a role among humans as it did in the days of Pieter de Hooch and as it does among vervet troops. Nowadays we'd speak of affiliative behavior, rather than the extravagant affiliative grooming. What is affiliative behavior? In humans it may be most easily understood through its association with friendship. The slow waiting that's connected with serotonergic emotions such as long-term pairing becomes quite clear when you look, without hurrying, at friendship. I'll be stressing here the obvious, if sometimes neglected, relationship between friendship and marriage such as that which the Hall Porter of the Berlin Grand Hotel enjoys. Infatuation and romantic love, which are usually understood as the basis, even the continuative basis, for modern marriage, are grounded on a rather transient and dangerous dopamine surge.

Lauren Brent, a young and prolific biologist working in the Centre for Animal Behavior at the University of Essex in the United Kingdom, leads a team that have produced a fascinating paper with the intriguing title of "The neuroethology of friendship."[8] Her work has a lot to say about the role of affiliative behavior and in the friendships that can exist in humans like Pieter de Hooch's duo as well as in animals like the vervet. Her paper also tells us a lot about the importance of waiting in friendship, although that is only incidental to her research. It's the initial definition of friendship provided by Dr. Brent that I find so helpful. Her definition makes it a lot easier to understand the vervets, but it makes it significantly easier to understand Pieter de Hooch and Mr. Senf. It also makes it easier to understand waiting and marriage and childbearing in the non-vervet world. Brent's and her team's definition is phenotypical. By this descriptor is meant that their definition of friendship is based not on how friends may feel, but rather on the observable characteristics or traits of creatures said to be friends. So it is that their definition is not grounded on the apparent observation of such imponderable, unrecordable, though real enough attributes of friendship such as affection, esteem, or reciprocity. Rather it is grounded on what characteristics are displayed by creatures that seek out one another's company. Lauren Brent's phenotypical description appears to work as well for animals as it does for humans—though without overstressing, or ignoring, the other-worldliness of vervet grooming.

This is how Lauren Brent understands friendship: friends are "pairs of individuals that engage in bi-directional affiliative (nonaggressive, non-reproductive) interactions with such frequency and consistency so as to differentiate them from non-friends... friends engage in affiliative interactions considerably more often and over greater periods of time." For me the most arresting part of the definition of friendship is how she places a handle on affiliation. Brent tells us "affiliation can include spending time together, conversing, vocalizing, grooming [no getting away from the admirable vervet], huddling, cooperatively foraging, and sharing food, as well as forming alliances against others." For humans I presume that cooperative foraging, the only one of these elements that seems on first sight to be a non-human habit, must entail such things as shopping together or even cooking together. Why not? But perhaps—and this is maybe more important—it may also entail, for humans, working together. The workplace is the basis for so many long-lasting friendships. And "forming alliances against others?" This is an aspect of friendship that we tend, perhaps churlily, to ignore. But, in my experience, it is at the very heart of friendship, for better or worse. We all like to plot, in my experience, and, more importantly, we rely on our friends for protection against those who would plot against us, especially when we are foraging around at work. Brent and her colleagues continue: "friendly interactions are non-reproductive so as to include sex that occurs in a non-reproductive context, as in bonobos." That was news to me, that bonobo chimps practice non-reproductive sex, just like humans (and married, paired up humans for that matter). The line between a sexual relationship based on friendship and love is so blurred as to be almost meaningless. Let's just stay with friendship. That's what Brent and her team appears to believe as well: "we acknowledge that reproductive and non-reproductive sex between heterosexual partners can be difficult to differentiate in practice." Amen to that. The species would rapidly vanish into a boring pit of indifference if all sex had to be strictly reproductive, though this is not necessarily the case for animals ("males and females that interact when the female is sexually receptive but not otherwise are not friends"). Brent and her friendly colleagues conclude their definition by suggesting, "sexual partners that consistently engage in affiliative interactions over time are friends (by this definition, married couples are often friends, which fits with folk wisdom that spouses should be best friends)." I'd add one last category to Brent's friendly cairn of wisdom. Kin can engage in bi-directional affiliative interactions just as much as non-kin. Your siblings may certainly be your best phenotypical friends. If that's to happen, kin or non-kin, you are going to have to spend an awful lot of time hanging around and waiting as you spend time together, converse, groom, huddle, forage, share food, and form alliances against your competitors.

Does all of this phenotypical hanging around encourage the production of serotonin? Does serotonin, as well as waiting, play a role in human friendship? Are serotonin levels encouraged as much by affiliative human *interaction* as they are by the vervets' affiliative *grooming*? Lauren Brent doesn't believe that there is a definitive experimental proof for this yet. She states: "the molecular processes underlying the association between serotonin and sociality are little understood and will require concerted future research efforts to disentangle." The less cautious Dominik Schoebi, a psychologist from the University of Fribourg, asserts that his team's experimental data supports "the contention that the serotonin system influences affective responses to social stimuli."[9] This is in humans. And even the skeptical Lauren Brent notes:

> Much of the work on serotonin, on the other hand, has been at the phenotypic level, exploring the association between serotonin and social behaviors. . . . The majority of research on the correlates of serotonin points to links between this neuromodulator and sensory inputs, including social stimuli. This has led to the proposition that serotonin modulates how individuals perceive and respond to social information.

There's a way to go yet, but it seems likely that affiliative interaction obtains, for paired-up humans, access to beneficial levels of serotonin. And then, in the reverse, the heightened serotonin assists the function of affiliative interaction. All of this displays itself through waiting.

Hall Porter Senf and his anxious, but endearing apprehension for his wife and for his soon-to-be born baby might be thought of as exhibiting affiliative interaction. Senf's waiting, his concern, and his friendship may represent the vital lubrication within the marital mechanism. It seems likely enough that serotonin and its capacity to encourage waiting are behind Senf's actions. It also seems that this sort of waiting behavior is as important for the stability of human marital and parenting relationships as it is for those of vervet monkeys. Waiting for marriage and waiting within marriage, waiting for babies, we might as well speculate, could be a form of torture without the assistance of serotonin. It looks like marriage (I am not referring necessarily to the legal or necessarily to the traditional gendered version here, just to long-term pairing) acts unsurprisingly as another variant of affiliative interaction. It's fostered and characterized by benign waiting.

Spencer Tracy, the two-time Academy Award winning actor, offers a real-life example that both tests and displays what I am trying to make clear.[10] Tracy began his very famous career in Hollywood about the same year that Hall Porter Senf was waiting for his baby to arrive in Berlin. Tracy, married to Louise Treadwell Tracy and later simultaneously paired up with Katharine Hepburn, offers another commentary on the experience of waiting in partnerships. How much the story of this trio and the Tracy's children can tell us about waiting and serotonin remains for you to decide. But their story is one that tested marital and partnerly waiting to within an inch of its existence and it's one Senf would have not wanted to understand at all. Listen to the enduring Louise Treadwell Tracy speaking here about a decade and half after the events at the Grand Hotel in Berlin: "I've repeatedly told him to go out with other people," she says of her film-star husband. "Occasionally he's gone out with some of the girls he's worked with. I haven't minded, because he always told me about it," she continued. "I can't truthfully say that Spencer and I are still madly, passionately in love with each other. I don't believe that kind of love ever lasts. But in its place comes a deep understanding, companionship and devotion."

Spencer Tracy met his future wife in early March 1923. Louise had joined the Leonard Wood Players in White Plains, New York, as a leading lady. She met Tracy in the same company, and they were married very soon after on September 12, 1923, in Cincinnati, Ohio. Tracy was 23 and Treadwell was 27. The first of their two children, John, was born almost nine months later. When John was 10 months old Louise discovered that he was totally deaf. She'd accidentally slammed a door near his crib, and it had not disturbed the boy in the least. In the summer of 1930, the year of the *Grand Hotel* movie, Spencer Tracy went to Hollywood to make his first film. John and Louise followed while Spencer was filming. On the return train journey back to New York, John, now aged six, suffered infantile paralysis. It seems to have been at this time that the remnants of the early marital dopamine began to be replaced by duty and, who knows, by a serotonergic capacity to wait. It looks to me like waiting was very important. A second child, Louise "Susie" Treadwell Tracy, was born in July 1932.

The Roman Catholic Spencer Tracy, by the time of Louise Treadwell Tracy's statement concerning understanding, companionship, and devotion, had begun his series of sexual infidelities with well-known actors—among others, Loretta Young, Joan Crawford, Myrna Loy, Ingrid Bergman, Gene Tierney, and with Katharine Hepburn. By the late 1930s, Spencer Tracy had begun to spend much of his time living in hotels rather than at home with his wife. It becomes even more difficult to say whether Louise Treadwell Tracy was telling the truth when she refers to "deep understanding . . . and devotion." But her words have the ring of sincerity, at least from her side of the marital duo. And who knows, perhaps Spencer Tracy and Louise Treadwell Tracy had shared enough interaction already to last them throughout any normal marriage. Spencer Tracy never divorced his wife. He kept on waiting. About a decade into their marriage Spencer Tracy responded to rumors of a parting between Louise and him like this: "If there is any blame to be attached, it is mine. Mrs. Tracy and I are still excellent friends, and perhaps living apart for a while will lead to a reunion." It certainly didn't lead to a split.

And, technically speaking, he never left her. He never ceased to support Louise and the children financially. It feels cheap to characterize their marriage merely as a compound of duty (on Spencer's side) and caution (on Louise's side). If I were gambling, I'd bet on the truth of Louise Treadwell Tracy's words.

Katharine Hepburn was also in the frame. Tracy and Hepburn worked together in 1941 and 1942 on the movie *The Woman of the Year*. They began their famous "marriage" that same year. Listen to Katharine Hepburn describe their encounter: "I found him irresistible—I would have done anything for him." But not marry him: "I was perfectly independent, never had any intention of getting married. I wanted to paddle my own canoe." Hepburn could wait and she did for their 26 years. They were friends in the same manner as Lauren Brent would have described it: they practiced an affiliation that involved "spending time together, conversing, vocalizing . . . huddling, cooperatively foraging, and sharing food, as well as forming alliances against others." Katharine Hepburn stayed loyal to a friend and probably didn't get much of a reward for it—beyond that friendship. When Spencer Tracy's health began to falter during the 1960s Katharine Hepburn took five years off from her own screen work to wait and to care for him. Tracy, though still married, had his own house by this time, and Hepburn moved in with him. She was there on June 10, 1967, when he died. She was asked, after Tracy's death, why she'd stuck with him so tightly and for so long. She responded: "I honestly don't know. I can only say that I could never have left him." Katharine Hepburn was a vervet. But so was Spencer Tracy. Perhaps he was more like Mr. Senf than we'd ever have imagined.

Louise Treadwell Tracy, a super vervet, was a woman to whom history may be kinder than to her actor husband Spencer, despite his seven nominations and two Academy Awards (not too many people these days watch *Boys' Town* and *Captains Courageous*, Tracy's two winners). While Spencer Tracy made 75 Hollywood movies (nine of them with Katharine Hepburn), Louise Treadwell started the first deaf school in Los Angeles. It was named after her son. It was designed for their son, John, and, to start with, was funded by Spencer Tracy's acting career. Not only did she provide her son John with opportunities often denied to the deaf, but she shared them with her community by starting this clinic. Louise received seven honorary degrees for her role in the foundation of the clinic. It is still going strong, 80 years later. The John Tracy Clinic these days describes itself as a "private, non-profit education center for infants and preschool children with hearing loss . . . it provides free, parent-centered services worldwide... the Clinic offers worldwide family services, local family services, professional education, preschool, hearing testing, and more." In 1963, Louise was appointed to the Neurological and Sensory Disease Advisory Committee of the federal Department of Housing, Education, and Welfare. Two years later she was appointed to the National Advisory Board of the National Technical Institute for the Deaf in Henrietta, New York. In the same year she agreed to a four-year term as a member of the National Advisory Council on Vocational Rehabilitation. Two years after her husband's death she accepted membership on the President's Task Force on the Physically Handicapped.

If ever there was a story about waiting in the world of affiliative interaction, the story of the two Tracy's, Katharine Hepburn, John, and Susie is it. Louise and Spencer stayed married until his death, for more than 40 years, an act of powerful waiting. Tracy poured money into his children for all of those years, and financially and socially didn't neglect Louise. Katharine Hepburn stuck with Tracy until his death as well, for 26 years. There must have been a lot of Mr. Senf in Spencer to earn this sort of serotonergic loyalty. Through it all Louise remained devoted to her children and to the disabled John, her first child. From his side, it seems that Spencer never stinted. It's a testing story about the power of waiting. It's testament to role of waiting in marriage, in friendship, and parenting. Each of the three adult players comes out well from this unusual story. But the two women, Louise and Katharine, never became reconciled to one another. A few days after Spencer's death Katharine called Louise to seek reconciliation. She's claimed to have said: "You know, Louise, you and I can be friends. . . . You knew him at the beginning, I at the end. I might be a help with the kids." Louise's response? "Well, yes. But you see, I thought you were only a rumor." The rebuff stands to reason. There'd never been any affiliative interaction between the two women.

Does partnership and friendship require fidelity, or does it need more loyalty and understanding? The strange marriage (and marriage is but a subset of friendship) between Spencer Tracy and Louise Treadwell Tracy, and the equally strange relationship between Spencer Tracy and Katharine Hepburn that came to coexist alongside the legal marriage (Tracy and Hepburn's friendship lasted steadily and decorously from 1942 to his death in 1967), both seem to have been admirable in their way, though unconventional. Both were defined and fueled by waiting. And both, over the long haul, seem to exhibit the traits that we've come to associate with Hall Porter Senf and those bibulous vervets. I believe that these two unusual relationships exhibit marriage and friendship and waiting in the most remarkable and unexpected of manners. Friendship in marriage really may require loyalty and understanding more than fidelity. Serotonin may help too.

One year after Spencer Tracy set off to start his career in Hollywood, Alice Neel lost her baby. I am sure that Spencer Tracy knew nothing of the theft. Alice Neel wasn't famous yet. The lost baby is one of saddest stories that you can think of. The tale highlights one of the more sorrowful aspects of waiting and of the lack of affiliative interaction. It was Alice Neel's artist and aristocrat husband from Cuba, Carlos Enriquez Gomez, who removed her daughter Isabetta (named officially Isabella Lillian). This was not Alice Neel's first brush with infant misfortune. Her first child, Santillana, was born the day after Christmas in Havana in 1926. One month before her first birthday Santillana died of diphtheria. Alice became pregnant with Isabetta soon after Santillana's death. Isabetta was born on November 24, 1928, in New York City. A year and a half later Enriquez intended for them to go to Europe to Paris. Isabetta was to stay with his parents. Short of money, he went alone and left the baby in Havana and his wife in Colwyn, near Philadelphia, with her parents. He didn't get as far as the Grand in Berlin. Alice Neel, ever waiting, had now lost two children and a husband. She suffered a severe nervous breakdown and unsuccessfully attempted suicide. She waited in the suicide clinic of the Philadelphia General Hospital for a year. She made in 1931 a harrowing and well-known sketch of the place entitled *Suicidal Ward, Philadelphia General Hospital*, 1931.[11] It's easy to find on the Internet.[12]

Alice never did get her daughter back. She was brought up by Enriquez's family. Isabetta visited and stayed with Alice Neel in 1934 and 1939 (the last meeting "for many years"). Alice Neel painted her "lost daughter" in 1934/5 (*Isabetta* aged six). She seems, for all that, to have had a close relationship with her two sons and their grandchildren. Alice Neel had her own mother living with her in the last year of her mother's life. She also painted her first granddaughter, Olivia (also aged six, as *Olivia in a Red Hat*, 1974). Olivia adopts a matching pose to that of Isabetta from 1934, 40 years previous. It feels as if Alice had never stopped waiting. She became, in passing, one of the greatest of the American portrait painters of the 20th century and definitely someone Spencer Tracy would have known about. Her paintings are infused with images of parents, of mothers (sometimes pregnant), and children. Many, many of them seem to be waiting. Alice Neel appears to have transformed the pain of her loss and her waiting—of waiting for birth and then waiting for the return of her family—into great art. *Margaret Evans Pregnant*, the painting I'd like to highlight here, represents one of her haunted, waiting mothers.[13] The waiter, Margaret Evans, was born in 1944. She was painted 51 years after Santillana died.

In Alice Neel's *Margaret Evans Pregnant* the subject is painted naked and bare-footed. Eight months pregnant with twins, Margaret Evans is seated uncomfortably on a very small and narrow stool. She grasps the edges of the stool with both of her hands as if to guarantee her stability and safety. It feels like she could fall off at any moment. The frozen, round blue eyes of Margaret Evans stare from her small expressionless face on its long neck. They appear to have many parallels in the reproductions of waiters within this book. Margaret looks without emotion at the painter, perhaps waiting for the vulnerable ordeal of posing without clothes on this narrow stool to be over, and perhaps waiting for some sort of response from Alice Neel. Margaret Evan's blurred shadow shows on the wall behind and to her right. There's also a double in the painting. This is Margaret Evans' reflection in the mirror positioned just behind her. It seems that the double, the woman in the mirror with her back to us, is also waiting for some sort of a response. Is that why there is the tear-like line on the double's right cheek? "The reflected image," maintains the artic critic Jeremy Lewison, "[and] the features in the reflection appear to be a combination of [Alice Neel's] and Evan's." The double, in other words, may be the painter herself, as well as her subject. So, while it is true to say that as this is a painting and that the response never comes from the double, Alice Neel could speak.[14]

I wish I could have shown you this painting. You could say that the painting still has me waiting. I was able to get permission for a reproduction of *Margaret Evans Pregnant* from its current owner, but not from the managers of the copyright to the painting. Too bad. That's why you'll have to make do with my awkward rendition of the image. But if you want to see the painting for yourselves, it's easily available online. Maybe there is more that's difficult about dealing with Alice Neel than I had anticipated. One of my friends backs this suspicion up. He promises me that he proposed to his wife on the property of Alice Neel's summer house in Spring Lake, New Jersey. (The marriage alas was not a waiter.) My friend also reckons that the property was haunted. Perhaps Alice Neel is still waiting in Spring Lake where she spent many summers and where she seems to have painted *Olivia in a Red Hat* looking just like Isabetta.

For those reasons, this might be the place to mention serotonin again. There can be unexpected complications relating to the operation of serotonin and to the waiting that it can encourage—to the families and friendships that it can assist. It is possible, and this is surprising, that too much serotonin, just as is the case for too much waiting, can act in a deleterious manner. Serotonin can go sour. It can make you agitated and restless, uncoordinated and confused. There's an element of that in *Margaret Evans*. There must have been a lot of that in the young Alice Neel. Dr. Tomas Furmark, an expert in abnormal psychology from Uppsala University in Sweden, argued in 2015 that anxiety disorders (which apparently trouble 25 million or more Americans) might owe their genesis to an individual's propensity to produce too much serotonin.[15] This is particularly the case in anxiety disorders that exhibit themselves as social phobias (feeling embarrassed, inferior, and ill at ease in public surroundings). You could speculate, therefore, that too much waiting, and even affiliative grooming might go wrong and produce phobic vervets and do the exact opposite of what is needed within the group.

Waiting was what made Alice Neel such a great artist. That is clear from Neel's paintings such as *Margaret Evans Pregnant*. The theme and the representation come back again and again in her art. Why? What was this artistic vervet waiting for? The impossible return of her daughters, especially Isabetta, and perhaps even of her husband, Carlos, that practitioner of a form of painterly magic realism who ended up losing a hand-to-mouth combat with the hooch. There is a happy ending, though a muted one. Alice Neel became one of America's best-known artists and a model, as it were, for feminists. Her portrait of the feminist writer and activist

Kate Millett, reproduced for the cover of *Time* magazine, was commissioned in 1970, in Alice Neel's 70th year. Nine years later President Jimmy Carter presented Alice Neel with a National Women's Caucus for Art award for outstanding achievement. Success came to her after all of that waiting. She produced by the end of her life a large body of painting. Focusing above all on the expressions on people's faces, she is a realist in the spirit of Edward Hopper and of Edgar Degas. You could place her cheek to cheek with her exact and neglected contemporary François Barraud who also appears in this book.

Waiting came at a terrible personal cost. That's how it feels. Alice Neel mastered waiting and she mastered her art. But perhaps all of the waiting came at a price. In 1978 the 50-year-old Isabetta, the lost child, came to see her mother for the first time in a long time. This was at one of Alice's shows. This was in the same year as Alice completed the portrait of Margaret Evans. Alice didn't recognize her daughter, then or afterwards.[16] Four years later Isabetta took her own life. You can't argue for cause and effect after four years. But perhaps Isabetta wanted an end to all of this waiting too. Is misery the product of the extinction of the possibility of waiting, as Roger Grenier believes?[17] Is a confused heart, as Alice Neel sometimes seems to display, the product of too great an ability to wait? We'll never know the answer. But perhaps an ability to persist in hopeless waiting, is something that too much serotonin enables. We've already seen how waiters have this neuromodulator in shovelfuls. Waiting for Alice Neel, the reflection of her personal tragedy, made her the great artist that she was, but perhaps it unsettled her, emotionally. When it relates to pairing, waiting may reward and punish.

If too much waiting can freeze the emotional arteries and damage a person's ability for attachment, what could be said of the direct opposite? What happens when an attempt at attachment is made where there's no waiting and, I can only presume, there's no serotonin involved at all?[18] You could put it another way—is attachment possible where affiliative interaction is not required? For marriage, for looking to babies, and for friendship it appears to be the case that you won't bother staying with your partners, babies, and friends—*wait* for them I mean—unless you've had a lot of practice. This is the point that I've been making again and again. One of the most startling of places to look at waiting and pairing relates to sexbots. There has been a lot of talk in the last decade or so about the possibilities of human and android emotional and sexual relations. For many people the biggest attraction of a sexbot, a robot purchased for sex, is that there is no waiting at all. They are the perfect individuals, the bots I mean, for speed dating and, if you find it necessary, for speed coupling. But, without the waiting and without the serotonin, would a sexbot be satisfactory for the likes of Senf—not to mention the vervets? No waiting, no pairing. You could marry a sexbot, no doubt about it, but then why would you bother?[19]

If you spend a little time reading David Levy's very entertaining *Love + Sex with Robots: The Evolution of the Human Robot Relationship*, it becomes pretty clear that sex with robots is already big business and that it will become even bigger business in the future.[20] It seems that attachment without affiliative interaction, or waiting or serotonin, is becoming profitable. And why not? If sex is all you want, what could possibly go wrong with a sexbot, short of circuitry failure? According to the *Japan Times* as far back as April 14, 2015, the Chinese sex toy market was estimated at up to

100 billion Yuan (£10 billion) per year by the business-to-business sex toy platform ChinaSexQ.com.[21] I suppose that if those customers could move on from sextoys to sexbots, there would be a lot of money to be made. In the same *Japan Times* report, one sextoy manufacturer, Zhang Han, maintained that business will boom, because of the gender imbalance in China. The *Japan Times* points out, "in the face of a traditional preference for sons and the one-child policy in the world's most populous country, sex-selective abortion is common—albeit illegal—and almost 116 boys are born for every 100 girls in China, far above the global average of 107." Perhaps Zhang Han is onto a winner. There is also a group called "friends of dolls" who, I reckon, have encouraged Zhang Han's entrepreneurial optimism. "Friends of dolls," that *Japan Times* report claims, "gather on dedicated online forums, sharing user reviews and advice. Their numbers have risen from a few hundred to more than 20,000 in recent years."

David Levy is as sanguine about the future of this sort of sexual activity as is Zhang Han. Levy includes the term "love" in his book title, and he devotes many pages to the notion. Love in his book is usually linked, to be blunt, with what used to be called wanton fornication. What Levy's really trying to say is why couldn't a person become infatuated or even sexually rooted to a robot? My response would be, first, serotonin and, second, that these android relationships are not connected via the two-way street of affiliative interaction. No waiting, no serotonin, and there can be no affiliation. So it is with dolls and androids. You may feel all of the surge of dopamine when you first meet, and you may, who knows, feel a strong sense of affiliation after the surge was gone away, but this is not how your doll, or your android will feel. Nor will you if the bot breaks down. You'll just buy a new one. Affiliation, to really work, benefits both parties (the groomer and the groomed will benefit) and it simply cannot here, in this situation. For what it's worth, I'd say that while people may be naturally and understandably impatient to experience sex, they are also just as anxious to form partnerships. Such partnerships result efficiently only from affiliative interaction and "grooming" and from the free play of serotonin—from the capacity and the practice of waiting. No waiting, no pairing.

So, if you can't find sexual satisfaction, why not buy a doll or, better still, a robot-like Ava the android in the movie *Ex Machina*? Why sexbots? If it's true that the average man is said to think of sex during his waking hours about 19 times a day,[22] that he will spend 48 days of his life having sex, then maybe there is something to be said for sexbots, for men at least.[23] The 48 days might become 96. If sexual relief is all that is at issue, well, any port in a storm. But don't go expecting to find a friend this way.[24] There was an Argentinian shepherd a few years back who had sex with a scarecrow, then froze to death. The scarecrow was a bucolic android, you could say. The story, which I reproduce here, indicates that people will do just about anything to avoid waiting. But we know that this can have unexpected outcomes.

> A lonely shepherd has been found dead alongside a scarecrow he had apparently had sex with after dressing it up in a longhaired wig and lipstick. The rotting remains of Jose Alberto, 58, were discovered after neighbors called their local council to report the smell coming from his house in the city of San Jose de Balcare in eastern Argentina. Rodolfo Moure, a spokesman for the prosecutor's office, said . . . "we are working

on the assumption that the man died during sex with the scarecrow. Straw had been stuffed inside the old clothes that had been sewn together to make the scarecrow."[25]

That must have been terribly embarrassing for his family at his funeral, if he had one. Perhaps he didn't. And I doubt that the shepherd would have wanted to marry the *espantapájaros*. Have people at any point in history married simply for the sake of having sex on tap? I wonder if this is the acid test—would you ever kill yourself because of the impending obsolescence of your robot partner? Would you wait around for her or his battery pack to be repaired? Or would you chuck the android out and go and buy a new one? Who waits for sexbots? Or am I wrong, and you'd form a suicide pact with your failing android? It's hard to imagine that. If you can't wait you can't affiliate.[26] It's very hard to imagine anyone forming a suicide pact with a robot in the way that seems to have happened with Arthur Koestler and his wife.

*Mr. Senf, anxiously at work in Berlin as hall porter in the Grand Hotel in 1929, began this chapter. What happened? Was the news good or was it bad? You probably know the answer but not the details. Let's hear them.

> At eight o'clock the hall porter, Senf, came on duty. His face was puffy, for he had spent the whole night sitting in the cold hospital corridor waiting to hear whether his wife would survive till morning.

This time the night nurse had let Mr. Senf stay in the hospital. The Grand Hotel, however, did not release him from work. Duty, after all, is duty.

> [Then] the hall porter ran past. . . . His blonde and dependable sergeant's face was wet with perspiration as after some gigantic exertion. He came to stop behind his desk, as though he had reached a haven. . . . "It's a little girl. They had to induce the delivery artificially. But she is here and weighs five pounds. No danger at all now. None at all. Both of them are alive and kicking," he panted, and took his cap off.

Herr Senf made such a good job of things because he'd obviously experienced a lot of affiliative interaction at home with his wife. Where marriage, and babies, and friendship are at issue, as I have been saying, the capacity to wait turns out to be very important. It appears to be the case, for marriage, for looking to babies, and for friendship that you won't stay with them—wait for them I mean—unless you've had a lot of practice at affiliative interaction. But then, if you haven't stayed—waited—you won't have managed any affiliative interaction. You'll be no Senf.

4

HAPPINESS—IS IT JUST A MATTER OF WAITING TO MEET YOUR DOUBLE?

A Chapter on the Life and the Lore of Waiting and Fulfillment

JUST BEHIND THE SEATED MARGARET Evans in Alice Neel's portrait sits her double, her reflection in the mirror on the wall behind.[1] For Alice Neel the mirror image seems to be one more example of the isolation that confronts many of her subjects—and Alice Neel as well, for she has been identified with the double. The waiting, unapproachable double with her back turned may echo how Alice felt at the loss of her daughters and at her isolation after her husband Carlos abandoned her. Could it say something else, that she felt somehow cut off even from a part of herself? If Margaret Evans or Alice Neel were able to communicate with that image, that double, if they could break down the sense of loss, then maybe the waiting and the unhappiness would be over. Does the painting suggest this? Would happiness then be possible? Would that frozen face of Margaret

Evans melt? Alice Neel too? It's as if these double images offer another chance at happiness, that's if only you can somehow get through to them. But, of course, you can't.

Doubles play an unexpected and strong role in the lore, in the imagery, and in the life of waiting. Perhaps, we shouldn't be surprised by the prominence of doubles for waiting. Is this because waiting is an experience that's built on pairs? You wait for someone or for something and just sometimes they are just like you or just like some part of you that you're missing. Maybe if you can understand that double you can understand that part of yourself. Of course, this can't really happen, can it?

Richard Anthony Jones shows that it can. An African-American from Kansas City, Jones was jailed in May 1999 for the aggravated armed robbery of Tamara Sherer in front of the Roeland Park Wal-Mart. He was set free after waiting in jail, innocently it turned out, for over 17 years. That was on Thursday June 8, 2017. His case was handled by the Johnson County judge, Kevin Moriarty. Jones was successful with his latest appeal because, adjudicated Judge Moriarty, there was not enough evidence to sustain the conviction. In the court's view there was a complete lack of physical evidence, of DNA or fingerprint evidence to tie Jones to the crime. What's more, Jones lived right on the other side of town from where the robbery took place. In Kansas City? Wasn't that where Mr. Lawrence John Ripple robbed the Bank of Labor and then waited in its lobby for the police to come and arrest him, all just to get away from his depressing home life? What is it with waiting in Kansas City?[2]

Richard Anthony Jones didn't complain about his home life. But he did appeal his case several times. The alibi? He insisted that he was with his girlfriend and other family members on a different side of town the day of the robbery. Jones' guilt was assumed until—and I am not fooling you—he discovered his double. After all of that time waiting in jail, Richard learned in 2015 that there was another man with the same first name, Ricky, who was also locked up and who looked just like him. He was Jones' identical pair. Richard took a punt and got in touch with the Midwest Innocence Project ("a non-profit organization that provides legal services to the wrongly-convicted") and the Paul E. Wilson Defender Project at the University of Kansas. They didn't wait around at all and agreed to help him. It was Jones' identical pair, Ricky Amos, who got him off. The Innocence Project attorneys showed the pictures of Richard and Ricky to the victim, two witnesses, and to the prosecutor of Jones' case. You can imagine the dopamine surge that Mr. Jones' brain must have experienced when he heard that this was taking place. It must have been as powerful as the feeling experienced by the diver in Kōshirō Onchi's *Diving* as she plummets from the high tower in 1932. All four witnesses agreed that they couldn't tell the difference between the pair of Richards. This was enough for Judge Kevin Moriarty. He ruled to the effect that Richard Anthony Jones should be released from jail. "Mr. Jones was convicted solely on eyewitness testimony that has been proven to be inherently flawed and unreliable," claimed Jones' attorneys. I should say so. I'd also say that it's not too often that your double appears to save you from the villainy for which you've been falsely accused. Or not as often as you'd think. But what a blast of opioids and endocannabinoids there must have been let loose in Mr. Jones' head when he heard the verdict.

This happy-ending story shows that sometimes you really can get in touch with your double. It also shows how happiness can be a matter of waiting to meet your double. It really was for Richard Anthony Jones, and his case shows how this can sometimes be true, even if it was not the case for Margaret Evans and Alice Neel. Richard Anthony Jones is now a free man and happily ensconced with his girlfriend and family—I hope he's just as happy with his family as our Mr. Ripple is now. He seems to sound that way. "When it comes to my kids," Richard Jones told the *Kansas City Star* (the best paper in the US for waiting reports), "it's been a rough ride, but they are now at an age where they can understand." The good news didn't end here. The state of Kansas "will pay more than $1 million to compensate Richard Anthony Jones."[3]

Doubles may seem like a pretty off-the-track topic even for an off-the-track book like this one.[4] That's because doubles, doppelgängers, identical pairs, look-alikes, twins, shadows, clones, bioidenticals, identicals, duplicates, reduplicates, mirrors, whatever you want to call them, are rightly viewed as a strangely sensational and as a strangely unbelievable subject. That's what makes the Richard Anthony Jones story such a good one—and that it was reprinted in newspapers all over the world in 2017 demonstrates the point. The Kansas City story really does make it seem as if the world is full of a large number of people who are very keen to *hear* about other people like Richard Anthony Jones setting their eyes on their identical pair. The stories are especially popular if they have a happy ending (or a very sensational one, like Jose Alberto dying in the arms of his amorous scarecrow double in San Jose de Balcare). Doubling and happiness, strange to say, can be as much a part of the story and of the lore of waiting, and

HAPPINESS | 91

of pairing, as are marriage, bonding, and producing babies. What I'd like to try to show to you is that this unexpected aspect of the lore and the life of waiting, doubles and happiness, really does exist, on the page (culturally) and on the tongue (real life), and that it is a very common and unexpectedly popular topic and one of remarkable power. The double in *Margaret Evans Pregnant*, you could say, is not a one-off. So it is that happiness gained, and happiness lost, is part of the theme of this chapter, just as it was in the last one. I don't believe that Hall Porter Senf would have drawn any solace at all from the prospect of meeting his double. On the other hand, he might've been very pleased to have become the father of twins.

Right beneath your fingertips is a good place to locate the operation of the waiting life of the double. You'll discover, if you let your fingertips roam, that there is quite a trade existing on the Internet for finding your fulfilling double.[5] All that you need to do is to type hard enough and happiness will become yours. This digital trade seems to show that double hunters reckon that finding your mirror image out there in our world will make you more fulfilled and happier. But it has to be fast. You've got to cut back on the waiting. They seem to reckon that they've been waiting too long. This shows just how impatient are Internet hunters of the feared wait. There are now sites that will charge you money for the digital experience of looking in the mirror, of ending the wait, and of finding a friend who will appear comfortingly to be just like you. "I couldn't get over her face, and some of the expressions she would pull." That's from Niamh Geaney, then 26, a student and TV presenter from Dublin, Ireland. "I would think . . . 'Oh my God that's my face.'" Ms. Geaney developed a remarkable enthusiasm for searching out her own identical pairs after she found her first, Karen Branigan, living only an hour from her in Dublin. Since then, Niamh Geaney has found two more.[6] She's even had one of the doppelgängers DNA tested to see if they are related. They're not. Or, better, they are, but they're not. When Ms. Geaney looks in the mirror, she must wonder whether she's looking at herself or one of her three doubles. There is a technical name for seeing more than one image of yourself, at least in psychological circles. It is called polyopic heautoscopy and it is sometimes associated with the presence of a brain tumor. But it wasn't in Niamh Geaney's case. Seeing all of these doubles made her very happy and fulfilled, though I am not quite sure why. Now she's in a rush to share her experience with the rest of us. If you ask me, the more you avoid the wait the less happy you'll be.

Niamh's story doesn't end here. Ms. Geaney set up a Facebook page to cater to this perplexing interest in hurrying to look for your mirror pairs. Her idea was to enable people not to have to wait so long to find their doubles. To this point (as I am writing) she has over 360,000 Facebook followers. To cope with the pairs-happiness boom, and to end the wait, Niamh has now set up a website, the fascinating "Twin Strangers," that you can join for $3.95 and, by using it, you can look for your own personal shadow image. "Now we have over three quarters of a million users on the site and 'Twin Strangers' are connecting through it every day," explains Niamh using different figures from mine. Her hunters reckon that quickly finding your mirror image out there in our world and ending the wait will make you happier. Why else pay Niamh Geaney $3.95 to join her Facebook search site "Twin Strangers" to look for your own personal double? There are no reliable statistics to indicate how popular double hunting has become nowadays, but Niamh Geaney's website in the year 2017 gives you some idea of how much public interest there is in this pursuit.

But let's be clear. We're dealing here with a cultural motif, not necessarily with the truth. It might be fun to find your double. It might make you feel that if there are two or even three of you that, er, you must be more important that you'd thought. Will that realization make you happier? It did for Richard Anthony Jones in Kansas City. I doubt it will for the rest of us. We'll be more like Margaret Evans. But lots of people reckon that stopping waiting and finding your double really will make you more fulfilled and who wants to argue with them? Maybe that's why the Richard Anthony Jones story became so crazily popular.

In the world of digital doubles things are changing pretty fast. This is just as you'd expect in a dopamine world of high-tower online doubles diving. It begins to appear, however, that more is involved that simply a pursuit of happiness. Finding or even producing a double becomes confused with the self-affirmation I alluded to in the last paragraph. Or could it be that self-affirmation is a version of the happiness that can be achieved if only you can avoid waiting? Here's two examples. The latest version of the Google Arts & Culture app (latest when I was writing this in mid-February 2018—the original app minus the double-hunter was released in 2016) has a feature that will allow you to "scour more than 1,200 museums in over 70 countries to find one's art doppelgänger."[7] "Take a selfie and discover if your portrait is in a museum," the *Washington Post* quotes from the app-description. This feature became, for a time, a viral hit. For those out there who are more interested in dating than in galleries and in finding other people's doubles there's now Badoo. It's a UK-based dating app that will enable you to search for future partners and friends without having to wait too long—the gimmick is that the future partners are the identical pairs of your favorite celebrity. Once your waiting is over and once you've found your celebrity double you swipe, and you hope that this dating double will fool your friends and make you happy. Badoo uses facial recognition to create its large and growing roster of celebrity doubles. In a report in the *Guardian* the makers of the pop app claimed then to have "1,405 Ed-Sheeran-a-likes, 345 David Gandys, 975 Jake Gyllenhaals, 751 Idris Elbas and 342 Kylie Jenners on the platform, while the most searched-for celebrities in the UK are Cara Delevingne, Robert Pattinson, and Fearne Cotton."[8] Who are all of these people? Peter Toohey didn't feature at all. No fulfillment for him. All the same, I reckon that the logic of this app is easier to understand than "Twin Strangers." Waiting and doubles and happiness have teamed up again to create the strangest of cultural lore. Lore? Yes. I don't know anyone who has found a credible double.

Doubles and waiting and happiness—they crop up in the most unexpected of place. It's always exciting. There's always a shove to do away with the waiting. This is not the serotonin-steady world of Alan Rabinowitz. Sometimes cosmetic surgery caters thrillingly to doubles, waiting, and happiness. Rather than engaging in a tedious quest for their own or someone else's doppelgänger on Internet search engines, some people like to take it into their own hands, or their doctor's, and make doubles of themselves as fast as they can. They shape themselves into Badoo look-alikes. They may reshape their bodies along the lines of the features of other people, or comic book characters, or even dolls such as Ken and Barbie. They're waiting and at the end of their wait, they hope, will be the surpassing contentment of their perfect double and the money and fame that may follow. One very endearing group is known as "Plastics of Hollywood." Marcela Iglesias and her business partner Patrik have set up a talent agency to represent these "modified human beings." They explain that there will be a reality TV show made starring 12 human doubles "including Ken Dolls Rodrigo Alves[9] and Justin Jedlica, Jessica Rabbit imitator Pixee Fox, Kim Kardashian wannabe Jennifer Pamplona and alien lookalike Vinny Ohh." There are possibly others: "Britney Spears emulator Bryan Ray, transgender model Aria Veach, Pop-Artist Sham Ibrahim, Brazilian Ken Doll Mauricio Galdi [who as I write is aiming to have four ribs removed], "anime doll Ophelia Vanity and real-life elf Luis Padron."[10] Some of these plastics even redouble. They move on from their original duplicates to create newer versions of themselves. Pixee Fox, who started out with Jessica Rabbit, now has different ideas. She wants to look like a superhero and is waiting fully to change her looks and to create a series of books based on her own superhero double. To this end Pixee has undergone a string of operations—"four breast augmentations, two liposuction surgeries, brow and butt lifts, and an implant to change her eye color." The latest, carried out by specialist Dr. Park of ID Hospital in Seoul, Korea (a doubles ID specialist hospital?), was "a painful jaw operation to give her a pointed chin just like a comic book character." This is called the V-line surgery and, she believes, will "achieve a more symmetrical look and have a jawline that looked more like a super-hero. The jaw surgery will make my face look smaller which will make my eyes appear bigger." The procedure sounds terrifying: "I had my cheek bones reduced, the chin re-centered, the shaving down of my jaw then moved back into place so it was a complete face and bone reconstruction." Good luck, brave Pixee.[11]

Marcela Iglesias describes her doubles like this: "From surgery and procedures, the dolls have spent over three million dollars altering how they look. Justin Jedlica has $500,000 of that alone and Rodrigo's body is insured for one million dollars." Marcela has even more to explain: "I am amazed by people who can achieve certain looks or turn themselves into characters.... A lot of my dolls have lived in the wrong body for most of their lives and through changing their appearance they are able to fulfill their dreams.... Who am I to judge any of my dolls for accomplishing their dreams too."[12] But their pursuit of their doubles allows no place for waiting. I'm not sure how much happiness the hasty but very appealing Plastics achieve. May it be plenty.

It is almost a letdown to turn from the inspiring Plastics to the lore of doubling and alternative medicine. There are no heroes here. But it is true that alternative medicine can offer a variant on doubling, though one that is much less dramatic, though no less hasty than that of the surgeries of the Dolls. It offers us a therapeutic double under the oddest of all names, the bioidentical. The idea of doubling, or at least the allure that seems to attach to it, is behind the naming of an anti-aging and menopause treatment called bioidentical hormone therapy (BHT). It's as if anything that is identical (that doubles, we would say here) is good for you and will restore happiness and will quickly end the painful wait for conditions such as menopause to end—or for death to occur. "The idea," explains Tom Blackburn, "is that the hormones—derived from plants such as soybeans and custom-compounded by pharmacists for individual patients—are almost identical in structure to those produced in women's bodies. And because of that, advocates say, they are safer and more effective than the conventional hormone treatment."[13] The BHT works, it seems like, because it is a hormonal double, an identical pair of what already exists within humans. Who knows whether this pharmaceutical mirror really will end the wait and offer happiness and fulfillment just as Ricky did for Richard? But the timeless, multimillionaire actress Suzanne Somers, aged 71 in 2018, swears by it and she has written two best sellers on the topic. The titles of both books display an unexpected enthusiasm for haste: *Ageless* and *I'm Too Young for This*. Me too.[14]

There's probably not much truth in any of this—Internet doubles, reconstructed bodies, or bioidenticals. There's only the accidental good fortune of a man like Richard Anthony Jones of Kansas City. For the rest of the time it is Margaret Evans. But truth is beside the point when you're dealing with cultural lore and with cultural motifs. All that I'm attempting to show, put really simply, is that this cultural lore exists and that it is frequent enough to represent an important aspect of the life of waiting. Does it work? The late Roger Grenier, writer, journalist, radio animator (whatever that is), and Regent of the *Collège de Pataphysique* ("a society committed to learned and inutilious research"), makes a helpful point in his essay "Waiting and Eternity" concerning the dangers of this hasty pursuit of fulfillment that we've been discussing. His comments could apply as well to the titles of Suzanne Somers' books. Grenier generalized that "misery is when no more waiting is possible." He went on to observe, "Jean Paulhan in a September 1923 letter to Marcel Ponge, writes about . . . a missionary, I think it was Father Bridaine, who claimed that the damned never stopped asking 'What time is it?' and that a horrific voice never stopped answering 'Eternity!'" I suppose this also means that if you still have the ability and the capacity to wait, then you'll still have a run at happiness. In Hell there's no waiting, because there's no time, just eternity. I'd say that if I were to try to draw a moral concerning the doubles and happiness and the avoidance of waiting that we've just been contemplating, then it would relate to Roger Grenier's formulation. All of these hasty doublings are based on a yearning for happiness, or should I also say, a yearning for fulfillment, that is doomed to disappointment because of the impatience with waiting.[15] What time is it? What time *is* it?

Doubling stories that involve waiting aren't all the product of a yearning for fulfillment. Nor are they all the product of the downright misery that Richard Anthony Jones went through in prison for 17 years because of his wrongful conviction. They can be happy.[16] Doubles can sometimes capture the serotonin-based pleasure displayed by people like the blonde-haired father-to-be Hall Porter Senf. One of the most beautiful examples doubling that I've encountered is to be found in an anonymous seventeenth-century painting of twin sisters. This one comes from real life and, like Herr Senf's world, it's also about babies.

The Cholmondeley Ladies (Figure 4.1), explains the Tate Gallery's online commentary, has "an inscription in gold lettering to the bottom left of the painting . . . [stating] 'Two Ladies of the Cholmondeley Family, Who were born on the same day, And brought to Bed on the same day.'" Same day of birth and same day of mothering—that is remarkable coincidence; it's even a remarkable instance of happy doubling. Are the women identical twins, maybe real-life doubles? They're

FIGURE 4.1. Twin mothers waiting happily in bed. *The Cholmondeley Ladies*, c. 1600–1610. Unknown Artist, Britain. Oil paint on wood, 886 mm × 1723 mm. Presented anonymously in 1955. Tate Gallery, London. Photo Credit © Tate, London 2019.

twins of course, but the sister on the viewer's left is little larger (and heavier—look at her pillow) than the one on the right and her hands are placed differently. She is definitely graver (her eyes and her mouth are slightly more downturned; the twin sisters also have different eye color, one blue, one brown). The contrast in their dress and jewelry is noticeable too, once you look harder (the sister on the left has a more ornate dress and a weightier necklace, for example). But you really do have to look hard and more than thrice to notice these differences.[17] At first, second, and third glance, the sisters look like near identical twins to me—doubles, that is.[18] *The Cholmondeley Ladies* is an almost perfect evocation of contented waiting, of happiness, and doubles, and fulfillment. Those two almost identical women are in bed with their almost identical babies and they are waiting all together for something even better and happier to happen, even if it's only for the children to shut their bug eyes and to put an end to the waking sojourn. There must surely be life for these twin sisters beyond the cot, though they don't seem to me to mind one bit where they are right now. The happiness, for viewer and for subject, that is enframed in this picture is as much as anything the product of the sisters being twins and their so contended waiting. If Roger Grenier were to ask these women the waiting question, "what time is it?" they'd consult a clock of some variety and give Grenier the correct answer.

What is it about identical twins and waiting and happiness?[19] There are lots of stories about troubles occurring between twins, but it's the other way around just as much. The links between twins are often idealized, as we've seen with the Cholmondeley sisters. Perhaps that's why there is an annual twin's festival held in the United States. Twins, identical and non-identical, modern-day versions of the Cholmondeley sisters, attend from all over the world—that's after a year of waiting for the festival to be staged so that they can participate in the pairing activities and find even more fulfillment again. Called the Twins Days Festival, this weekend celebration of doubles and near doubles is held in Twinsburg, Ohio. The town was named after the identical twins Moses and Aaron Wilcox, who were early settlers of the hamlet. The year 2016 marked the 40th anniversary for the festival and it attracted more than 2,000 sets of twins to celebrate the Twins Days in Twinsburg, Ohio. The festival began in 1976 (a year in which, on September 10, two passenger jets collided disastrously over Zagreb) and is held annually on the first full weekend in August. Some people say that it is the biggest gathering of twins in the world. One regular attendee, who waits all year for this pairing jamboree, is quoted as saying that the main attraction for him of the Twins Days is "meeting people from all walks of life who understand what it's like having a double in the world."[20]

It makes sense that the life of identical twins is as prominent on the page as in lived life. There are many plays and movies about twins who've been separated. Although not all of them end with reunion and happiness, many of them do. The ancient Roman comic writer, Plautus, wrote a play in Latin in the second century BCE about two identical twins, called *The Brothers Menaechmi*. The play describes the separation and waiting of two now middle-aged brothers, both named confusingly Menaechmus. The identical twins had been separated at birth, with one ending up in Syracuse and the other ending up in what is now Durres in Albania (the port town is called Epidamnus in the play). The play ends the long wait for the reunion of the twins. They both move to Syracuse in Sicily, their birthplace, to spend the rest of their days together. Finding happiness by finding your twin double is also the theme of William Shakespeare's *A Comedy of Errors*. Little wonder, for the play, dated usually to the 1590s, is based on Plautus' original. There are two sets of identical twins in this play and they both finish up happily reunited after their wait at the end of the play in the Ionian city of Ephesus. My favorite twins mix-up, despite my profession (I try to teach Plautus regularly and the *Brothers Menaechmi* is one of the plays we read), is the 1942 *Palm Beach Story*. The movie has some echoes of Shakespeare's version of the theme. *The Palm Beach Story* was directed by Preston Sturges, the on-again off-again US director, who specialized in very funny screwball movies in the 1930s and in the early 1940s. Preston Sturges uses the motif of doubles, identical twins in this story, to bring his movie to a happy close after a long wait. Tom (Joel McCrea, one of the most serious money savers in Hollywood history—his waiting was all financial) and his wife Gerry (the beautiful Claudette Colbert—who was gay and spent much of her life waiting anxiously not to be outed) seem set to end their marriage after a period of waiting and trying—he's an engineer with impractical ideas and he's unable to support Gerry, who can't cook or sew, or so she complains. As the film unfolds, the mesmeric Gerry is pursued by the millionaire John D. Hackensacker III (played by Rudy Vallée who seems in real life, up until his downfall, to have waited for nothing, especially a party). His sister, the Princess Centimillia (the silent movie actor Mary Astor, who never in her life waited for anything either) is after Tom. But Tom and Gerry can't really live without one another. The solution is identical twins, and Tom and Gerry each have one. When the Hackensackers' pursuit of Tom and Gerry fails, they give up waiting and settle for the identical twins. ("I don't suppose you have a sister," asks Hackensacker. "Only a twin sister," replies Gerry. "Well, what's she doing." "Well, nothing. You see. . . .") The film ends with John D. Hackensacker III teamed up with Gerry's identical twin sister, and the Princess Centimillia with Tom's identical twin brother—getting married.[21] And they all lived happily ever after—or did they?

The lore relating to waiting, doubles, and happiness can be found in unexpected places. I wonder if it's not too farfetched to think of some planets as being identical twins. The vision of other earths, of other habitable planets just like ours, appears to be real enough and it is something that is in the news a lot. Could we think of these exo-planets as doubles of our own planet? More and more of these planets seem to be being discovered. Here's one. "Scientists have discovered what they believe to be a new planet, the closest one ever detected outside our solar system. It is a small rocky planet not unlike our own, orbiting the sun's closest stellar neighbor. Astronomers have long suspected that the star Proxima Centauri would be home to a planet, but proof had been elusive. Dim red dwarf stars like Proxima have been found to host billions of small, closely orbiting planets throughout the galaxy. Now a [recent] study ... provides the best evidence yet for a tantalizingly close target on which to seek alien life."[22]

That's the double. We've been waiting a long time to find a planet like this. But where's the happiness and where's the fulfillment? You could have asked the late Stephen Hawking. He claimed in 2017 on a BBC science TV show, *Tomorrow's World*, that we have 100 years to get off the earth and colonize a planetary Earth Double if the human species is to survive. If we wait too long a pandemic could wipe us out. That's the biggest threat according to Dirk Schulze-Makuch and David Darling in their book, *Megacatastropies! Nine Strange Ways the World Could End*. Or "carbon emissions [could] continue to fuel global warming which could unleash dangerous climate change." Dirk Schulze-Makuch from the Technical University of Berlin thinks Stephen Hawking is right, but that we should really hurry up with the colonization and stop waiting, if we are to find happiness with our planetary double. But he fears the twin life that the computer simulation of real life can produce may hold us back. Of this dangerous doubling Schulze-Makuch speculates: "I agree that we should colonize a planet within the next 100 years, but see a more mundane reason to get on with it: the risk posed by an increasingly virtual world. Why bother building a spaceship and making the arduous journey to Mars when you can experience anything in simulation?"[23] That new planet, one of the earthly doubles that we have so long awaited, becomes more and more attractive, more and more a possible source of happiness. There'll be no fulfillment with a life in a facsimile world. That would mean settling for the lore of doubles rather than the reality of doubles.

Let's hear another little report on life and planetary doubling. Does it entail happiness? You can be the judge? It certainly entails waiting. The story begins when Rhoda Williams crashed her car drunk after a party. She was just 17. This happened outside New Haven, Connecticut, in the summer of 2006. Of the four people in the car that Rhoda Williams hit, a couple and their two children, three were killed. This was a pregnant mother and her children, a boy and a girl. The father, John Burroughs, a head of music from Yale University, survived the collision but remained in a coma. Although Rhoda was a minor and her identity was protected from the public, she was sentenced to a four-year juvenile prison sentence. On the night of the accident Rhoda had been drinking with her friends at a party to celebrate her acceptance into university. What happened to Rhoda after her prison sentence? She took a job as a janitor at a local school. She wanted to work "physically" and maybe even to punish herself for her crime. Anonymity, you might guess, was all she felt she deserved. No matter how long she lived, Rhoda didn't believe that she'd ever deserve happiness. Rhoda also wanted desperately to apologize to John Burroughs, the sole survivor of his family. The musician had, since the crash, apparently lost interest in life, had become depressed, and neglected himself, despite recovering from his coma. Burroughs lived alone in grimy disorder and had quit his job at Yale University.

It all happens, not in the *Kansas City Star*, but in the enthralling 2011 Indie movie, *Another Earth*, directed by

Mike Cahill (and written by Brit Marling and Mike Cahill— neither of whom are from Kansas). Rhoda Williams (played by Brit Marling) did confront John Burroughs (played by Tom Cruise's first cousin, William Mapother), but she lost her nerve and couldn't confess to who she was. The apology wasn't made. Instead, using a ruse, Rhoda became John's housekeeper and eventually his lover. But all of this is only part of the story. *Another Earth* is a science fiction movie. Visible in the sky above New Haven is a huge second planet that appears to be orbiting Earth. This is Earth 2, a mirror or double of our planet. It's just the place for Stephen Hawking or Dirk Schulze-Makuch. We learn that a respectable scientist believes that Earth 2 mirrors our Earth in every manner. That will be the case until the moment that the two planets make contact. From then on, the individuals on the two planets will probably begin slowly to deviate and the doubles will gradually cease to be doubles. I know what you are thinking, that I've oozed back to the imaginary life, the lore of my theme. It's true and you're right. But even the imaginary has to have a proper basis in real life. That's what I'm trying to suggest. (And I also hope that you'll enjoy the movie—it one of the best of the early 2000s.)

Sounds silly? It works in the film but remember what we're looking for is a parallel for the predicament of Richard Anthony Jones, a link between doubles, waiting, and happiness. *Another Earth* offers this sort of lore. Rhoda enters an essay contest that is sponsored by an Elon Musk figure with an Australian rather than a South African accent. The winner will be given a flight on one of his rockets to the Earth double, to Earth 2. You've guessed it. Rhoda wins, but, in a selfless act, she gives her ticket to, you've probably guessed it again, John Burroughs so that he can reunite with his family who may be still alive on Earth 2. Burroughs takes the chance. The film ends four months later. Rhoda is returning home gloomily to her parents' house. She looks up to the sky, but Earth 2 is blurred by fog. She peers down and, near the back door to her parent's house, stands her double. Rhoda's long wait is finally over. Happiness, you see, is not just around the corner. It's just a matter of waiting to meet your double.[24]

The identical twins that we've just been discussing a few paragraphs back are part of real life, no doubt about it, and their link with happiness seems to be firmly based on waiting. Maybe because twins so easily become sentimentalized, they often ooze over into the fantasy world of Plautus and Shakespeare, into the fantasy world of what I have termed discourse or lore or the cultural motif. That's especially what we've just been looking at in the movie *Another Earth*. In the paragraphs to follow I'll aim to keep my focus more firmly on the daily life and the real apparitions of my theme. We'll be back here to something that is closer to the experience of Margaret Evans. I hope that this will convince you, just a little more, of the importance of my theme. Who trusts motifs? Who trusts lore? Maybe you should, even from me.

In scientific circles meeting your double is claimed not to be a good sign at all.[25] Medical research stresses the sheer psychopathy of the experience of encountering your double. Some doctors speak of it, as I have already mentioned, as "heautoscopy." And what a wonderful and unexpected word for such an apparently dangerous experience—it's Greek based and means looking at yourself. It's the technical expression used in psychiatry and in neurology for the "reduplicative hallucination" (itself a pretty impressive phrase) of seeing one's own body at a distance. This is not you in a mirror or you in a photograph or you on a computer screen, but the real thing. A You that's walking about but that's not You. Heautoscopy can occur as a symptom in schizophrenia and in epilepsy, it's said. And it can get worse. There is a condition called polyopic heautoscopy. As you might not have guessed, this means encountering several personal doubles as did Niamh Geaney. Professor Peter Brugger is a psychologist from the University of Zurich, and he is well known for linking paranormal experiences, such as Saint Paul's vision on the Road to Damascus, with abnormal psychology. Brugger lately described the case of a man who caught sight of no less than five of his own pairs.[26] That would be a truly confusing event and surely would not betoken happiness, however long was the period of waiting. Brugger's polyopic heautoscopist was neither epileptic nor schizophrenic. The poor man was not happy at all to have encountered his identical pairs. He was suffering from a brain tumor in the insular region of his left temporal lobe. It's almost as if, in cases like this one, that the removal of waiting period by illness is in some way associated with the diminution of the capacity for happiness.

Sosia was a Greek slave from the ancient Greek city of Thebes. As you can see, we're now back to the cultural lore—but, surprisingly, this is a striking instance of the cultural motif (discourse) matching real life and I will show you why in just a moment. Just wait—the link will reside in the strange illness termed Capgras Syndrome that in French at least is named after Sosia, the Theban Greek.[27] Sosia had the misfortune of suddenly encountering a famous double. He has just returned home from war with his mythological master Amphitryo. At the front door to his house he meets his exact double. There is no waiting involved at all in this encounter.

It's the god Mercury and he's taken on Sosia's perfect likeness. Mercury, through persuasion and aggression, manages to convince Sosia that he is not, I mean, just not himself. It's Mercury who is. He's the real Sosia. The slave Sosia gives in and reluctantly agrees with the god. Slaves aren't allowed to argue. And meeting your double, as you can see in this famous Greek myth legend, doesn't always work out as well as it does for Richard Anthony Jones or even the Plastics. Some doubles are just very bad news, as Jason McClure has explained to me, though they don't necessarily lead to madness or brain tumors. But when this is the case the encounter is often sudden and devoid of waiting.

Let's stay with the myth for just a moment longer. Jupiter, the king of the gods, wanted to sleep with Alcmene, the loyal wife of Amphitryo. Jupiter reckoned that the only way to do this was to become Amphitryo's double. It worked and that's why he had Mercury on guard by the front door. This was to stop Amphitryo blundering in on the act. Amphitryo eventually met his double, Jupiter, too, and he was as flummoxed as Sosia. His innocent wife Alcmene has slept with Jupiter by then and she never gets the chance to say, "you are not the man I married." Amphitryo was very jealous. But then how can you be jealous of "yourself"?

Now for the real life analogue: this, you'll see, is why I have brought Sosia into the mix, When the French psychiatrists Joseph Capgras (1873–1950) and Jean Reboul-Lachaux encountered the 53-year-old "Madame M" in the 1920s, she was seeing doubles all over the place.[28] This was not just polyopic heautoscopy, for she didn't merely see multiples of herself, but she also saw doubles of the members of her family. Her husband, her children, and her neighbors—and even herself—had been replaced by exact "doubles." It was all part of a jealous plot to purloin her property, she deduced. Madame M was in Sosia's predicament. Seeing doubles also appears to have been something that came on her without too much warning. What I am trying to illustrate with this Greek legend and with Joseph Capgras' Madame M is, first, that not all doubling, particularly when it is in real life, works out as well as it did for Richard Anthony Jones. Sosia and Madame M's encounter with doubles did not bring them happiness at all. My second point relates to waiting. In both of these unhappy events waiting looks to have been out of the question. Perhaps it really is true that waiting is the element that allows the emergence of happiness and fulfillment in our encounters with doubles. Remove the waiting and you are liable to end up in strife.

The unexpected element in this little story lies here. When Joseph Capgras and Jean Reboul-Lachaux encountered Madame M they turned to the mythological legend of Amphitryo, Alcmene, and Sosia to understand their perplexing patient. They must have known Plautus' first version in Latin (dating from some time after 200 BCE) as well as Jean-Baptiste Molière's 1668 version. They named Madame M's illness after the poor victimized slave Sosia. In 1923 the illness became *"l'illusion des sosies"* ("the illusion of the Sosias"). These days the psychological problem takes its name from the lead author of the study. Now it's termed Capgras Syndrome, or, sometimes, "delusional misidentification syndrome," or even the "syndrome of subjective doubles." But *"l'illusion des sosies"* certainly does prove that the lore relating to doubles can suddenly insert itself into real life.

What causes Capgras Syndrome? This is interesting in its own right and well worth hearing about, though this may lead us temporarily from the topic of waiting and happiness and doubles. For the psychoanalysts of the earlier 20th century, especially Anna Freud, the daughter of Sigmund Freud, Capgras Syndrome appears to have involved a jealous guilt, or better, a guilt over jealousy. To assuage this guilt you create a double, as a sort of a scapegoat. Then you reject the double as an imposter and let yourself off the jealous or guilty hook—subconsciously—because the double is not the real person giving you the grief. It would be good if this line of evidence-poor, though fascinating speculation were true. Professor Peter Brugger of the University of Zurich certainly wouldn't think so. Nor do I. Just recently I had a man write to me who said his wife suffered from bipolar disorder and Capgras Syndrome at the same time. He did not know how to cope with it. The man's wife's problem may suggest that biology is at the base of Capgras Syndrome and that in his wife's case it may have been linked with the bipolar disorder. Anna Freud's philosophical speculation is of no help in a complex neurological situation like this one. Brain, rather than Anna Freud's logic-driven version of the mind, has been the focus of the most recent work. Dr. Chris Fiacconi, a neuroscientist from Guelph University in Ontario, looked lately at what happens when people believe that someone they're close to—usually a spouse—has been replaced by a double.[29] Fiacconi speculates that we recognize people using two linked neural systems. One deals with the structural content of the face, the other with the emotional connection you have built up with the person (their "interoceptive awareness"). It's this second emotional pathway that's possibly damaged in people with Capgras. Someone with Capgras will think that their wife looks like their wife, but that it can't be her. This is because her emotional "glow" isn't right.[30]

Capgras and doubles, heautoscopy and polyopic heautoscopy, in these cases I can't help but think that it's the removal of waiting from the package that literally makes them so shocking. By shocking I really mean just that. Without any proper warning, sufferers of these conditions are cast into the wildly confusing situation, the shock-inducing condition of the completely unexpected appearance of a double. It's as if in Capgras, heautoscopy, and polyopic heautoscopy the removal of waiting period means the removal the buffer, the lubrication in the joint, as it were, that allows shock to be diminished and even to become happiness. I can't prove this of course. But this is consistent with the way we've been seeing waiting work so far.

Waiting, it appears, has nothing to do with doubles when brain damage is involved. Perhaps this is why they become so painful. Let's therefore stay with the biology of doubles for just a little bit longer and illustrate the point even more clearly. In this case there'll be a mirror involved and, just as was the case for Margaret Evans, there's a double in it.

"You've got another woman here" is something a sufferer of Capgras Syndrome like Madame M might say to their husband when he was absent-mindedly talking to the cat. In the case I am going to speak of now he didn't have a cat or another woman there and it wasn't a typical case of Capgras Syndrome at all. The man was 75. But the woman was convinced her husband had a girlfriend in the house despite his age. She was mid-way with the vascular dementia that had got to her in her mid-60s. There was certainly no other woman in the house and there was no cat either. It was the vascular dementia that caused her unfortunate experience of doubling. It took about eight years for her to die. But why would my poor vervet mother have accused my determinedly waiting and patient father of having a girlfriend in the house? He was the most caring of men and she used to know that too. One of my colleagues, a psychiatric epidemiologist named Andy Bulloch, suggested an answer. It had nothing to do with waiting and everything to do with brain damage. Andy Bulloch asked me if there were mirrors in the room where the change took place. There were mirrors close by. My friend wondered if she might have seen herself in a mirror just before she delivered the wild accusation.

A mirror? Here is how Professor Bulloch understood it. When my mother saw herself in that mirror, she may not have recognized herself. It's true that by that point in her life she recognized very few of the people she had ever known. Her image, as far as she knew, might as well have been that of another person. All she saw was a woman that she did not recognize, and that woman was in her bedroom. That was the girlfriend. My mother was the girlfriend and she was made so by the reflection in the mirror. She'd become someone else. She had become face blind, a victim of prosopagnosia.[31] Her reflection was no longer the self-image it is for the rest of us. It was a living and breathing double. Although no amount of waiting would have helped my mother, she in fact didn't even have the option of waiting. Her version of Capgras Syndrome was the result of all of those strokes destroying her brain.[32] When dementia becomes bad enough, you can't tell the time, and you can't sense that you're waiting. The vision of doubles was something that came on suddenly in the course of her illness and it didn't last. That double was a source of profound unhappiness for all of us. We hadn't been waiting for it.

Perhaps my mother's experiences were a little like the vision of the Belgian artist René Magritte (whose mother drowned herself when the artist was just 13 years old).

HAPPINESS | 113

Magritte conjures a man looking at himself in the mirror in his well-known painting *Not to Be Reproduced* (Figure 4.2).³³ In *Not to Be Reproduced* a man (it's said to be Magritte's patron Edward James) looks in the mirror and he sees himself. But his image has crazily turned its back on itself. The figure in the mirror looks familiar, insofar as your back ever looks familiar. By turning its back on him, the image in the

FIGURE 4.2. You've got another person here. René Magritte (1898–1967), *La reproduction interdite (Not to Be Reproduced)*, 1937. Museum Boijmans van Beuningen, Rotterdam, Netherlands. © Estate of René Magritte/SOCAN (2019). Image: Peter Horre/Alamy Stock Photos.

mirror has assumed a life of its own. It's become someone else, the equivalent of my father's girlfriend. Magritte's image is funny and poignant at the same time. (And let me assert too that *Not to Be Reproduced* isn't an example of surrealism. It's real life.) Although my mother had no interest in Magritte, *Not to Be Reproduced* catches the confusion that she may have suffered. Her misrecognition was the product of the brain damage incurred from all of those mini-strokes that precipitated her vascular dementia. The girlfriend in her room was certainly "not to be reproduced."

Magritte's painting captures the drama of what I've been speaking of here, of the loss of the sense of self that can happen with these doubles when illness is involved. My mother didn't see the back of her head when she looked in the mirror, she saw another person altogether, but she might as well have seen the back of her head. Magritte's painting gets this idea very well. Your double has turned away, so it can't be you, but then again. . . . You must be looking at yourself, but then it is the back of your head you're seeing. It would help if the image had a mouth, then you could ask they if they were you. But you don't have a mouth. The viewer, my mother if you wish, can't wait because her brain will no longer allow this. Without waiting a moment, she utters, "you've got another woman here."

It feels almost as if we are back in the world of Margaret Evans, doesn't it? I wonder if Alice Neel had *Not to Be Reproduced* in mind when she painted *Margaret Evans Pregnant*? Magritte's figure waits, Margaret Evans waits, Alice Neel waits. My mother did not wait. The illness stopped her. But her double was a foreigner like Magritte's. Margaret Evan's double seems to weep because she can't make contact with Margaret. Who is in the mirror?

Richard Anthony Jones' experience with doubling and with waiting had a very heart-warming ending. It was the complete opposite for Alexander Jheferson Delgado Herrera when he got out of jail. His story took place in January 2017 and within the Lima province of Peru. It was here that Alexander Jheferson Delgado Herrera, 27, managed to escape from the Piedras Gordas Prison.[34] He'd served two years of a 16-year sentence for robbery and sexual assault. Unlike Jones he really was guilty. Herrera's breakout was all down to his double, in this case his twin named Giancarlo Steven Delgado Herrera. Alexander Delgado Herrera had invited his twin brother, Giancarlo, to visit him at Piedras Gordas and "to bring some of his favorite snacks and treats." The visit appears to have gone rather well and without much interference from the guards, because an hour after Giancarlo arrived, Alexander was able to take his twin for a visit to his cell. There he offered him a drugged drink, which Giancarlo unsuspectingly accepted. It sent him straight to sleep. Alexander immediately swapped clothes with his comatose brother and, disguised as his double, strolled out through "six internal doors manned by prison guards as well as the outside gates of the jail." It took the screws several hours to twig to what had happened. It was only after they had taken Giancarlo's fingerprints that they realized they had the wrong man in the cell. Giancarlo was released some hours later after convincing the guards that he "knew nothing about the escape." Alexander remained happily on the lam for a full year.

I'm not so sure that this almost happy-ending story—happy for Alexander at least for a while—offers an answer to my chapter's query either. I don't think that it clears it up whether happiness is just a matter of waiting to meet your double at all. It does say something about the bad luck that can be associated with doubles and waiting. Alexander was recaptured. But then he did have a year off from the dreary life in the Piedras Gordas Prison. He probably doesn't see it that way now, as he faces at least a 14-year wait inside the jail. I suppose that this just goes to prove, as Jason McClure believes, that to see your double is not all that it could be, despite Richard Anthony Jones' experience.

There are certainly a good number of doubles in the United States. Currently there's about 5.5 million people who suffer from dementia and who may have seen the sort of double that my mother did.[35] You don't have to be demented to be face-blind. Oliver Sacks suggests, "severe congenital prosopagnosia is estimated to affect two to two and a half percent of the population—six to eight million people in the United States alone." If you added in the double hunters on "Twin Strangers," the Plastics, and the 2,000 sets of twins attending the Twinsburg Twins Days Festival the number would go up even higher.[36] Some of this doubling ends up with an experience like that of Rhoda Williams or even Richard Anthony Jones. But some of it ends up like that of Margaret Evans and Alice Neel. Doubling, it looks like, is no panacea for unhappiness—but sometimes it can be. Maybe this is as it should be for waiting. Everyone is just waiting. But when it comes to pairing and to doubles, waiting may reward and punish.

THE PAUSE

5

MILES DAVIS BREAKS

FOR A SMOKE

The Power and the Pleasure in Pausing

HE CAN'T HAVE BEEN MORE than 33 at the time. You can watch him playing that year on a Vevo recording. It was *So What* for US network TV and the year was 1959.[1] That must have been a very big moment for Miles Davis' musical career. Jazz, and Miles' music, is speaking to an audience that didn't always hear them. Miles Davis' posture during the broadcast is almost as remarkable as the music (which to date has been viewed on Vevo 17,067,107 times). He plays and improvises as usual with his eyes open, wide open, as intensely as you could imagine, and just a little angry. It's as if he's waiting and watching to see what he can come up with. He's watching and waiting to figure out how his group will work out too. Miles is almost curious, but still fiercely concentrated. He appears as well to want to challenge the audience, to dare it to dislike what he's playing. He's waiting for opposition. Miles Davis was always like that as far as I can tell. As well as challenging the audience I reckon he wants to show them that what he's doing is easy. *So What* became the first track of the biggest selling jazz record in history and a permanent moment of American art. The album is *Kind of Blue* (1959).[2] It's still as bracing as the Jackson Pollock painting *Blue Poles* (1952) from which it apparently drew the inspiration for its name.

When Miles Davis finishes his opening solo on *So What*, John Coltrane takes over. Coltrane was just as great a player as Miles Davis. Perhaps he died too young to be able really to consolidate the point. Perhaps John Coltrane was also a much more polite man than Miles Davis.[3] Is that why he closed his eyes when he played his solo? Eyes closed is just what you might expect of an improvising jazz musician. It makes it easier to concentrate unless you're Miles Davis. John Coltrane is maybe too reticent a man to challenge an audience on network TV and to show them how he is waiting for their correct response (proof? he was eventually canonized as a saint by the African Orthodox Church). Not Miles Davis. While Coltrane plays, Miles Davis steps to the back and to the right side of his band. He then lights up and smokes a cigarette while he pauses and waits (Figure 5.1). It is an astonishing moment. Vevo viewers remark on it. Smokes a cigarette? Why does Miles Davis do it? Shouldn't he be concentrating on what Coltrane is playing? The easy explanation is that Miles wanted a smoke and that he could smoke and concentrate perfectly well. But that cigarette is just like the eyes open while he solos. It's a challenge to the way that things are normally done. Miles is trying to be so in control that he can pause and wait and smoke and seem almost to ignore his environs. Does it work? The cool, the apparent indifference that Miles Davis exhibits here matches perfectly the title of the song, *So What*. But watch the video

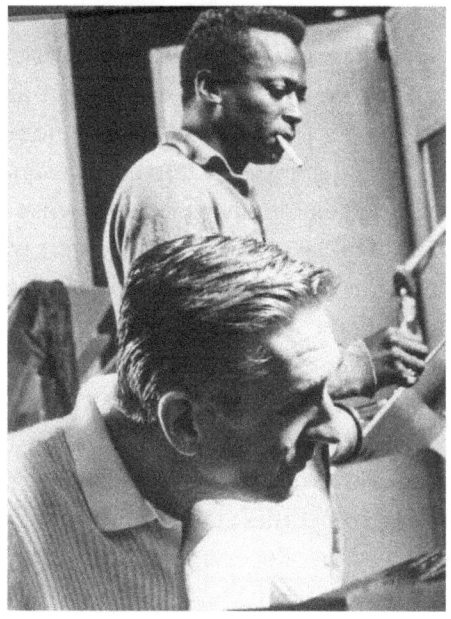

FIGURE 5.1. Miles Davis smoking and getting ready to play (the pianist and arranger Gil Evans is in the foreground) in 1957. © Bridgeman Images.

again. Miles hesitates just a little. People who ostentatiously pause always do.

Miles Davis' pause, his version of waiting, is what I've been terming a strategy. It's using waiting, in his case pausing, to get something—it adds a slightly insolent flavor to the performance and provokes the audience to react. You couldn't speak much of Miles Davis' experience of waiting, of pausing, because the open eyes and the smoke are all about performance. It's not like that for the audience. The pause, the version of waiting, is an experience for them, and it can be a very exciting, a pleasurable, but even a confronting one.

This chapter will be about pausing—it will focus mostly on waiting in performance and how this strategy can benefit the performance, and how as well it can benefit an audience's experience of the performance—and how the power of the pausing can engender pleasure in the listeners.[4] What do I mean by pausing? I'm not using it in the sense of a "break" ("let's pause for breakfast," says the early shift worker), or a moment of rest ("let's pause from our work for an hour," says the exhausted laborer), or a moment for reflection ("let's take a pause and reconsider our options," says the surgeon), or just plain stopping ("let's pause, let's stop now," says conductor to his tired, rehearsing orchestra). Pausing looks to the resumption of activity and is a period of waiting that takes place within, and sometimes at the beginning of some longer activity. That could be, for example, Miles Davis waiting it out smoking (or improvising with his eyes wide open) while the other members of his band perform their solos during *So What*. This sort of pausing is characterized by choice and by some degree of individual control. Miles Davis chose to pause, and he chose the manner and length of his pause. Because he was the bandleader, it was something under his power. This sort of pause also seems to be characterized by concentration. Even when he's smoking, Miles Davis looks very intent. This sort of pausing is also characterized by anticipation. That's something the performer may feel, but it's something that the audience seem to feel just as much, sometimes even more. This pause is very like the freeze-frame vision of diving evoked by the Japanese artist Kōshirō Onchi. This sort of a pause is a very exciting experience for the listener and the viewer, in music and in art and in the water.

In music, pausing can contribute to how it is that a piece is performed. Pausing can catch the mood of a song like *So*

What just as much as it can project the horn player's attitude to life. There is, or there was, something mildly antisocial in the title of Miles Davis' song. You can see now how waiting and pausing in the performance of *So What* worked so well for Miles. His disdain for the TV audience and for the venue in which he was playing is highlighted in the emphatic and indifferent manner by which he pauses with that cigarette in his hand. And I believe that he lights a second smoke. But he doesn't get time to finish that one. The music is great, but performance in the screen version of the song, the strategy, is just as great. The performance is captured perfectly in that waiting cigarette and the player's wide-open eyes.

Miles' dramatic pause may match the title of his song. But it elicits a different reaction from the audience. That reaction works in the opposite manner. It encourages them to listen all the harder. It seems to ask of them, what is Miles going to do next? It'd be fascinating to know not just how the audience really reacts, but how the brains of the audience might experience the strategic pausing that Miles Davis powerfully manipulated. There's some evidence that could help us to answer this question. And it's provided by Valorie N. Salimpoor. She was a young post-doctoral researcher at the Baycrest Centre in the University of Toronto when she published a report in *Nature Neuroscience* in 2011 looking at the way dopamine is released when people listen to or are about to listen to music.[5] (Dopamine primes you for a future reward by offering a pleasurable reward right now.) Using brain imaging, Salimpoor discovered that different parts of the brain showed dopamine action when music was played. She discovered that dopaminergic action was present primarily in the portion of the brain called the caudate during the anticipation of the playing of a favorite piece of music. But when actual listening is involved the dopamine reaction is present in the nucleus accumbens. This is, she explains, at the time of "peak emotional responses to music." Both of these parts of the brain belong to the striatal system and both displayed dopamine activity during her experiment, but not at the same time. Salimpoor's conclusion, put neatly and unemotionally, is: "the anticipation of an abstract reward can result in dopamine release in an anatomical pathway distinct from that associated with the peak pleasure itself." For the listener the experience of waiting—pausing—has its own pleasurable reward. No wonder Miles Davis' cigarette makes such an impression.

So it is that dopamine produces pleasure, but it acts on different parts of the brain when musical pleasure is involved. It depends on whether you are waiting to listen, as Miles Davis' cigarette made you do—it forced you to anticipate his final solo, despite the playing of the sainted John Coltrane. There was another very instructive experiment relating to the pause in performance that was carried out at McGill University in Montreal where Valorie Salimpoor completed her PhD. The Canadian neurologist and music expert Daniel Levetin and his colleagues took Salimpoor's work a step further.[6] Levetin showed how opioid signals, allied to dopamine, can increase the intensity of the "peak emotional responses to music." Dr. Levetin demonstrated that, by blocking the opioid signals in the brain just as people were listening to music, he was able to decrease the pleasure they gained from their musical experience. To achieve this result, he gave his research subjects a drug that is prescribed to help with the management of opioid and alcohol dependence. This was Naltrex and it diminished the pleasure of Levetin's listeners by reducing their opioid signals. Levetin showed, therefore, that when you listen to music it's not just dopamine that's active in your brain, but there are in addition opium- or heroin-like signals within the nucleus accumbens.

David Levetin's experiment didn't end there. What happens when you are paused and waiting for the playing of your favorite song? Is there an opioid signal operating then in the caudate region? To unravel this puzzle, Levetin and his team also gave Naltrex to his research subjects when they were paused, waiting to listen to one of their favorite songs. There was a dopamine release in the caudate when they were paused and waiting. Just like Salimpoor and her team, he could see this using brain imaging scans. But the pleasure that the subjects gained as they paused anticipating the music was in no way diminished by the Naltrex. The opioid blocker Naltrex, he concluded, may reduce the amount of pleasure that listeners get from actually listening to their favorite song, but they still enjoy just as much being paused, waiting to hear their favorite song, all thanks to the dopamine release. It makes you think again of those hungry quayside cats that we met in Chapter 2.

Maybe musicians like Miles Davis have always instinctively understood the power of the pause and how it can produce a pleasurable experience for listeners. And maybe that's really why Miles Davis smoked so nonchalantly on stage while his group performed. He was stroking the collective nucleus accumbens of his TV audience. It comes as no surprise that it's not just musicians who use pausing to enhance performance. When the Swedish filmmaker Ingmar Bergman made his award-winning 1974 screen version of Mozart's opera, *The Magic Flute*, he used a trick that was very like Miles Davis' with the cigarette. This is how it worked. Helene Friberg, then aged 13 years, was sitting in the audience of the old baroque theatre, the eighteenth-century Drottningholm Palace Theatre in downtown Stockholm. Helene was paused and waiting with anticipation for the beginning of the performance of the opera. The young actress is almost smiling. But she's also tense as she sits paused during the overture to *The Magic Flute*. I can tell you this with confidence because Bergman filmed Helene's reactions and blended them into the beginning of his version of the opera. Bergman didn't leave it with just the pausing Helene. He panned out to other members of the audience, who were also paused. The Swedish Film Institute lists some of the other people who appear very briefly during the overture: Ingmar Bergman himself is there, as is his son Daniel and his wife Ingrid; in addition, there's his old friend the actor Erland Josephson and the actor Lisabeth Zachrisson. There's also the film's cinematographer Sven Nykvist, János Herskó, Magnus Blomkvist, the film's choreographer Donya Fewuer, and the moneybags Lars-Owe Carlberg. They're all paused and waiting for the same thing, the start of the opera in which they are appearing as audience members. It is a remarkable evocation of the pleasure of people paused and waiting for the dramatic action to begin. And of course, this pleasurable experience, this excitement is powerfully transmitted to the viewers of his cinematic version of the opera, in much the same way as Miles Davis transmitted the excitement of *So What* to his studio and home audience. Ingmar Bergman regularly has the camera return to Helene Friberg's young face as the action of the opera develops. Sometimes Helene Friberg expresses pleasure and even smiles, but on most occasions, she seems to show pleasure at what is *about* to take place. She is paused as she waits for the story and the singing to unfold. Helene Friberg appeared one year later as an actor in Bergman's movie *Face to Face* (released in 1975). She was Anna, the daughter of Dr. Jenny Isaksson (Liv Ullmann), the lead character in this film. Bergman knew it in 1974 and he knows we know it now. Is he tempting us towards the experience of *Face to Face*?

Cigarettes, let's take them up again. The use of the smoke to create the pause and to create a sense of waiting isn't something that Miles Davis invented. He just did it better than most other people. In the same year as *So What* Frank Sinatra recorded a version of the standard *Here's That Rainy Day* by Jimmy Van Heusen (with lyrics by Johnny Burke). The song was published in 1953. Frank Sinatra's version was recorded on March 25, 1959. It was for the Capitol album *No One Cares*. Sinatra performed *Here's That Rainy Day* on a Timex-sponsored program entitled *The Frank Sinatra Timex Show: An Afternoon with Frank Sinatra*, broadcast on December 13, 1959. You can watch it on YouTube if you like Frank's voice. Sinatra smokes as he sings the TV version. He uses the cigarette to create a dramatic pause within the song. It punctuates his performance like a doleful exclamation point. It is a very soulful version of the ballad, no doubt about it. But the smoking is absolutely contrived—you cannot sing with a mouthful of cigarette smoke. I dare say that it also could have ruined his phrasing on this version—but he never inhales, as you'll see when you watch his rendition. Miles Davis was much more careful when he broke for a smoke and he only inhaled when he wasn't actually performing. It was different for Miles Davis. He had to be cautious as he was trying to break in as a celebrity, while Sinatra, after a pretty rough patch with Ava Gardner, was getting back. *No One Cares.*

If you wait or pause *within* a musical piece, like Frank Sinatra, are the same emotional reactions of excitement and pleasure produced as when you wait for a favorite piece of music to begin? Can the same dopamine-fueled experience of waiting occur *within* a musical piece as *before* it? It feels as if this is the case. Everybody will have their own favorite example of this sort of dopamine-driven pause. It's sometimes called the "stop-start" song. The English daily, *The Guardian*, ran a reader survey on the topic of "classic song writing [that] often utilizes one of the key elements in the composer's toolbox: the pause." This was in 2014. I will reproduce the list of winners, despite Herb Alpert coming top of the list.[7]

> *A Taste of Honey*—Herb Alpert & Tijuana Brass
> *I Want You So Bad*—James Brown
> *Roxanne*—The Police
> *Horse with a Freeze Pts. 1&2*—Roy Ward/Eddie Bo
> *Buddy Bye*—Johnny Osbourne/Prince Jammy
> *The Adventures of Grandmaster Flash on the Wheels of Steel*—
>   Grandmaster Flash & The Furious Five
> *Breathe and Stop*—Q-Tip
> *Birdy*—22-Pistepirkko
> *Time*—David Bowie
> *Hard to Explain*—The Strokes
> *Breathe Me*—Sia
> *I Will Always Love You*—Whitney Houston
> *String Quartet in E Flat Major: "The Joke"*—Josef Haydn

Make of that list as you wish. But my own favorite stop-start comes from the last movement of Bach's *Sonata No. 6 in G Major* for violin and piano. (Yes, I'm afraid this is the sort of music that I listen to.) Two-thirds of the way through this piece (please don't ask me to be any more precise than this—I am an ignoramus of such technical matters as bar counts) the piano and violin, both playing at a fair clip, suddenly cadence then stop playing altogether. You know they'll soon resume, so this is definitely a pause. When I first heard this pause, I thought it was immensely exciting. What would the piece produce next, the pause seemed to say? I mentioned this pause to a friend, Bazza Simpkins, who is also a Bach enthusiast. I said that the pause was about 10 seconds long and it was terribly exciting. He agreed that the pause was a real dopamine driver. So, there's the answer to the query I made at the beginning of this paragraph. But we can go a bit further with this observation. Simpkins was a little puzzled about the length of this pause and went away to check. Ten seconds? The pause in the version I was listening to, he came back to tell me, lasts barely two seconds, maybe even one second. It feels much longer than this to me, but I was definitely wrong. I know this because I went and timed the pause myself after I'd been corrected. I can only conclude that this is another example of the distinction between what the psychologist of time Marc Wittmann calls "felt time" and the time that's measured by watches.[8] The exciting pause, which can't really be measured, works as an example of felt time. It feels much longer than it really is and this feeling, maybe, is in proportion to the amount of dopamine and excitement that it produces. So, yes, pauses within a piece of music can be every bit as exciting as pauses at before a piece starts. Sometimes it's possible that they are even more exciting.

I checked this notion of the artificial lengthening of time in Claudia Hammond's *Time Warped*. Hammond doesn't address the musical passage to which I'm referring. Perhaps she doesn't like Bach as much as I do. Claudia Hammond does have a lot to say about how the experience of felt time can entail the sense of the deceleration of time. She relates this particularly to dread, but perhaps it works as well with dread's opposite, strong pleasure. She explains:

> We know from many laboratory studies conducted . . . that emotions do alter time perception. Just as fear makes time go slowly, so does looking at pictures of mutilated bodies or listening to the sound of a woman sobbing. It seems that when faced with distressing images, your body and your mind ready themselves for fight or flight, so the clock goes faster, more pulses accumulate, and it feels as though time went slowly.

I wonder if what Claudia Hammond speaks of here could as easily be applied to suspense generally? Perhaps we could think of it like this. Suspense makes the body clock run more slowly, or at least we perceive time to run more slowly. If the suspense entails something dangerous, then dread or fear seems to be responsible for the deceleration of felt time. But if the suspense entails something very pleasurable, such as music, then excitement and pleasure seem to be responsible for the deceleration of time. Could that be the explanation, perhaps, for the situation that I experienced in Bach's *Sonata No. 6 in G Major*? That may explain, as well, the skepticism of my friend. He hadn't heard the piece of music recently, but he knew that a 10-second pause is extremely uncommon. Perhaps all this may offer a little more help in understanding Miles Davis' break for a smoke. Maybe it also shows how we feel time. It makes the pleasurable pause seem to last even longer.

Can my Bach experience be depicted visually? That might seem like a strange question, but we've already seen Kōshirō Onchi's version of the exciting pause in diving. Can you repeat this with the depiction of non-diving scenes as well? Can you see time pausing in music? Edgar Degas, who really is a master of all things emotional, created a remarkable picture of a singer whom he captures when she is, it looks to me, paused in mid note (much more realistically than even Kōshirō Onchi's diver paused in free fall). It feels, from the shape of the singer's mouth and the raised and gloved arm that the woman is holding, a very long note. This is, you could say, a sort of a pause within the music. The singer's listeners, and I admit that I am guessing, are waiting for this pause to end and for her to resume the melody. This is not quite what happened in Bach, where the music actually stopped altogether. But it is very close, and anyhow if the singer had stopped, well, she would not be singing. Degas loves images such as this one, images that today would more normally be caught by a camera. That was not so possible in 1878.

In *The Singer with the Glove* (Figure 5.2) the emphasis is not so much on the imagined experience of the singer's audience as it is on that of the viewer. Degas freezes the experience for the person viewing his work. What will come out of the singer's mouth when sound returns? Will it be the song that we all love best? We are caught forever waiting for this singer to resume, or at least that is how it feels for me when I look at the work. The singer can of course never resume, because she's just pigment on canvas. But it feels as if she really and suddenly could burst back into song. The work creates an artificial but believable situation. That's also part of what Degas is getting at here. It's the suspenseful experience of the imagined audience projected onto us, the viewers. The work is all about the pause and the suspense and the anticipation

FIGURE 5.2. Is this a musical pause visualized? Hilaire-Germaine-Edgar Degas (1834–1917), *Singer with the Glove,* about 1878. Pastel on canvas. 53.2 cm × 41 cm. Harvard Art Museums/Fogg Museum, Bequest from the Collection of Maurice Wertheim, Class of 1906. Photo: © President and Fellows of Harvard College.

that is involved in a period of waiting within a piece of music. But I am starting to become a little too speculative.

Let's stay with musical performances and pauses for just a little longer. During a concert with his band, the Boomtown Rats, of their well-known pop song from the 1979 *I Don't Like Mondays,* Sir Bob Geldof, then aged 64, "paused and stayed silent for 90 seconds." This was in July 2016 at a two-day musical event, The Brentwood Festival in Essex in the United Kingdom. Geldof, reportedly worth £32 million in 2012 and who knows how much by 2016, subsequently accused the family event that his band was headlining of being "boring and tame." It probably was and, like me, the audience was very glad about it. Before his performance-pause Geldof explained to this audience, in vivid language, that he didn't like the way the family revelers were dressed. They weren't "edgy enough for a music festival and . . . [were all] wearing Primark clothes." Not him. Sir Bob was garbed in a "£350 snakeskin suit . . . made by a tailor on London's Brick Lane." He complained to his suburban audience, "I am wearing a fuck off pretend snakeskin suit and [you] are wearing fuck off cowboy shirts even though [you] live in London."[9] I suppose Sir Bob must live in a viper's nest. The 90-second musical pause came after the complaints. Maybe Sir Bob Geldof and the Boomtown Rats couldn't get the Essex audience excited enough. To push them into the Boomtown spirit of things, he insulted them and then, when that didn't work, he paused—he used what you could think of as a very extreme variant of the pause in Bach's *Sonata No. 6 in G Major*, BMV 1019. Phew. Surprisingly this didn't work either, although you'd imagine it should have. "One festival-goer . . . said, 'We were just thinking we probably wouldn't bother staying to hear *I Don't Like Mondays* as it didn't look like it would be worth the wait when Bob launched into an extraordinary, expletive-laden rant. As he launched into another dreadful song, we, along with hordes of others, headed for the exit and I found myself in a queue [paused and waiting] to leave in the middle of the headline set.'"

Ninety-second pauses, if you ask me, don't really work very well. By the end of the 90 seconds the neuromodulator dopamine has all but drained away and the listeners are feeling just deflated. Brevity encourages surprise and suspense. Here is one more example of the long-winded musical pause. Opinions vary on its effectiveness, but you'll know that I don't think it works. Some of you will already guess that I am referring to John Cage and his famous piece from 1952. This is entitled *4'33"*. To perform this classical piece of music, all that the musicians need to do is to raise their violins to their shoulders and to hold the bows poised to strike for four minutes and thirty-three seconds. Or they could do nothing at all, and do this on any instrument that they choose. The musicians give the impression of waiting for the music to start. The audience is definitely waiting for the music to start. It never does. It is sometimes claimed that this piece is not "four minutes and 33 seconds of silence," but an opportunity for the audience to listen to the sounds by which they are surrounded. Maybe. I think that most of us hear these anyway and don't need a musicologist or a composer to tell us this is what we do. Cage wrote this piece in a decade that was full of works of waiting (not just Miles Davis; Samuel Beckett's *Waiting for Godot* aired first in 1953.) Cage needs to be placed firmly within the pause category. He was also a Zen Buddhist and may have heard silence differently from most of us. (Cage published a book in 1961 entitled *Silence: Lectures and Notes*).[10] Miles Davis is sometimes said to be "famous for his dramatic silences in performance: the notes he chose *not* to play were almost as meaningful as those he did."[11] I wish that I could say that I understand what this means, but I do not. Cage, on the other hand, works best if his *4'33"* is surrounded by other pieces where music is played. It would probably be best if *4'33"* were not advertised on the program. Cage's piece works within a context of noise and won't work so well on its own; *4'33"* definitely does not bear repetition. Once you know the trick, there's no more dopamine. That's unless you believe that dopamine can be produced by being able to hear the person next to you shuffle their program. The point of *4'33"* is not so much silence as it is pausing. When I encounter John Cage's *4'33"* I can't help but think of a room full of people at a silent disco. The dancers can hear and understand and react to the music for sure. But this won't work for someone who is unconnected to the occasion and who walks into a room full of silent ravers. Apparently, the silent disco has become popular these days in old age homes.[12] It is felt to be therapeutic and for all I know it probably is, though I can't say that I am looking forward to practicing it when I move into Autumn Lodge. Imagine, one of my family visitors walks into Autumn Lodge and sees me dancing wildly, apparently to no sound at all. She or he looks around and wonders—what's the strange and vigorous pause? When will the music start? No dopamine here. Toohey's lost it.

The trick seems to be to know just how long you can be silent without losing the attention of the audience. Surprisingly, or perhaps not surprisingly, you can get a little help on the subject from research on public speaking and on conversation. This is not a place to which John Cage might have looked, and understandably. I promise you, however, that this really is more interesting than might be expected, so do please wait. Danielle Duez, a French phonetics specialist attached to the Centre National de la Récherche Scientifique in France, examined during the 1990s the modes by which some French politicians effectively or not so effectively used the pause within their public speeches.[13] Duez's analysis was particularly illuminating on the former president Francois Mitterrand and on three of his four-minute-long speeches. Danielle Duez found that in 1974, when Mitterrand was president but lost, he spoke relatively quicker "with about 30 per cent of his speech taken up by pauses." Ten years later he was president, but he was overtaken by a crisis over education. In that year 40 percent of his speech consisted of pauses. Four years later he was fighting for re-election as president and "just over 36 per cent of his speech was taken up by pauses."

For Danielle Duez the pause is all about power—not pleasure. In everyday speech pauses are not long and are used as an opportunity for us to gather our thoughts or to punctuate what we're trying to say. Not so, she believes, for powerful politicians. Tara Patel, in her report on Duez' work, states: "The differences [in the way pauses are used] reflect Mitterrand's changing status. In 1974 he was forced to argue the case for his party's policies in a few minutes, whereas in 1984 he had reached the peak of political power." Duez believes in that election Mitterrand's presidential power "is symbolized by his silence." You could compare the pause frequency between '74 and '84. "In 1974, Mitterrand paused at the end of each sentence for an average of 0.8 seconds; in 1984, he paused for 2.1 seconds," Patel explains. In 1988 Mitterrand used the pause less. Danielle Duez believes that Mitterrand was trying then to sound more like he had in 1974. He was aiming to sound like a "a president who happened to be a candidate."

Or it is possible that the use of the pause has nothing to do with the exercise of power and everything to do with pleasure? Listeners enjoy encountering the pause, if it is of the right length, and this encourages the production of dopamine within their brains. It engenders pleasure. So it is for Bach and so it could be for Francois Mitterrand. The trick again is to get the length of pause right. I suspect that Georges Pompidou, president of France from 1969 until his death in 1974, might have reflected his reputation for being ponderous with his weaker ability to produce pleasure in his use of the pause. Patel tells us that "In a speech he gave in 1973, 53 per cent of the speech was taken up by pauses, with those at the ends of sentences lasting 2.2 seconds on average." That is getting into Geldof territory.

Is there an optimal pause for pleasure? Maybe we don't know the answer to that yet, but Kristina Lundholm Fors of the University of Gothenburg, Sweden, who thinks that former US president Barack Obama gets the performance pause just about right, reckons that she has the answer to this question, at least as it applies to speaking.[14] She argued for this in a 2015 doctoral Gothenburg dissertation, where she used "eye tracking to study the processing of sentences with long pauses, sentences containing pauses of typical duration and sentences without pauses. Her results show that sentences with unusually long pauses tend to be more difficult to process. The long pauses in her study were four seconds long."[15] Kristina Lundholm Fors tells us, "four seconds doesn't sound like a long time, but when you are talking to somebody it can feel like an eternity. A typical pause in speech lasts only about a quarter to half a second." Obama, she believes, uses the optimal pause. He avoids the long pauses favored by Mitterrand and Sir Bob Geldof that "can affect communication negatively." His optimal pause is half a second.

If the four-second pause, or even the mighty 90-second pause bothers you as much as it does Kristina Lundholm Fors, then one solution would be to coach the performer to better manage his or her use of waiting. One unexpected, or should I say alarming, method of achieving this is to ingest stimulants. Do amphetamines help the pause? I haven't knowingly tried them, so I can't really answer that query, but others have opinions. Amphetamines are said to assist some performers of music and even some writers and mathematicians. How do we know this? They tell us. It's as simple as that. The pause in their cases is not quite the same thing as Lundholm Fors is concerned with. In their instances the pause is a mental state of slowing that seems to improve their ability to compose. It's possible that stimulants such as amphetamines create a sort of an intellectual or mental pause, an experience during which they're able to plan in advance their work. The beneficiaries of their mental pausing are us, their audience. The musicians, writers, and mathematicians strategize the pause, their use of waiting, to produce a better experience for their audience or readers.

I've spoken occasionally with people who've known working jazz musicians and they've told me about the value of stimulants for their playing. As they see it. How are these drugs supposed to help? The musicians don't play pieces from memory or from sheet music. They have to embellish, to improvise their solos often at great length on the song that they began with. This requires many skills, mastery of your instrument, being able to play exactly what you can hear in your head (the improvised solo), and being able to hear something in your head that translates well into sound. It seems that once you've got the manual skills and the ability to "play by ear," time becomes crucial for the person who is improvising. The musician has to compose quickly and on the spot. That's what Miles Davis and John Coltrane do in *So What*. But what if nothing comes? Or what if nothing decent comes? You'd think that if time could slow down for these players, if it could give them a pause in which to put the notes together for their solo before the tunes come out their instruments, then they'd play all the better. There'd be fewer situations when nothing decent comes or when nothing decent at all comes. That's how it's been explained to me and it seems to be how some players think. Amphetamines, it's claimed, can help by offering the jazz performer more time for planning. The musician needs to feel two minutes, you could say, while the audience is hearing one minute by clock time. The slowing of felt time would give the musicians the time to wait, double the time in this scenario, and it would allow them the pause in which to plan the pleasure with which they are going to treat us. Or maybe you could understand it like this: the slowing of time, the pause, would allow them to compose in a sort of slow motion, but to play in real time. It is all about controlling time if you are trying to strategize the pause in performance, and stimulants like amphetamines are sometimes claimed to give you more "time."

Can time really slow down like this? Can amphetamines really offer such an advantage through this version of the pause? Or is this just the wishful thinking of amateurs like me who are trying to explain and to imagine how jazz musicians manage to improvise with such ease? Some assistance with the puzzle can be drawn from the ever-helpful Claudia Hammond. She explains how the wife of the American psychologist Hudson Hoagland was sick in bed with a bad flu. She complained to her husband that he wasn't being attentive enough to her. His periods of absence were becoming longer and longer in their duration. Hoagland explains, in his report, that they weren't becoming longer at all. He suspected that his wife's increasing body temperature might be changing the way felt time operated for her. As her temperature rose, therefore, he persuaded his wife to count out the seconds to one minute. He decided to perform a little experiment with time. Hoagland sat by his wife with a stopwatch to gauge clock time. "The higher her temperature,"

Hammond explains, "the sooner she thought a minute had passed. When her temperature reached 103 degrees, time had slowed to the extent that she thought a whole minute has passed after just 34 seconds." Claudia Hammond insists that there are a variety of other ways that felt time can be made to decelerate in this manner. Hudson Hoagland's wife was getting nearly double the value from time when her illness peaked. This is just the sort of advantage that these musicians are looking for with their drugs. Illness of course would be of no help to them, as then they couldn't play. But it seems that concentration or "attention" (or "task salience" as some scientists describe it) can provide some of the same advantages.[16] Concentration is what these musicians need. The psychologist Amelia Hunt tries to explain concentration "attention" like this: "when we focus our attention on an event, even one as brief as looking at the clock, it creates the impression that it lasted longer than it did."[17]

Concentration is, maybe, the answer to the conundrum concerning the jazz musicians, their improvisation, their claimed interest in amphetamines—and how the pause operates to increase the players' capability and our pleasure. What these musicians are after is the deceleration of time, the mental pause that comes with concentration and attention. Naturally they're keen to get this when they need it most. So, they buy it from a dealer. This provides them with the capacity to pause mentally and to wait whenever they want and to allow their ideas to form and play out in slow motion on demand. Amphetamines aren't the only performance helpers. Ritalin especially (which is used for sufferers of ADHD), as well as cocaine and heroin, can slow time down. There was a systematic analysis of the existing literature relating to the possible cognitive improvement offered by the consumption of amphetamine and methylphenidate (Ritalin) done in 2015 by a team from Department of Psychology, University of Wisconsin, Madison, led by Robert Spencer.[18] The group's results were positive. There were improvements in cognition, memory, and in inhibitory control in healthy adults provided by these psychostimulants and, the researchers maintained, the drugs also increase a person's arousal. I guess that this translates to the capacity to concentrate effectively. Amphetamine and methylphenidate (Ritalin) also improve functioning on difficult and on boring tasks. (Some students use them to improve their performances in exams.[19]) Amphetamine and Ritalin secure their effect, it seems, by means of our old friend, the neurochemical dopamine. These pills inhibit dopamine reuptake and as a result cause a concentration in the brain (they act as dopamine reuptake inhibitors). It's likely that this concentration is what enables the slowing of time and, not surprisingly, the capacity to wait—the pause. This may be the slow motion that assists some musicians to improvise. This is the pause that can be so beneficial for composition and, if all goes well, pleasurable for the listener.

It's not just musicians who use drugs to increase their performance by enhancing their ability to concentrate and to pause mentally and to plan and execute what they are doing with great speed.[20] The British novelist Graham Greene used amphetamines to help him complete two novels at the one time. This was in 1939 when he was writing *The Power and the Glory*, for posterity as it's said, and *The Confidential Agent* as quickly as he could for money. According to his biographers it was speed and endurance that Greene was after in 1939. He completed *The Confidential Agent* in six weeks, working at 2,000 words per morning (the afternoons were for *The Power and the Glory*). That is probably as close to improvisation as it is possible to get with the written word. To achieve this improvisatory feat, Graham Greene took Benzedrine pills at breakfast and at lunch. Benzedrine, or "Bennies" as they used to be known, is a trade name for amphetamines and it was available over the counter in the United States, for example, until 1959. They are, I believe, less potent versions of the contemporary variety of methamphetamines that are smoked or snorted or injected or ingested. This variety is known as "speed," "meth," or "chalk." Graham Greene's Bennies worked. He was able to cut them out completely after he'd finished the two books.

Just as well. Bennies are not good for the health when taken over the long term. They are blamed for the French novelist, philosopher, and celebrity Jean-Paul Sartre going blind, among other things. "In the 1950s, already exhausted from too much work on too little sleep—plus too much wine and cigarettes—the philosopher turned to Corydrane, a mix of amphetamine and aspirin then fashionable among Parisian students, intellectuals, and artists. The prescribed dose was one or two tablets in the morning and at noon. Sartre took 20 a day, beginning with his morning coffee, and slowly chewed one pill after another as he worked. For each tablet, he could produce a page or two of his second major philosophical work, *The Critique of Dialectical Reason*." The conservative novelist and philosopher Ayn Rand fared no better or worse with Bennies. "In 1942 Ayn Rand took up Benzedrine to help her finish her novel, *The Fountainhead*. She had spent years planning and composing the first third of the novel; over the next 12 months, thanks to the new pills, she averaged a chapter a week. But the drug quickly became a crutch. Rand would continue to use amphetamines for the next three decades, even as her overuse led to mood swings, irritability, emotional outbursts, and paranoia—traits Rand was susceptible to even without drugs." Benzedrine and Ritalin don't seem to have bothered the famous Hungarian mathematician, Paul Erdös. It's been said, "He owed his phenomenal stamina to espresso shots, caffeine tablets, and amphetamines—he took 10 to 20 milligrams of Benzedrine or Ritalin daily." There is a good story told about his narcotics habit. A friend, Ron Gorman, bet him $500 that he could not give up amphetamines for a month. His hope was that this would cure Erdös of his habit. Erdös won his $500 then resumed his amphetamine habit. "You've showed me I'm not an addict," he explained to Gorman. "But I didn't get any work done. I'd get up in the morning and stare at a blank piece of paper. I'd have no ideas, just like an ordinary person. You've set mathematics back a month."[21]

Paul Erdös was lucky. He didn't become addicted. He didn't go blind like Jean-Paul Sartre. The right amount seems to help, but how do you know what that is? The German psychologist Marc Wittmann, whom we've met a number of times (I have used his term "felt time" repeatedly), has done work on the relationship of time and psychostimulants. He concludes: "This investigation showed that stimulant-dependent subjects (SDI) show impairments in time perception and in sensorimotor timing."[22] So this notion of the deceleration of time, of the intellectual pause seems to work, but Wittmann goes on to stress the damage it can do. Miles Davis and Bill Evans, the pianist on *Kind of Blue*, and John Coltrane all suffered from drug addiction at various times. The drug doesn't seem to have harmed *So What* but it did damage their lives. Miles Davis' career had gone into a slump because of heroin before *Kind of Blue*. Miles Davis was able to manage his addictions, periodically, and he lived until he was 65. His pianist Bill Evans was just 51 when he died, it's said, suffering a peptic ulcer, cirrhosis, bronchial pneumonia, and untreated hepatitis. It's been claimed that at the time of his death his hands were swollen from injecting speedballs into them. The Canadian lyricist Gene Lees described Evans' life with drugs as "the longest suicide in history."[23] Hepatitis appears to have been the official reason for the death of John Coltrane, but the hepatitis has been linked to his heroin addiction. Naltrex wasn't invented in 1959. What a shame for Miles Davis, Bill Evans, and John Coltrane. Naltrex might have helped Jackson Pollock too. His famous 1952 painting, *Blue Poles*, was, as I have said, part of the inspiration for the title of the album *Kind of Blue*. On August 11, 1956, at 10:15 p.m., Jackson Pollock died in a single-car crash. He was driving drunk.

Paul Erdös, with his constitution of pure iron, lived to 83 on that diet of amphetamines and Ritalin and espresso coffee. He never touched Naltrex. Most of us could not manage a feat like that. The good news, however, is that it is possible to achieve such feats of pausing, waiting, and of concentration without doping up. Practice really does appear to make the brain of the musician better at improvising. I presume that this is also the case for writers and for mathematicians. I hope so. The parts of the brain that enable self-control—that you might link with the strategizing of waiting and pausing—seem to disappear from the scene when musicians like Miles Davis improvise. This was argued in 2008 in a famous experiment carried out at Johns Hopkins University by Charles Limb, a jazz musician and professor of otolaryngoly, in conjunction with Allen Braun.[24] They believe that the dorsolateral prefrontal cortex, "a broad portion of the front of the brain that extends to the sides, showed a slowdown in activity during improvisation." The dorsolateral prefrontal cortex is a brain region that is sometimes linked to "planned actions and self-censoring." Limb and Braun have suggested that shutting down this area could lead to lowered inhibitions and therefore to an increased capacity to improvise. This does rather make improvisation sound like musical squawking without self-control, but it is another way of looking at things. Perhaps it plays a role along with the deceleration of time. The report on Limb and Braun's work also observes, "the researchers also saw increased activity in the medial prefrontal cortex, which sits in the center of the brain's frontal lobe. This area has been linked with self-expression and activities that convey individuality, such as telling a story about yourself." But what's missing in Limb and Braun's understanding is the lit cigarette. The dramatic pause that the creator manipulates, both to please their audience and heighten the power of their music—or even their political speech. It leaves the pause out of the inspiration.

The control of time has received a lot of attention in this chapter. Control during performance enabled the specific version of waiting, the pause that can so unexpectedly enable pleasure for the audience. That's how Miles Davis' lit cigarette worked for the experience of the audience in Vevo's *So What*. Let's finish this chapter with the wide-open mouth of Edgar Degas' *Singer with the Glove*. I suggested of Degas' canvas that the artist freezes the experience of time for the viewer of his work. The viewer seems to wonder what will come out of the singer's mouth when sound returns, when the pause is over. Will it be the song that we all love best? We're caught waiting for this singer to resume, but the performer can of course never resume, because she's just a pigment paused on canvas. This is a little how it feels as well with Onchi's frozen diver. What will it be like, we wonder, when the diver hits the water?

Barbara Hepworth is one of the most recognizable of twentieth-century British sculptors. Her large, abstract creations made of polished stone, or of bronze, or of wood, often included a circular hole, a great eye, within their mass.[25] You can see this for yourself in Figure 5.3. There are three or even four eyes in *The Family of Man*. The eyes or the holes within Barbara Hepworth's sculpture seem to work in very much the same manner as I've been suggesting for the "o" of the mouth of Degas' singer. Barbara Hepworth's viewer seems to wonder what will come out of these great

FIGURE 5.3. Is this a musician's pause in stone? Barbara Hepworth (1903–1975), *Family of Man*, sculpture created in 1970. Snape Maltings, Suffolk, England. Geophotos/Alamy Stock Photos.

holes when their pause is over. We're caught waiting for the resumption of something—but what? The power and the pleasure evoked by Hepworth's sculptural holes is often the product of the pause they embody, and of their stillness, and of the waiting that they evoke.

6

DITHERING

A Chapter on the Strategic Advantages of Indecisive Waiting

IN THOMPSON STREET, BENDIGO, A 53-year-old was woman stopped in her car by the police at a Random Breath Testing (RBT) site. These RBTs aim to check, randomly, motorists' blood alcohol levels.[1] They can be placed anywhere on any road at any time in Australia. You're obliged to pull over and take the breath test by puffing into a "breathalyzer" instrument that registers the driver's alcohol levels. This particular evening in Bendigo, the 53-year-old woman blew into the breathalyzer and registered a blood alcohol percentage of 0.098. That's nearly double the local legal limit of 0.05%. It's about the equivalent of six small glasses of wine in an hour. This unfortunate woman (the newspaper reports didn't release her name) was transporting her trusting but none too innocent 55-year-old husband home. She had her driver's license canceled on the spot by the police for six months and was fined $443.00 for a D.U.I. This expensive incident happened at 9.00 p.m. on Saturday March 7, 2015. I suspect the couple was on the way home from a social club, but I cannot be sure. Bendigo is a town of about 150,000 people and is situated in the very center of the state of Victoria in

Australia. I don't believe that it's an especially boozy place, though I could be wrong.[2]

The husband should have hesitated before getting into the car with his sozzled wife. Maybe he should also have tried to stop her from driving. But he was drunk too. In fact, he was a lot drunker than she was, and that's perhaps why his wife chose to drive. I guess he didn't think to dither or to hesitate or to wait to try to stop his wife from driving. Instead of pausing, he got straight into the car with his wife at the steering wheel. Perhaps, after drinking, his judgment was not all it should have been. I'm sure it wasn't. That, anyhow, was his first big mistake, getting into that car. After the police had picked up his wife and taken her back to the station for further testing, the 55-year-old reveler, left alone in his car, called a taxi to take him home. He must have been waiting for a long time because that's where he made his second mistake. After some dithering, but not near enough at all of a pause, he decided to drive his car home. This was because the taxi failed to pick him up. That was at 10.00 p.m., one hour after his wife had been charged. It was only 50 meters down Thompson Street from the Random Breath Testing site. The police at the RBT site spotted him getting into his car at once and pulled him over. He was checked and registered a blood alcohol reading of 0.125 % even an hour or more after his drinking had ended. That blood alcohol reading must have been the product of about nine or so small glasses of wine. The intoxicated driver had his license suspended for 12 months and was fined $627.00. Husband and wife were booked at the same spot on the same street in Bendigo and within one hour of one another. That is a remarkable instance of doubling. The newspaper reporting on this couple's very expensive night out also noted, "both drivers will have an alcohol interlock device fitted to their car for a minimum period of six months from the date their license is restored."[3]

Ditherers don't make up their minds quickly. They hesitate too much. They are prone to confused pausing and they seem to wait forever to decide what to do. There wasn't too much of that in Bendigo. What does Bendigo have to do with the strategic advantages of dithering? There really are consolations to be had from dithering and from indecision and from pausing if they can keep you out of a car like that one in Thompson Street. The biggest error that the sozzled husband made was not just drinking too much but being sufficiently decisive as to have his wife drive and then confidently to get into his car with his inebriated wife when he was even more inebriated than her. He'd have been better to make no decision at all. The solution here was not to act, a decision that is easy to make if you are soused. The best decision would have been no decision and to wait and to remain in a blotto and semi-permanent state of bedithered pausing. When should this benighted man have made a decision to act? Not then, though his inebriated state must have made any form of sensible decision difficult to make. Frank Partnoy, whom we'll meet soon, would have advised him that he had all night to wait if he wanted. A taxi would have come eventually. If not, the police might have driven him home. Or he could have slept in his car until the police left, when the coast would have been clear to drive himself home illegally—he may even have been sober enough by that point, though I doubt it. Dithering often represents the most judicious course. Dithering is often a very advantageous strategy. So here you can see my very first example of one of the alarming advantages of dithering.

The great city of Bendigo offers three really useful lessons concerning dithering. The first lesson concerns what's called proception, the second concerns delay discounting, and the third self-handicapping. Each of these important modes of decision-making, while not obviously entailing dithering, is offered a decisive leg-up by the pause. Let's start with *proception* (or delayed gratification), the first of the trio.[4] It's an emotional ability, part learned part innate, which encourages a person to be willing to wait for a bigger reward that will come later, rather than a smaller reward that will come right now. The Bendigo couple took the choice of a smaller reward now, a quick trip home, a cup of tea, and an early night, instead of aiming for the bigger reward of a slower and more expensive trip home without the distressing worry over the loss of driving license, the fines, and the alcohol interlock device. Strategic dithering was not one of the Bendigo couple's strong qualities.

Delay discounting is the converse of proception. This version of decision-making is also based upon the notion of people looking forward to maximize future benefit. It's often argued that if most people are faced with a disadvantage (paying for a taxi, for example, instead of driving home free but sozzled) or a punishment ($1,070 in fines, 18 months of combined license suspension, and the embarrassing interlock), they will decisively opt to deal with their disadvantage sooner than later. Most people, it's also argued, like to avoid punishment, but if they must suffer it, they prefer this sooner rather than later. Tell that to the Bendigo drivers. Delay discounting would have had the Bendigo duo leaving their car at the club or in Thomson Street and waiting for a taxi no matter how long it took. Maybe they could even have walked home. Bendigo was a safe city last time I visited.

Self-handicapping represents the third of Bendigo's lessons. It provides a strange mode by which humans and animals will procure personal advantage. Some people and some creatures will deliberately self-handicap, deliberately and decisively lose or deliberately appear less than competent and, by so doing, attempt to gain personal benefit. There is the potential for an awful lot of dithering in self-handicapping. This tactic of self-handicapping is one of my favorite varieties of apparent dithering. The husband could have tried to employ this on Saturday, March 7, 2015. He could have approached the police at the RBT site on Thompson Street and said, "I'm just an old dopey drunk, constable, and now I don't know what to do, fool that I am. I'm stuck here. Can you help a penitent?"

Proception may have its simplest illustration with marshmallows. The late Walter Mischel, who even at age 88 was still working as the Robert Johnston Niven Professor of Humane Letters in the Department of Psychology at Columbia University, was an expert in the subject. I think that he must have loved marshmallows. They were one of the things that made him famous. And, anyhow, why else would he have chosen marshmallows for his very renowned marshmallow test?[5] This was administered to small children in the early 1960s, a more righteous era than ours, and it involved marshmallows and proception.[6] In Professor Mischel's test, young children were offered what has now become a very well-known choice (that the psychologist, behavioral economist, and Nobel Prize winner Daniel Kahneman calls a "cruel dilemma"). The children were presented with a marshmallow. They could eat it now or, if they could wait 15 minutes before eating it, they'd get a second marshmallow.

Then they could eat both of the marshmallows. Most children couldn't wait. But Walter Mischel discovered that those who could wait, those who were blessed not merely with the willpower to keep their jawbone wired together, but with a better than average capacity for proception, fared better in later life. Mischel and his successors kept records on the marshmallow children as they aged. They discovered that those who could wait for the second marshmallow enjoyed better life-outcomes—better results at school, more friends, and less drug and alcohol use, and especially higher IQs. The two-marshmallow children seem to have lived their lives just like those dopamine-doused quayside cats.[7] Those cats knew it was better to wait for the boats to come in rather than wandering off chasing mice on the quay and maybe missing out on the big reward. So, they stayed put and waited for their "second marshmallow." Dopamine helped them to do it and I am quite sure that, unless Professor Mischel is fooling us, it helped those successful little two-marshmallow children.

What would you have done with Professor Mischel's first marshmallow? A talented proceptor hesitates, then says no. I guess I'd have golloped down that first marshmallow without even a thought. But that, recent research says, may not have mattered after all. My innate inability to manage strategic dithering as a child mightn't have predicted my future after all—especially as I'm still dithering. Recent research by New York University's Tyler Watts and the University of California, Irvine's Greg Duncan and Hoanan Quan, entitled "Revisiting the Marshmallow Test," attempted to replicate Mischel's experiment.[8] This time, instead of using 90 children from the Stanford University preschool, they used a sample of more than 900 children who, they claim, represent more accurately the general population in terms of race, ethnicity, and parental education. Their conclusion in their replication was that "the capacity to hold out for a second marshmallow is shaped in large part by a child's social and economic background—and, in turn, that that background, not the ability to delay gratification, is what's behind kids' long-term success."[9] They also maintain that Mischel's children's advantage, tested against the history of their larger sample, doesn't last.[10] It's maybe a bit easy to lose sight of the wood for the trees here. Marshmallows or no, there is an advantage in being able to hold out for the larger payback. Just ask those drivers from Bendigo. I am still inclined to trust in the advantages of strategic dithering, and I would say that the two-marshmallow children, irritatingly worthy as they are, have mastered the art.

Watts, Duncan, and Quan weren't the first ones to cast a leery eye on proception and on the strategic advantages of dithering, The 2005 bestseller *Blink: The Power of Thinking Without Thinking* by the enigmatic Canadian writer from the *New Yorker* magazine, Malcolm Gladwell, offers a very dramatic and quite unexpected blast at the idea of proception. Raising self-help almost to the realm of moral philosophy, *Blink* argues for the strength and the reliability of instant decisions—gut reactions, I suppose you'd call them. Drive, don't taxi! Taxi, don't drive! Be careful in Bendigo! Not one ounce of dithering here. It's all about fast decisions. Gladwell's book concerns itself with decisions that are made in the time that it takes you to "blink." They are definitely not the sorts of decisions that are typical of ditherers. There's no need to consider which of two rewards is best, the littler one now or the larger one later. Just decide. That will invariably get you to the bigger reward. Gladwell's own description of some of the contents of *Blink* will give you an idea of book: "we meet the psychologist who has learned to predict whether a marriage will last, based on a few minutes of observing a couple; the tennis coach who knows when a player will double-fault before the racket even makes contact with the ball; the antiquities experts who recognize a fake at a glance."

Malcolm Gladwell would like to demonstrate that humans, without any dithering and without any waiting, and without any conscious proception, are able to reach correct conclusions from a narrow range of information and experience.[11] He adopts the term "thin slicing" for this process of snap decision-making. Thin slicing is a descriptor sometimes used by psychologists and philosophers to describe the knack of being able to find logical patterns that are based only on "thin slices," or narrow ranges and collections of knowledge or experience. Snap decisions work well, Gladwell believes, although dislikes, prejudices, and stereotypes can sometimes spoil a person's capacity to slice thin, just as can having too much knowledge or a blunt knife. This encourages "analysis paralysis," something that indecisive folk like me are always bothered by. Snap judgments are in most cases the most reliable, Gladwell maintains. But as well as being a very good-hearted man, Gladwell is an honest one. He does document the "great failures of 'blink': the election of Warren Harding [until recently ranked as the worst of all American presidents]; "New Coke" [it did not sell]; and the shooting of Amadou Diallo by police [41 bullets were confidently pumped by four policeman into the wrong man]." I'd also like to tell Gladwell about when I confidently took up Forex day trading [I lost my shirt].

Gladwell is often motivated in his volumes to demonstrate that the small person, the David to the governmental or commercial or academic Goliath, can triumph unexpectedly. The popularity of his very good books and his novel arguments are based on the enthusiastic message than we too can become a David, if we have faith and if we slice a bit thin. So one of his bestselling books, aiming to demonstrate that very impossible dream, is called *David and Goliath* and it shows how Davids can do well in a competitive world of Goliaths, while another is called *Outliers* and it attempts to show how people who are not born to privilege or in the center of things often can triumph in the world of the insider. Bendigo beats New York, you could say. Gladwell, a David from Toronto, is now said on the Net to be worth many millions of dollars. David triumphs and moves to New York and makes a bundle. And so it is with decision-making. Instinct and a modicum of training are often as successful as the labored opinions of experts in the matter of getting it right fast. That's a little of what we learn in *Blink*.

Frank Partnoy, now a professor of law at Berkeley and formerly the George E. Barrett Professor of Law and Finance and founding director of the Center on Corporate and Securities Law at the University of San Diego (which suggests that decision-making theorists get long dithery titles associated with their names and places of employ), will have none of this. Partnoy offers a rebuttal of Gladwell's *Blink* and provides a defense that holds out some hope to the ditherers of this confusing planet.[12] In 2012 Professor Partnoy wrote a book entitled *WAIT: The Art and Science of Delay* that unashamedly has Gladwell in its crosshairs.[13] He explains, "I interviewed a number of former senior executives at Lehman Brothers and discovered a remarkable story. Lehman Brothers had arranged for a decision-making class in the fall of 2005" and "for the capstone lecture, they brought in Malcolm Gladwell, who had just published *Blink*."

Lehman's president, Joe Gregory, was one of the prominent casualties of that firm when it failed in the crash of 2008. Joe Gregory loved Gladwell's book and had been passing out copies on the trading floor. "The executives took this class," Partnoy continues, "and then hurriedly marched back to their headquarters and proceeded to make the worst snap decisions in the history of financial markets."[14]

What is Frank Partnoy's alternative to the Malcolm Gladwell blink? And does it really demonstrate the strategic advantages in dithering? As an alternative to blinking, Partnoy argues for an active, a beneficial form of procrastination.[15] Procrastination? Now that is the ditherer's lodestar. It sounds very good to me, even if Partnoy's procrastination does not represent quite the same failing that people like me are frequently prone to. His procrastination is more of a strategy, than it is an experience. Partnoy's strategy of procrastination is characterized by two decision-making steps. The first step is to determine "what is the longest amount of time I can take before doing this?" In this phase Partnoy believes you will gather information relevant to the decision. To maximize the information-gathering phase, his second step, Partnoy suggests delaying "the response or the decision until the very last possible moment. If it is a year, wait 364 days. If it's an hour, wait 59 minutes." He adds, "This is a process that is used by successful decision makers such as professional athletes at the level of milliseconds . . . the military at the level of minutes [and by] . . . professional dating services at the level of about an hour." Partnoy aims to show that in each of these pursuits there exists a window, shorter or longer, during which they can gather information before acting. He maintains, for example, of professional tennis players, "studies of superfast athletes show that they are better because they are slow. They are able to perfect their stroke and response to free up as much time as possible between the actual service of the ball and the last possible millisecond when they have to return it." This is, in his mind, a version of productive procrastination. He believes we can all benefit from it, not just professional decision-makers: "Just take a breath. Take more pauses. Stare off into the distance. Ask yourself the first question of this two-step process: What is the maximum amount of time I have available to respond?"

The Bendigo couple seems to have relied more on the blink than on productive procrastination—or proception if you prefer. I guess they were too intoxicated for the distinction to have mattered. There is, of course, a much simpler version of procrastination and that would have helped them too. If you are indecisive and put things off too much (a specialized version of dithering, you might say) then you might have instinctively stayed in the club until a cab came or until a sober friend was leaving who could help you out. This version of procrastination may be the most famous and, maybe, is the most common form of dithering. It's a habit or *experience* that's generally and most often rightly disapproved of. There is even a whiff of immorality attached to this type of procrastination, as if it represents a failure of personal control. Frank Partnoy believes that the moral opprobrium attached to this type of procrastination dates to the "Puritanical era with Jonathan Edwards's sermon against procrastination and then the American embrace of 'a stitch in time saves nine,' and this sort of work ethic that required immediate and diligent action." It is a habit that would have saved the Bendigo couple $1,070.00.

The attractions and the dangers of procrastination (and of the blink) are dramatized unexpectedly in Edgar Degas,

DITHERING | **159**

Monsieur and Madame Edouard Manet (Figure 6.1). Perhaps the Bendigo couple might have gained from viewing it. I certainly could. The procrastination painting is from Paris in the 1860s, well before Bendigo was indelibly stamped on the map. The image may be one of the strangest in the visual history of procrastination.

What we should be seeing in this image is Degas' friend, the artist Edouard Manet, and Manet's wife Suzanne Leenhoff. That is Manet sprawled on the couch, looking too comfortable for his own good. To his left is Suzanne seated.

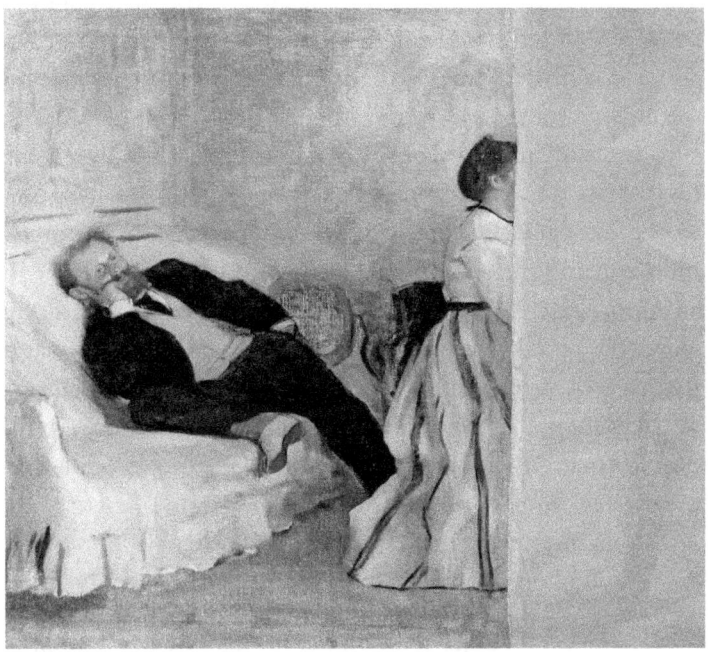

FIGURE 6.1. "Get on with it, Edgar." Hilaire-Germaine-Edgar Degas (1834–1917), *Monsieur and Madame Edouard Manet*, 1868–1869. Oil on canvas. Municipal Museum of Art, Kitakyushu, Japan. Asar Studios/Alamy Stock Photo.

She was supposed to be playing the piano in the picture and she was said to be a very good pianist. But some of Suzanne has disappeared. Her face, most of her arms, and the front part of her body have been removed from the canvas. Degas had given the painting to his friend Manet as a gift. But Manet did not like what Degas had done with his wife's face. He'd made Suzanne look too ugly. After Degas had left, in a blink he angrily slashed the right quarter of the painting away to disguise his wife's face and left it at that. When, on his next visit to the Manets' apartment, Degas discovered what Edouard had done to his painting, he "stormed from the apartment with the painting under his arm." His intention, he later told his art dealer Ambroise Vollard, was this: "I'm going to 'restore' Mme. Manet." But he never did get around to the restoration. He procrastinated and left the picture to survive as a "mutilated relic" of the friendship between the two artists. (They did become friends again.) It's hard not to like the painting the way it is. When you see it, Suzanne, Edouard, and Edgar, and their turbulent friendship, come to life almost despite the intentions of the canvas.[16] The painting may now be flawed, but, thanks to procrastination, what a story it tells. I suspect as well that the painting now sells for much more than it is worth because of this mutilation. Degas' procrastination may have provided an unexpected financial windfall for future collectors.

What a slob is Manet. That's the other aspect of the painting that needs to be mentioned. This is Manet's posture. It is hard to imagine the man ever getting around to doing anything. Otto Friedrich wonders whether Manet is "lolling dreamily" as he listens to Suzanne's playing or whether he is bored. I suspect that it's Manet's head-on-the-hand posture that makes Otto Friedrich wonder whether the painter is bored. He's not alone. The painting was used as an illustration of Oblomov. This was on the cover of an Italian edition of Ivan Goncharov's novel, *Oblomov*.[17] Goncharov's story concerns the most bored and dithering procrastinator in western literature. Who wouldn't like Oblomov? My point here is that other people have had the same impression of Manet in *Monsieur and Madame Edouard Manet* as did Otto Friedrich. It really does make you wonder whether Degas caught the condition of procrastination from viewing his own painting. I can't tell you, though, whether Manet was a procrastinator.[18]

Procrastination, the simple version, the experience of Degas rather than the strategy or process enjoined by Professor Partnoy, may be infuriating at times, both for the perpetrators and for the victims. It isn't usual to suggest that there is much to be said for the habit. But Degas' version of things has been defended at some length by the American philosopher John Perry in his lavishly titled book, *The Art of Procrastination: A Guide to Effective Dawdling, Lollygagging and Postponing, Including an Ingenious Program for Getting Things Done by Putting Them Off.* [19] John Perry's defense of procrastination is something that's pretty simple to put into operation. If you know you're a procrastinator, he suggests, it's not a good idea to commit to too many things, because the procrastinator will pick out the easiest thing to do, and that will distract them from the most important and pressing tasks. But all is not necessarily lost. Although you'll have neglected the most important of the tasks, it's likely that, as the deadline approaches for the important task you have been putting off, unconscionably, you'll burst into action and finish it. This way you'll find that you'll get a lot of tasks done, the easy ones and probably the important one too. He calls this structured procrastination. Or, we could say, that's strategic dithering for you.

"You've got to face death, so it's a lot easier if you've got the coffin ready," he said. That's Russell Game speaking with Carla Howarth of Australia's ABCNEWS.[20] Russell Game offers one of the strangest versions of *delay discounting* that you could encounter. Delay discounting? When most people are faced with something awful, they'll opt to deal with it sooner than later. Most people, it's also argued, like to avoid punishment, but if they must suffer it, they prefer it sooner than later. Russell Game and Carla Howarth were speaking about death and coffins. They met at the Community Coffin Club in Ulverstone, an attractive, but not so well-known town of about 14,000 people on the north coast of Tasmania. We've heard enough about Bendigo, so it's good to move a little south. Ulverstone's Coffin Club offers a curious illustration for delay discounting. We will learn, however, that all is not as it seems with delay discounting.

At the Coffin Club, reports Carla Howarth, they don't buy and sell coffins, they build them themselves for themselves while they are in good health. That's the users, not the undertakers. Why would anyone choose such a strange hobby? Russell Game explains. This club member believes that his hobby of making caskets will have the benefit of getting him used to the idea of death. Staring your own future death in the face, in the form of a coffin, may not be the most pleasant experience, but it's one way of getting ready for the Big One. If that's not delay discounting, I don't know what it is. Russell Game is taking on a bit of death now, so that the full sentence will be easier to take later. But of course, like many delay discounters, Russell Game is keen to save a dollar. Of the homemade coffin Game explained to Carla Howarth, "I don't know what the funeral directors think about it, but we can make them for probably a tenth of the cost." Mr. Game will make his coffin for about AUD$200, quite a save on the $2,000 for the average North American commercial casket. If you factor in inflation, then this is a real bargain. Other members of Ulverstone's Community Coffin Club place utility above cost benefits. Carla Howarth spoke to Sheree Whittington and she doesn't look like she's at retirement age yet. She plans to use her coffin as a CD and DVD rack until her final day comes. "It's an actual, functional piece of furniture," she bravely claims. And Declan Banim, another enthusiastic Coffin Club member, will boldly use his version as a bookcase. "It'll be in my lounge room," he calmly explains. Mr. Banim did hint that if one of his friends needed the coffin that he'd be glad to oblige. That's backtracking a bit on the idea of delay discounting.

As far as I can tell the Coffin Clubs started in New Zealand. It's here maybe that you'll get a sense where the dithering comes in. A *Guardian* report on September 22, 2016 by Eleanor Ainge Roy suggested that the clubs might have begun in New Zealand's north island, in the town of Rotorua. This was in 2010. Katie Williams, aged 77 in 2016, is a former palliative care nurse and she founded the Coffin Club movement in New Zealand as an act of psychological palliative care for the aged. Since then a dozen clubs have popped up. Katie Williams' initial aim was to personalize funerals. Her goal was also practical: New Zealand Coffin Club caskets fetch in at NZ$250, not much more than the Australian copies. But, according to Ms. Williams, the biggest attraction of the Coffin Club movement for her mainly older members is not delay discounting nor saving money but companionship.

"There is a lot of loneliness among the elderly," Ms. Williams states, "but at the coffin club people feel useful, and it is very social. We have morning tea and lunch, and music blaring, and cuddles." Couldn't they just as effectively have been making wooden toys for their grandchildren? Why coffins? Part of the answer to that is, children don't go much for homemade wooden toys anymore, not when they can visit inexpensive and glossy places like Toys R Us. It sounds as if the Ulverstone idea of building your own coffin and facing your own mortality is incidental, in Rotorua, to gaining a little pleasure with woodwork, saving some money (eventually), and making some new friends. Friends and carpentry and a quirky hobby come first, and delay discounting death comes a pretty weak second. Coffin Club members in New Zealand maybe, can't really decide why they do it. Ditherers.

It seems to me that you can overdo this idea of strict delay discounting. Some psychologists have claimed that experimental subjects when faced with the prospect of an unavoidable small electric shock now or one later, will go for it now. People like to get their punishments over quickly, the psychologists claim. Do they? When I was a secondary school student in the state of Victoria I was educated by the Christian Brothers. Some were very amiable, very intelligent, and even holy men. Others were less intelligent, of dubious holiness, and were very violent. Some of those men, the ones with a taste for violence, seemed to enjoy nothing more than belting us, either on the spot or later in the day. We often had it coming. But I can say with all honesty that everyone I knew preferred a form of inverted *delay discounting* that entailed later in the day, or even the next day, or better still the next week. Our hope, I vividly recall, was that if we waited long enough the punishment might be forgotten, forgiven, and even just go away. Just as often it did too after a new target for the brotherly ire had been found. Aren't all people fueled by such a hope? This version of waiting, then, may be the real-life method for facing future unpleasantness. Dithering, once again, and waiting and pausing come to the rescue with a strategic benefit. In Solzhenitsyn's 1966 novel, *Cancer Ward*, the tale of Ward 13, a cancer ward in Soviet Central Asia, we learn of the very ill Pavel Nikolayevich Rusanov, a bullying "personnel officer" and nark. He's no devotee of delay discounting either and prefers long-term treatment to the more decisive, delay discounted operation: "'And an operation . . . Impossible'?" he tells his doctor. Alexandr Solzhenitsyn, the fearless Russian dissident, comments, "Behind the question lay an overriding fear—of being stretched out on the operating table. Like all patients, he preferred any other long-term treatment." As you can see from Pavel Nikolayevich Rusanov and from my schoolboy illustration, dithering and procrastination are perfectly natural and perfectly helpful ways of avoiding the worst. Dithering can save you from the immediate punishment of delay discounting. It's seems to me that if you can put your punishment off, you'll be a happier person. And there, if you like, is another strategic advantage of dithering. It's inverted discount delaying.

Self-handicapping, my third version of dithering, is something that gorillas are good at. Maybe it's not too different for humans. The gorillas will invite other gorillas "through gaze and gesture . . . to share interest in and attention to objects" when they play. This was observed by the primate psychologists Joanne Tanner, a Californian, and Richard Byrne, a Scot.[21] These gorillas, Tanner and Byrne observe, "share patterns of play . . . and re-engage after breaks. . . . Sometimes, gorillas . . . assist others in their efforts to engage in collaborative play." How do they do this? Here's the part that I like best. Occasionally "older gorillas encouraged younger partners [to continue to play] by 'self-handicapping' their own actions." The older apes will deliberately lose in the game to keep their younger partners stimulated. What is this but using for one's own advantage a calculated form of dithering, of indecisive waiting? It is also a type of procrastination, I suppose, where you deliberately put off the inevitable victory just for the sake of the pleasure of the game. If animals will self-handicap to gain personal advantage, then how much more might we expect this version of dithering of human beings?

Play, for Joanne Tanner and Richard Byrne in their 2010 article, is frequently a triangular or, as they put it, a triadic experience. It's one that is exercised by two individuals with some object. The play situation they have in mind could be, for example, two individuals with a ball. The two creatures know what they are going to do with the ball—probably a competitive game in which one or the other of them will somehow win by trying to keep the ball. But Tanner and Byrne report that for gorillas, when they play, "winning is not [always] the point." Just as important is the "continuation of the game." That's the reason why some of the great apes will deliberately lose. It keeps the ball rolling. This sort of "self-handicapping" is not common, as far they know, in other apes or animals. Compare dogs. In a game of tug with a human companion, dogs always play to win. Once they have the rope, they usually run away with it. That's what my dogs have done. Many humans are like this too. But not the ditherers. They prefer to wait indecisively and to keep things going.

They'll dither and deliberately lose, the gorillas, in Joanne Tanner's and Richard Byrne's report. These apes seem to understand that the game is more enjoyable than the victory. What about humans then? Do they ever do the same sort of thing just to keep the ball rolling? Here is a rather intriguing example. Leland Carlson and 17 of his friends established a club called the Dull Men's Club (DMC) within the New York Athletic Club. Leland Carlson explains why: "the Dull Men's Club began in New York when Grover Click was sitting with friends at the Long Bar . . . reading about the clubs-within-the-club—clubs for squash, sailing, skiing, judo—in the club's monthly magazine, *The Winged Foot*. 'We don't do any of those things,' one of them said. 'That's right, we are rather dull, wouldn't you say?' said another. 'Let's start a club-within-the-club for *dull men*,' said Grover." The idea was a club that would be "free from glitz and glam, free from pressures to be in and trendy—free instead to enjoy simple, ordinary things." The Dull Men's Club soon followed with its bans on exclamations points, its preference for "dull-lights" over highlights and its refusal to allow any office member to rank higher than assistant vice president. What can I say? The Dull Men's Club insisted not only on being dull, but also on institutional losing. There'd be a group of confirmed ditherers gaining great consolation from the lack of presidents in their lives. No one wins. They all self-handicap. The game dithers on.

Unfortunately, it wouldn't be fair to say that the Dull Men's Club has dithered indecisively from strength to strength. It is a rather specialist club and its membership seems to be steady and not virally growing. But Leland Carlson, the real-life version of Grover Click from the DMC, has an interesting website, members, newsletters, and in 2017 he produced a DMC book telling the stories of various waiters, ditherers, and insistently indecisive losers, in Joanne Tanner's and Richard Byrne's sense, called *Dull Men of Great Britain*. Among these waiters, ditherers, and losers there's Keith Jackson, for example, a waiter if ever there was one. He is a paint-drying expert ("a job that dull men everywhere would love to have"). There's also Nick West, a beer can collector, who has 7,522 cans all carefully displayed, and who speaks of "that special buzz I get whenever I find a new can." There's also a drainspotter (Archie Workman and his "life in the gutter"—Archie collects cast iron drain covers), a golf ball collector (Martyn Vallance has "more than 70,000 golf balls tucked away in his garden shed and attic"), a milk bottle collector ("I don't even like milk," says Steve Wheeler of his 20,000 bottle collection), a traffic cone collector ("nothing warms David [Morgan's] heart more than a traffic cone"), and a vacuum cleaner collector: "James [Brown] was a child prodigy in vacuuming" explains Leland Carlson. "He started the activity aged four, and had his own vacuum cleaner by the age of eight."

It's not just men. Amy-Louise Allen isn't a member of the DMC. She's a shoe designer from Walthamstow, northeast London, who was 31 years old when I wrote this paragraph and has been amassing Hello Kitty memorabilia ("Now, Amy's home in Walthamstow, London is full of items branded with the little white kitten, including 150 handbags, 50 cuddly toys, clothing, bedding and a 40 piece dinner set") since she was 11. In that 20 years she reckons she has spent about £30,000 on her obsession. Great for her. Amy-Louise has apparently spent £800 decking out her scooter as a Hello Kitty vehicle. I think she sounds wonderful. In self-defense she says: " 'My life is just a bit bonkers and I look a bit bonkers—but I'm not a total idiot.'"[22]

Amy-Louise Allen is a ditherer, a waiter, a hoarder, and a collector. She rivals any of the eccentric dull men in Leyland Carlson's book in sheer wanton strangeness. But her version of dithering and of hoarding and of pausing is probably as healthy as a two-mile jog followed by a cold shower enjoyed to the accompaniment of J. S. Bach's *Goldberg Variations* played by Glenn Gould. If ever you doubted the efficacy, if not necessarily the consolation, of focused hoarding, Amy-Louise Allen should be enough to stop your doubt. Unusual she may be, but her happiness is not in question.

There's more to Amy-Louise Allen's Hello Kitty collection and Leland Carlson's list of ditherers than mere British eccentricity. The cast of *Dull Men of Great Britain* and Amy-Louise Allen seem to make a virtue out of public self-handicapping. It's not for them to brag about their exploits on the bourse or in real estate deals. They are all keen on a world without presidents. They are laughed at and sneered at in equal measure for their ditherer's choices. Their gain from their version of self-handicapping is a type of honesty that is easily lost in the public world of ambition. Leland Carlson's self-handicapping celebration of dithering and of the ordinary is not as singular or as unusual as you might think. There's also James Ward who founded an annual "Boring Conference" in London: "a one-day celebration of the . . . ordinary and the overlooked—subjects which are often considered trivial and pointless." To make his pointless point more firmly, James Ward published a well-received book entitled *Adventures in Stationery: A Journey Through Your Pencil Case*. Ink, paper, pens, rulers, erasers, all are worthy of Ward's benign gaze. James Ward explains that he is, and his book shows it, a devotee of the infra-ordinary. And there's Pieter Hoexum. His most recent book shares the enthusiasm for the ordinary of Leland Carlson and James Ward. The book, *A Small Philosophy of the Row House* (2015), is, in its way, an example of the archaeology of the ordinary. Pieter Hoexum lives in a terraced house (a *rijtjeshus*) in a suburb of Purmerend in the Netherlands. He writes with feeling about mundane everyday little things: "the garden gate, the meaning of the sidewalk, the difference between an avenue and a street and their relationship to the row house."

When collections like Amy-Louise Allen's Hello Kitty assemblage get out of hand it's usual to drop the term collecting and to speak of hoarding.[23] Amy-Louise Allen's collection seems to sit on the border-line between collecting and hoarding, the border-line between hobby and obsession. Her version of collecting seems to be what you might call an active version of hoarding, one that seeks and acquires unnecessary things, usually quite decisively. I do this with books and with the music of Miriam Feuersinger and Margot Oitzinger. This sort of collecting, this active hoarding, can get out of hand. What I mean by "out of hand?" It's when the collection grows beyond a manageable size, isn't kept in place and clean, and tends to overwhelm the owner's life. Dithering, you could say, has suddenly become dangerous. The term that's used to describe this version of collecting is "compulsive hoarding." There are other names for this personality problem such as Hoarding Disorder, Diogenes Syndrome, Syllogomania (used more in French), Disposophobia (I am not joking), or Messie Syndrome (used more in German). I rather like the term Obsessive Compulsive Dithering (OCDi), which, you're right, I just invented. I include a brief discussion of hoarding here as a warning to all enthusiastic ditherers that things can get out of hand and that they should beware.

What is, to a degree, a strategy (good dithering and active hoarding) can become an overwhelming experience (bad hoarding). Where OCDi is involved the alarming advantages of indecisive waiting can transform themselves into alarming disadvantages.

The Mayo Clinic, in its discussion of hoarding, points out that: "Hoarding often creates such cramped living conditions that homes may be filled to capacity, with only narrow pathways winding through stacks of clutter." Hoarding like this can also be life threatening, because of the fire risk entailed by the presence so many moldering possessions, because of the risk of infection through the vermin those shopping bags may breed, and because of the risk of eviction that such a mess may inspire in a landlord. I wonder if one of the fundamental distinctions between humans and other animals is the capacity of humans for this dangerous version of hoarding? Collecting, whether it's stamps, money in the bank, or books, is a habit that seems to be rooted in proception, delay discounting, and even self-handicapping. But when this benign version of hoarding goes wrong it's called compulsive hoarding.

Hoarders are like collectors, but they dither in a self-destructive manner.[24] They self-handicap, but without intending to do so and without aiming to or gaining pleasure or advantage from their collection. They wait and wait to see when something might prove its value. Collectors such as the deliberately self-handicapping enthusiasts of *Dull Men of Great Britain* shouldn't be confused with hoarders. It would be easy, I'll admit, to confuse a man with "more than 70,000 golf balls tucked away in [a] garden shed and attic" with a hoarder. If you were to read the description of the hoarding personality provided by, say, the Mayo Clinic you might be more easily able to distinguish between hoarding and golf ball collecting. "Hoarding disorder," the Mayo explains, "is a persistent difficulty discarding or parting with possessions because of a perceived need to save them. A person with hoarding disorder experiences distress at the thought of getting rid of the items. Excessive accumulation of items, regardless of actual value, occurs." Many hoarders don't just keep things, they compulsively and uncontrollably accumulate. The golf ball collector is in control and can see a value, even if it is only a social value in the collection. A distinction between collecting and hoarding that is based on actively accumulating (collecting vacuum cleaners, for example) and being unable to part with any possession, no matter how minor (hoarding just about every household possession you've ever owned) shows the difference collecting and hoarding. Hoarding Disorder, so named, is a variant of Obsessive-Compulsive Disorder and that is a psychological illness. It is something over which a person has no easy control. The Dull Men are certainly in control.

The copperplate by Thomas Rowlandson (Figure 6.2) presents a bleak version of the life of the hoarder. It's nothing like Amy-Louise Allen's bedroom (which you can see in the article I've cited describing her all-consuming hobby). Rowlandson envisages hoarding as such a dangerous thing that it is beset by death—the threatening skeleton at the end of the hoarder's bed. And maybe this is how it is. I'd be a liar if I didn't admit this version of waiting has its attractions. I'll admit to finding something attractive about this awful room. But that is my problem, not yours. You can see why I'm writing this book.

Why do some people, such as our antiquarian hoarder, dither so much over divesting themselves of possessions? Why do they hoard? Why does their version of waiting become

DITHERING | 173

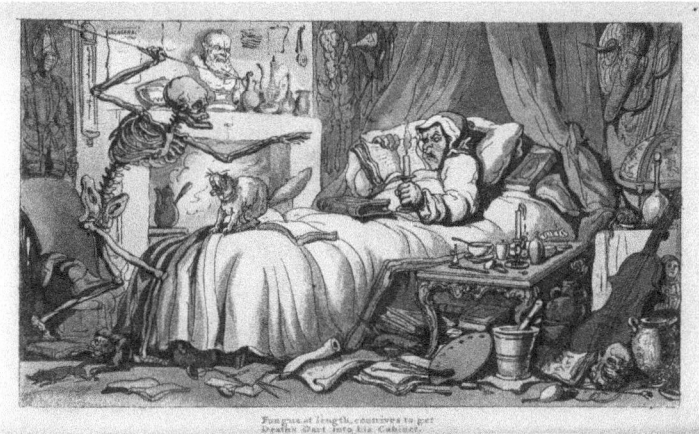

FIGURE 6.2. The skeleton of Death with the antiquarian hoarder in a bedroom filled with musical instruments, books, manuscripts, armor, a globe, a bust, rats, etc. Hand colored copperplate drawn and engraved by Thomas Rowlandson from *The English Dance of Death*, Ackermann, London, 1816. © Florilegibus/Bridgeman Images

so self-destructive? Paul Salkovskis and Sinead Lambe, both psychologists from the University of Bath, believe "that some people learn, very early in their life, that things they receive from others are more reliable and consistent than the people they came from."[25] They hoard therefore to make themselves more secure. They hoard as a way of consoling themselves. Salkovskis and Lambe suggest three other reasons for this compulsive version of dithering. Obsessive Compulsive Disorder (OCD) comes first—common activities of the obsessive may include hand washing, the enumeration of their possessions, checking to see if a door is locked, making sure a door is locked by pointless and repetitive activities—and of course a difficulty throwing things out; about 1.2% of the population suffer this illness. "Those with OCD who hoard often report having worries that their rubbish will contaminate or otherwise harm others, or that throwing away a possession connected to somebody will cause something bad to happen to that person." Fear of loss comes second: "For others, the experience of having nothing, or losing everything, seems to be important." And, third, some people have experienced the loss as a child of the family home. "For these people, holding on to possessions can provide insurance against future deprivation or losses." The hoarding, however injurious, can offer solace for the wounded personality, they suggest. It is strange to say it, but even this version of waiting, this sad form of dithering, compulsive hoarding, may have its advantages.

Everyone sympathizes with a ditherer—not that you'd necessarily want to be one. Given a choice between a decisive friend and a hesitant and dithering friend, most people will go for the hesitant and dithering friend. Perhaps some people will draw the line at procrastinators, who tend sometimes to infuriate. But many of us are sympathetic even with our procrastinating friends. There are considerable emotional advantages to be gained by being a ditherer or even a procrastinator—or even a hoarder. I am not for a minute suggesting that these personal qualities represent underpraised virtues. When they are too pronounced, the individuals who show such qualities can be maddening or even dangerous. But the humility that most ditherers display is an endearing quality in any person. Just read Professor Perry's book on procrastination if you doubt this.

There's another really good thing about dithering. It slows down time, allows us more time to contemplate what is about to or liable to happen, and to make the decision at the appropriate time. That's probably the very latest minute. This is Partnoy's conclusion as it relates to decision-making and as it relates to being effective in business. This version of dithering, a process rather than an emotional experience, is almost a competitive strategy—that's a very good reason for thinking of dithering as being alarming. But my aim in this book, of course, is much different, because I'm more concerned with the experience than with the strategy. Most of us, I believe, are prone to dithering and to procrastination. It may be that most of these apparent failings make all of us better people. Maybe we need to relax more about our failings. I don't think we should worry for one moment about good and bad business decisions. Most of us don't inhabit that world. Ours is one of friendly incompetence and of pausing. But maybe, just maybe, we're doing it right and that's the best world to live in.

The last two chapters have taken as their focus the idea of the pause. I have been trying to show that the pause can sometimes be a very beneficial thing indeed. In the next two chapters I'll turn the relation of waiting from the pause to dread and to death, and to loss. In Chapter 1 the image for these qualities that I highlighted was the empty chair. My next chapter will concentrate on the "empty chairs" of the human soul—death, religion, and dread.

DEATH, RELIGION, AND DREAD

7

HEAVEN CAN WAIT

That Empty Chair, Waiting, and the Beyond

THE ARTIST OF POP BANAL, Wilhelm Sasnal from Krakow, Poland, makes real sense out of the well-known painting in Figure 7.1. Here's what Sasnal thinks of Lucio Fontana's *Spatial Concept "Waiting"*:

> I'm surprised, looking very closely, that I can't see the wall behind the slash in the canvas. Some obstacle, something black, has been put behind the hole. It's not actually open. If you took this painting off the wall, the back would be blocked by this black linen, painted black. I have to say, I'm disappointed. I'd always believed that there was a void in this work—a gap—and not reality. Instead, Fontana created black.[1]

I *believe* I know what Sasnal is getting at. He seems to be saying that behind the slash in the painting there should be some sort of a super Reality (with a capital "R," the Real Thing, not just the Usual Thing, reality with little "r," the reality that we inhabit day by day). He calls what he'd hoped to see a void (that's what I've called Reality with the capital "R"). It's something that's not part of the mundane world in

DEATH, RELIGION, AND DREAD

FIGURE 7.1. Lucio Fontana (1899–1968), *Spatial Concept "Waiting,"* 1960. Tate Gallery, London. Photo Credit: © Tate, London 2019.

which we live. It's not the black linen Fontana placed on the back of the painting, nor is it the white wall on which the painting hangs, and which might have been visible without the black linen. According to the way that Sasnal imagines his *Spatial Concept "Waiting"* it's almost as if you could slip your hand right inside the slash and on into the void, on into the hyper-Reality.

Yes, Sasnal knows there's no Reality behind the canvas. All the same, like Sasnal, who wouldn't hope? So, when he finds out that it's just black linen and that his hand if inserted wouldn't go anywhere, he's disappointed.[2] It's possible that this is what Fontana wants his viewers to feel too. It's as if for

Sasnal and for Fontana the painting should offer the viewer a hint at the Real world or the non-ephemeral world, the transcendental world maybe Fontana would say, that some people hope exists behind the banal and mundane surface of the painting—or, what really matters, behind the banal and mundane surface of the world in which the mostly cheerful but mostly ignorant creatures like me, and maybe some of you, live.

All of that may sound a little fancy. But don't go taking the pistol to this dispatcher's head. My job is just to report on the state of the performance and to indicate to you whether it's liable or not to actually work. Let's then continue with this strange evocation of Reality and see whether or not it does work. Maybe it'd be easier to understand Sasnal's insight if you were to liken his Reality simply to the afterlife, or to the beyond. Many people believe in an afterlife. Many feel that it is an almost parallel world alongside of us all here on the earth. It's an afterlife where all of our lost relatives and friends, dogs, cats, budgies, and horses are waiting for us. Maybe they're even watching us from this place. It's there where we'll eventually go to join them. I'm not too sure that I believe this myself, but a lot of people do, and, well, good luck to them. I wish I could. This idea of the afterlife is more or less the same as that which some people term the beyond or the transcendental. I think that this may be what Sasnal and Fontana are getting at. The slash, the hint of Sasnal's void, offers (or denies) the possibility of Reality. Maybe what is behind this idea really is a dread of death—the empty chair that we encountered in Strandgade 30, Copenhagen. Maybe it's the fear of personal extinction, but also of never seeing again our lost relatives and friends, dogs, cats, budgies, and horses that makes Sasnal and Fontana want to wait for

Reality (again, the capital "R" Reality). And maybe all of this is what Sasnal is pointing at when he expresses his regret at there being nothing but black linen behind the slash. Wilhelm Sasnal was hoping for and waiting for a glimpse of the beyond, of the transcendental. I believe that's what he meant by "void." And perhaps this is what Lucio Fontana meant too. When Wilhelm Sasnal sees nothing but black cloth perhaps he fears that there's no beyond, no lost relatives and friends, dogs, cats, budgies, and horses. The waiting is in vain. You insert your hand into the slash and, bang, you hit the gallery wall.

How does all of this relate to the Waiting that's in the title of Fontana's painting and the Waiting that's in the title of this book? It'd be tempting to compare those empty round eyes in Barbara Hepworth's *The Family of Man*. When you look through those eyes it's also appealing to think that it's *Another Earth* behind them. But maybe not the Real. Does Fontana's title tell us any more about this glimpse of the Real (big "R") behind the real (little r) and, at the same time, can it tell us anything more about the nature of being on hold—of the waiting to which Fontana and to which I refer? I suspect that Fontana is trying to say that humans are all waiting for an understanding of the beyond, the transcendental, the Reality behind reality. They're waiting for someplace that might let us come to terms with death and with the empty chair. Fontana's slash, in just the way that Wilhelm Sasnal explains, dramatizes this "waiting." I believe that what Sasnal and Fontana are getting at is this: the experience of examining the painting entails in the viewer an experience of waiting. This is waiting for the reality of the void, the reality of Reality (the one with the big "R") to declare itself. Wilhelm Sasnal is disappointed because he's left permanently waiting for the appearance of Reality—or is forced to abandon the wait altogether. Sasnal's savvy interpretation of the painting is, in my opinion, probably just what Lucio Fontana meant by his title.

When you're trying to understand Lucio Fontana's painting and its evocation of waiting, the distinction between experience and situation is helpful once again. I mention this here because Fontana's picture aims to conjure a *situation* that will encourage the viewer to wait and to think about the big "R" behind the little "r." Remember the fish shop queue in Rochester? Those people in the fish queue in Kent were waiting for sure. But how did they feel? Some were bored, some were happy, and some seemed just nothing. The situation of waiting tells you zero about the experience of waiting. Back to Fontana: the situation that he envisages may entail waiting, if he insists on this, and if we can be bothered to believe him. It may even tell us something about being afraid of death, the door to the great beyond. But it certainly doesn't necessarily embody the *experience* of waiting. That's unless Lucio Fontana or Wilhelm Sasnal explain that this is the case and we, the viewers, agree on it. Maybe the way to describe Fontana's version of waiting is to say that it's an intellectual *strategy*, not unlike those waiting strategies of Frank Partnoy or of Daniel Kahneman or of Jason Farman. The waiting strategy in Fontana's case is aiming to help the viewer see beyond reality. It has nothing much to do with the experience of waiting or with how people actually feel with waiting. (Nor, for that matter, does it tell us convincingly that people yearn for "Reality" and are fed up to the gills with "reality" (little "r," the here and now).) As I keep on saying, this is a book mostly about experience. Experience entails, among other things, grief, unhappiness, and happiness. Situation is neutral or, at its very best, it's functional. It can get you some place (N. Hill & Son's fish shop, for example), but you mightn't feel very good about that place. You might think fish tastes rotten. Or you may even like it.

Two final observations need to be made about *Spatial Concept "Waiting."* Lucio Fontana's slashes have been linked with vaginas. Some people see this as a good and exciting use of sexualization, to paint holes in canvases like vaginas.[3] Others think not. One of my female colleagues characterizes these *Spatial Concept* paintings of Fontana as commercial sub-pornography. She has a good point, and just how validly she does I'll return to later. I believe, as well, that her opinion says something about the worth of all of this transcendental— no, religious—strategizing. Second, and even more importantly, is that Fontana's vision of waiting may be a sexualized one. I'll also return to this version as well. But for now, let's take a step back to another evocation of the spatial slash. This evocation will occur in Scandinavia.

"Our waiting has been a time of joy," says Karin when she finally sees God through a slash not in a painting, but in the wall of an old attic bedroom on an old Swedish island, Fårö, within the Baltic Sea. Within that slash in the wall Karin encounters God not once but twice. On the first occasion she falls to her knees then to her hips. The experience is ecstatic in the religious sense, but perhaps also orgasmic and even sexualized, though God does not actually appear to her, at least on this first occasion. She faints after seeming to hear voices behind the slash, within Fontana's and Sasnal's void. On her second, fixated viewing of the slash, God comes through the wall. "I came as quickly as I could, but it wasn't easy," she speaks towards the slash, "there are many who would stop me. I am so happy. Yes, I understand, I understand. Yes. I know it won't be long now. It's a great comfort to know that, but our waiting has been a time of joy." The last words that Karin says sum up the experience: "our waiting has been a time of joy." That's not the reaction to waiting we've become accustomed to encounter, though it might be one we'd like to be hearing and to be experiencing ourselves. Karin is speaking about the experience, not about the situation. Karin's reaction is certainly not how some would describe waiting in that queue in Rochester, Kent—though some might if they like fresh fish enough and they're in no rush. There are no strategies here on Fårö. Then, at the same time as Karin speaks to the wall, a small closet in that wall of the room swings open. "No God is going to walk through that door," Karin's doctor husband Martin tells her. Martin has just entered the room. She snaps back, "He'll be here any moment now. And I must be here." Karin is convinced that this time God actually will enter the room. What appears instead is a large black spider that emerges from the *Spatial Concept* slash. Karin screams and "I was frightened, the door opened but the god that came out was a spider. He came towards me and I saw his face. It was a terrible stony face. He crawled up and forced himself on me. But I fought him. The whole time I saw his eyes they were cold and calm. When he couldn't penetrate me he continued up my chest, up onto my face and up onto the wall." When she calms herself enough to speak again, she announces, "I have seen God."[4]

This strange, sexualized apparition happened in the year after Fontana had completed his *Spatial Concept "Waiting."* The apparition, including the slash in the wall that confronted Karin, appeared in a very famous movie

186 | DEATH, RELIGION, AND DREAD

FIGURE 7.2. This is 29 minutes and about 15 seconds into *Through a Glass Darkly* and Karin [Harriet Andersson] has her first divine encounter. A whispering voice of God comes through the slash in the wall next to her right hand. Karin is not quite Jenny Didier, but close. Harriet Andersson in Ingmar Bergman's *Sasom i En Spegel/ Through a Glass Darkly*, 1961. Photo 12/Alamy Stock Photo.

(Figure 7.2). The film was *Through a Glass Darkly* (1961) by the same Swedish director, Ingmar Bergman who made last chapter's *The Magic Flute*. Harriet Andersson played Karin. *Through a Glass Darkly* won an Academy Award in April 1962 for the Best Foreign Language Film.

Was Bergman "quoting" Fontana? I like to believe that he was, though he doesn't mention this in his autobiography, *The Magic Lantern*. Does the link between Bergman's slash and that of Fontana help us to understand the thinking behind *Spatial Concept "Waiting"*? It certainly makes it clearer. It shows again the link between waiting and the vision of a transcendent Reality, or God as Karin has it. It also shows again that there's no escaping sex when you meet up with this image of the slash. More important still is that Lucio Fontana's notion, that behind *reality* there is *Reality*, is precisely what Karin is getting at. The Reality for her is more exact than that of Fontana. For Fontana it's the beyond, the afterlife, the transcendent—one or another or all of those. For Karin it is God.

Ingmar Bergman doesn't think very much of this sort of a divine vision. He associates it with mental illness. He doesn't view it as a means for coming to terms with the empty chair. Karin is usually said to be suffering from schizophrenia. Her husband in the movie, Martin (played by Max von Sydow), says the illness is incurable. Bergman doesn't commend Karin's estimation of waiting for God when she claims, "our waiting has been a time of joy." Not for Bergman is the view of the writer of Psalms in the Old Testament who announces, "I waited patiently for the Lord: and He inclined unto me, and heard my calling." Karin's vision of God ends up being just a large, scary, and banal black spider that crawls haplessly through the slash and frightens the life out of her after trying to ravish her. At the end of *Through a Glass Darkly*, Karin is taken by helicopter to an asylum. This is at her own request. She wants to remain at her hospital because, she says, she can't go back and forth between the two realities (reality and Reality, we could say now). She opts for the hospital rather than the banal life with her husband, her father, David, and her brother, Minus. She doesn't really seem to have learned much at all from the slash. Ingmar Bergman's own sister Margareta suffered serious mental troubles too, though these don't appear to have led her to experience a dispiriting vision of God like Karin. Margareta Bergman appears to have used her own mental troubles as the backdrop to her novel *Mirror Mirror*... about the mental illness suffered by Jenny Didier. Jenny Didier, maybe you can recall, got us started. Margareta Bergman's other novel to have been translated into English is entitled *Karin*. Karin was also the name of Ingmar and Margareta's mother.[5] Margareta, minus God, is the real-life figure behind the schizophrenic Karin of *Through a Glass Darkly*.

Through a Glass Darkly, released just a year after *Spatial Concept "Waiting,"* provides a very moving but a very firm commentary on Lucio Fontana's 1960 painting. The Swedish director, Ingmar Bergman, insists to us that no amount of waiting and no amount of wishing will make God and Reality burst into your life. The experience may be ecstatic, the experience may be sexualized as well, but it will not reveal God, the Reality behind reality. Ingmar Bergman in this case attributes Karin's experience to a neurological disorder and to nothing more than a scary spider.

Simone Weil was not a movie character, like Karin, and she doesn't speak about slashes and about black spiders coming through walls. Though she does speak about her experience of waiting, if not her strategy for waiting. Her waiting is a time of joy and it is for God, the Reality behind reality. I don't believe that Simone Weil would have much sympathy for Karin, though she might have for Lucio Fontana. Simone Weil was a young Jewish French woman who finished her life, aged just 34, in 1943 in Ashford, Kent, not so far from Evelyn Dunbar in Rochester, working for the Free French during World War II. She died of tuberculosis as she prepared herself for a return to France and work with the Resistance. Simone Weil's celebrated work, *Waiting for God*, was published posthumously in French in 1950 and in English in 1951, 10 years before Karin saw God on Fårö. Her famous book shows that it's not just in the movies that individuals experience an encounter with God—with Reality. Simone was born into an agnostic Jewish household and grew more and more religious as she grew older. She was, by her own reckoning, waiting for God. And, just like Karin, she had an ecstatic encounter with God. This waiting confirmed itself in three strong religious experiences, not two like Karin.[6] The first of these experiences seems to have been in 1935. She had entered a small Portuguese village "on the very day of the festival of its patron saint." It was the procession and the singing of the fishermen's wives that so moved her. "I have never heard anything so poignant," she writes. "There the conviction was suddenly borne in upon me that Christianity is pre-eminently the religion of slaves, that slaves cannot help belong to it, and I among others." Weil's politics had always been left wing. This may explain her fervor for slaves. In 1932, for example, she visited Germany to help the Marxist activists in their battles against the nascent Nazis. In 1936 she visited the Republican forces in Spain to witness their battles against the Fascists. In 1937 the second, this time ecstatic religious experience took place in Italy in Assisi. In "the twelfth-century Romanesque chapel of Santa Maria degli Angeli . . . something stronger than I was, compelled me for the first time in my life to go down on my knees." This is what happened to Karin during her first vision of the slash in the wall. Both Simone and Karin had been waiting for God and both ended up on their knees. Weil's third experience occurred in 1938 at the Solesmes Abbey, a French religious community famous for Gregorian chant.

It was Easter and Simone Weil was suffering a terrible migraine. Migraines are often linked to mystical experiences—the famous medieval Christian mystic Hildegard of Bingen suffered from them too.[7] Simone Weil claims that, listening to the music, she was able "to find a pure and perfect joy in the unimaginable beauty of the chanting and the words." She later describes these experiences as "this sudden possession of me by Christ." Her waiting had been a time of joy. Had she found the Reality behind reality that eluded Wilhelm Sasnal in Lucio Fontana's *Spatial Concept "Waiting"*?

The ecstatic religious experiences of Karin in *Through a Glass Darkly* in Fårø in 1961 and of Simone Weil in Portugal in 1935, in Italy in 1937, and in northwest France in 1938 were provided with a very startling parallel just recently in Spain. *Live Science* reported a case of a 60-year-old Spanish woman who began to claim that she'd been not just speaking with the Virgin Mary, the Santa Maria, but also seeing and feeling her.[8] Before her religious experiences the woman is reported to have been "a happy, positive person who was not particularly religious." During the two months before her mystical experiences started, the woman "appeared sad and withdrawn, and also showed increasing interest in the Bible and other sacred writings." Not unlike Simone Weil, the Spaniard would spend many hours a day reading the Bible and "reciting religious writings." Her doctors performed an fMRI scan and discovered lesions within her brain. They performed a biopsy and concluded that she was suffering with a glioblastoma multiforme, a very nasty version of brain cancer. They followed up with chemotherapy and radiotherapy (the tumor was too large for surgery). They also prescribed antipsychotics, which are claimed sometimes to have an anti-cancer effect.[9] This treatment lasted for five weeks and during this period the mystical experiences with the Virgin Mary ceased. Sadly, the cancer did not cease along with the mystical visions. The woman "experienced a stroke two months after she started treatment . . . [and] eight months after her cancer diagnosis she died due to the progression of her tumor."

Karin was a schizophrenic. Simone Weil did not have a brain tumor, although she did suffer from migraines. Migraines, as I've just indicated, are sometimes linked with mystical experiences. Could her visions have been physical rather than supernatural? Do her strange mental conditions have a physical basis? Was Simone Weil ill, like Karin or like the Spanish woman, rather than seeing the Reality behind reality? Let's go back to the Spanish visionary for a moment longer. In her case the unexpected religious behavior came on very suddenly and represented an abrupt break from her previous behavioral patterns. Her religious behavior was "not preceded by a gradual change in her thinking and acting," the researchers, from the Hospital General Universitario Morales Meseguer in Murcia, Spain, wrote.[10] "Nor," they noted, "was there any kind of trigger or reason [for the behavioral change] except for the disease, and hence, it can be considered a clearly pathological experience." The Spanish research team also observed that the lesions in the woman's brain were on the right temporal lobe, a region of the brain that has sometimes been linked with mystical experiences. There was a final point: "before her cancer diagnosis, the patient may have experienced non-convulsive seizures, possibly as a result of her brain tumor. They suspected this because of particular changes they saw in her brain scan. Some cases of hyper-religious behavior have also been reported in people with epilepsy."[11] It would be rash to write off Simone

Weil's experience of waiting as something caused by mental illness or by physiological problems. Many Christians find her waiting inspiring and I have no intention of demeaning their understanding. I earn my living in a university department that includes Religious Studies. Some of my colleagues have the greatest of admiration for Simone Weil, just as I do for them. But, I suppose, we owe physiology the same cautious respect that we do the mystical experience.

Does the most famous piece of writing in the twentieth century concerning waiting have anything to do with mystical experiences? Nothing at all? Or is that rejection just on the surface of it? Samuel Beckett's *Waiting for Godot*, despite its beautiful title, shows a stealthy dependence on the same sources of inspiration that we've come to observe with Simone Weil and probably with the slashing Lucio Fontana. Weil's *Waiting for God* (as *En attendant Dieu*) was published in French in 1947. The French version of Irish émigré Samuel Beckett's play (as *En attendant Godot*), composed between October 9, 1948, and January 29,1949, was premiered on January 5, 1953, in the Théâtre de Babylone, Paris. The English *Godot* premiered in London at the Arts Theatre on August 3, 1955. *Waiting for Godot*, as well, may be the most famous piece of literature devoted to waiting in any century.[12] Here is what I'm getting at: *Waiting for Godot* was published about three and a half years after Simone Weil's posthumous *Waiting for God* and I don't believe it can have been produced in ignorance of Weil's book. The 1969 Nobel Prize winner Beckett lived in France from the early 1930s until his death in 1989. You can't easily avoid cultural influence when you're living and reading in that sort of intellectual and national proximity. There, then, is a hint of an answer to the query concerning the link between mysticism and the most famous piece of writing in the twentieth century about waiting.

But what is the story of *Waiting for Godot*? Here is Samuel Beckett's biographer Deidre Bair's summary of the play.[13]

> It is the story of two men, Vladimir and Estragon, who amuse themselves with conversation that alternates between hope and despair while they wait for a person called Godot to keep his appointment. In each of the two acts of uneven length, they encounter a man called Pozzo and his slave, Lucky.... In each act a young boy tells them that Godot will not come today but will surely keep his appointment tomorrow. In the second act a tree which has been bare in the first act suddenly sprouts leaves.

What isn't said here is just how funny the play can be. The English version was translated by Beckett himself and is subtitled "a tragicomedy in two acts." The black humor of *Waiting for Godot* is perhaps what makes such a bleak and spare piece of theatre so enjoyable. That's not all. As Dr. Seuss pointed out, "Everyone is just waiting." You may find that a little flippant, to compare the philosophical point of a Nobel Prize winner with the poetry of a best-selling children's author. But both writers make a very simple and similar point. And anyhow, if ever there was a play that ennobles Dr. Seuss, *Waiting for Godot* is it. And: don't most friends kid one another like the pair of waiters Vladimir and Estragon? (*Est*: "Now let's make up." *V*: "Gogo!" *Est*: "Didi!" *V*: "Your hand!" *Est*. "Take it!" *V*: "Come to my arms!" *Est*: "Your arms?" *V*: "My breast!" *Est*: "Off we go." They *embrace. They separate. Silence.* *V*: "How time flies when one has fun!" *Silence. Est*: "What do we do now?" *V*: "While waiting." *Est*: "While waiting." *Silence.* *V*: "We could do our exercises.") Aren't they just like us? And don't most viewers identify closely with the skeptical and ever pessimistic Estragon? Or is it just me? The play is also very popular because it appeals, dare I say it, to an adolescent strain in many of us that sees the world as something where you wait without expectation and in which waiting without hope is the dominant characterizer (of Lucky's name in the play Beckett comments, according to Deidre Bair: "I suppose he is lucky to have no more expectations . . ."). Godot, representing some sort of a miserable and unattainable hope, never gets around to appearing. Isn't that just how it is? No wonder the play is so perennially popular. But what has it got to do with mysticism and Simone Weil?

This is a simple way to understand the genesis of *Waiting for Godot*. This may help to provide an answer to the question concerning mysticism. The name Godot, though having nothing to do with God in French, does in English. The echo in the title, at least in English, of Simone Weil's recent and famous *Waiting for God* is pretty hard to overlook. Beckett's Godot never arrives to see Vladimir and Estragon and we all know he won't be coming. That offers some estimation of our chances with God in Beckett's opinion. He or She won't be coming any time soon. We'll likely be waiting in vain. That's what Ingmar Bergman, in his serious Swedish manner, is saying too in *Through the Glass Darkly*. You could even make this a little less religious and a little more palatable by thinking of Godot as the Reality (the big "R" one) that so intrigued Lucio Fontana—or the afterlife or the beyond or the transcendent that was signified by the slash on the canvas. Beckett is saying in his very funny play that your chances of linking up with Reality or with the afterlife or the beyond or the transcendent are Buckley's. Most people, as I've already said, believe in an afterlife that exists alongside of us all here. This idea of the afterlife is more or less the same as what some people term the transcendental or the beyond. Beckett appears to think, then, that everyone is *Waiting for Godot*. But She or He won't be coming, and you'd better get used to the idea of death. So much for Simone Weil's three mystical experiences, he could be saying. Samuel Beckett's play, you might interpret, is in full agreement with the diagnosis of that unfortunate sick Spanish woman: the mystical experience is probably the product of illness—the visions were physical rather than supernatural. Beckett is perhaps saying that this applies to the lot of us. God won't be coming. Your chances of meeting Him or Her are as good as Didi's and Gogo's of meeting Godot (or Godet or Godin). There's no Reality behind reality. This makes Beckett's likely attitude to Simone Weil easier to understand—if we can presume to guess at it. He thinks the mystical link with the divine that she'd been waiting for and that she believed she'd experienced would come to nothing. Godot will never arrive, so you'd better enjoy the company of Vladimir.

Of course, there's more to *Waiting for Godot* than just a commentary on mystical visions of Reality. *Waiting for Godot* was composed in a period during which waiting without hope seemed to be understood as the defining characteristic of what it was to be human. It was a period that played on easy alienation and existential waiting. Eugene O'Neil's mammoth, four-hour play about waiting for Hickey (another disappointing Reality figure) in *The Iceman Cometh* was played first in 1946. Saul Bellow's waiting novel *The Dangling Man*, in which a young, unemployed man named Joseph waits to be drafted to service in World War II, dates from 1947, six years before Beckett's play was first produced. So does Malcolm Lowry's alcoholic masterpiece that dramatizes a fruitless anticipation of death and resurrection. That's *Under the Volcano* and it is all about coming to terms with death. This was also the year of Albert Camus' *The Plague*—the citizens of the plague-ridden city Oran wait for death or cure—and it was the year of that terrible of tract of hopeless waiting, *The Diary of Anne Frank*. And 1947 was the *annus horribilis* when the famous Doomsday Clock was first set ticking. The clock was set up by the Board of Atomic Scientists (BAS) in response to the development of atomic weapons and it aims to dramatize the nearness of Armageddon. The clock is claimed to represent an accurate indicator of the vulnerability of the planet to destruction by nuclear weapons, climate change, and the deleterious new technologies in the life sciences. This was the beginning of the Cold War and the sense that nuclear destruction really might be just around the corner for the planet. It's not just global nuclear destruction—the hopeless of the 1930s Great Depression is behind *The Dangling Man*, just as it is behind *The Iceman Cometh* in which a cast of firm-minded drunks in the Bowery await the arrival of Hickey, their disappointing deliverance. The modernist allure of such big-picture hopelessness seems to have faded a little, even if the Doomsday Clock still ticks on vigorously. Who would say it's lucky to live without expectations? And who finds much solace with John Cage? As a purposeful activity, waiting seems more related to personality these days than it does to the human condition. Beckett, these days, is as easily understood as a brilliant depressive, and *Waiting for Godot* is the ultimate depressive's play. Wasn't it Peggy Guggenheim who used to call Samuel Beckett Oblomov, after the bored and melancholy hero of Ivan Goncharov's novel, *Oblomov*?[14] Or maybe it was after Edouard Manet.

Martin Heidegger (1889–1976), that periodically infamous German philosopher, may be perhaps the strongest influence behind both Simone Weil's and Samuel Beckett's thinking. Weil reverberates in tune with Heidegger, while Beckett dissonates with Heidegger. The philosopher has a very influential take on waiting (which he tends to see through the lens of boredom).[15] The vision of waiting is based on his philosophical understanding of time. Heidegger was concerned for most of his career with answering the question, "what is Being?" By Being (with a capital "B") he means more or less the same thing that I have intended by Reality (with a big "R"). The philosopher's most significant take on the "Being Problem" came in 1927 with his most influential book, *Being and Time*. The monograph has had a very powerful influence on the ways that waiting, time, and especially boredom have been understood.[16] It is squarely behind the ideas not just of Simone Weil and Samuel Beckett but also of the slash artist, Lucio Fontana. The "Being Problem," just as you would expect from a famous German moral philosopher, is vigorously thought through. It is a view that has had enormous influence on left-liberal and even socialist politics. I am not sure how this influence on the Left came about. Until 1915 Heidegger was a reasonably conservative Catholic thinker and, but for poor health, it's said, he would have become a Jesuit (he left the novitiate because of a psychosomatic heart condition, apparently). Heidegger had a successful university career for a time and was elected rector (president or vice-chancellor) of the University of Freiburg in 1933. The philosopher's enthusiasm for Hitler allowed him to join, in the same year, the National Socialist German Workers' Party (the Nazi Party). He expressed his interest in the ideals of the National Socialist Party in his inaugural address as rector in 1933. Heidegger lasted but one year in this position, although he remained a member of the Nazi Party until the end of World War II and the Nazi defeat. In the post-war period the philosopher was banned from university teaching because of his involvement with the Nazi Party. By 1951 Martin Heidegger was deemed to have paid reparation and was allowed to resume university instruction. He died in 1967 and had what seems to have been a Catholic funeral. Perhaps Heidegger's popularity is in part the result of the French philosopher and writer, Jean-Paul Sartre. The communist Jean-Paul appears to have been one of the earliest of the many French thinkers of the Left to be influenced by Heidegger's ideas. The German-American intellectual and political scientist Hannah Arendt also plays a role here. Along with left and left-leaning liberals like Sartre, she had considerable influence in the United States where she championed the philosopher's work. (Arendt greatly admired Simone Weil as well as Heidegger.[17]) Such has been the influence garnered to Heidegger's enterprise until recently, especially if you work in a university, that to doubt it is tantamount to farting in church.

The Kent fish shop queue might help us again, but this time to understand Martin Heidegger just a little. I say just a little with due caution, because Heidegger's thought and expression are notoriously difficult to comprehend. Imagine that you are standing on your own in that fish shop queue. Time is passing and it seems to be passing more and more slowly. The longer you wait the more bored you may become—let's just assume this experience. The wait may be becoming so long that the situation may seem like a complete waste of time. To distract yourself from this tedium you look for things to kill time with—maybe your phone? But that helps for only so long and besides it's too cold on your

fingers in winter in Rochester to be messing with a phone—
yes, I know they weren't invented in 1944, but you get my
meaning. Heidegger seems to believe that this sort of waiting
and the boredom that it may engender helps us to understand our genuine selves better. How is this? Deprived of
distractions such as phones (it's too cold for them) and talk
with friends (you don't know anyone) you become alarmed
by the experience of time slowing and weighing so crushingly
on you. We are, Heidegger believes, encountering raw time,
thanks to waiting and boredom. Lars Svendsen explains that
in this situation "the self is brought into a naked encounter
with itself, as the self that is there and left to its own devices."
This is, interprets Svendsen, a moment of "liberation" for the
individual or, as Heidegger puts it, a "moment of vision." This
fish shop waiting and its boredom "removes a veil . . . from
things," continues Svendsen, "and allows them to appear
empty and ephemeral." What remains after the veil of triviality has been removed from our lives is "nothing less than
Being."[18] We are back to Reality, with a capital "R." Heidegger
never terms this Being or Reality "God," but it would be easy
to make the equation, as I am sure Simone Weil and Martin
Heidegger may have done. The American-English critic
George Steiner observes, "the substitution of . . . 'God' for
Sein [Being] in many key passages in Heidegger's texts is un-
deniably plausible."[19]

Heidegger's vision of Being, thanks to waiting and
boredom, possibly may have allowed him to come to terms
with death more satisfactorily. Perhaps this is also the case for
the famous French philosopher and writer Jean-Paul Sartre
(1905–1980).[20] Sartre studied in Germany before World War
II and seems to have been come into contact with Heidegger's
work in this period and as well during the time he was a

German prisoner of war (1940–1941). This idea of Being or Reality is usually said to have influenced Sartre's most famous philosophical text, *Being and Nothingness* (1943). Sartre maintained, a little like Heidegger, that in everyday life our business, that "veil of triviality," blinds us to the true nature of our existence. In those times we are merely playing at existing, much as an actor plays at a role. Self-awareness is encouraged by waiting and boredom, Sartre believes, in much the same way as it was for Heidegger. There follows, he maintained, a gap between the self-knowledge waiting and boredom can produce and that which is lost when we are merely acting our roles. That self-awareness can be painful and disgusting, Sartre believed. Jean-Paul's mode of understanding time and waiting and boredom is also dramatized in his novel *Nausea*. For Sartre, however, there is not the solace of Being, of a sort of an encounter with Reality. An honest encounter with self-awareness is about as good as it gets. Death is still a problem. Ho hum.

In the same year that Karin confronted the divine spider on the island of Fårö and two years before Jean-Paul Sartre was offered the Nobel Prize, a short novel entitled *Awaiting Oblivion* was produced by the greatly admired Maurice Blanchot.[21] Here is a portion of the Kirkus review of this much esteemed tract:

> a man and woman alone in a sparsely furnished hotel room who try to remember what has happened to bring them there as they apprehensively await whatever will happen next. Their reserved confusion and quiet desperation eventually impress upon them (and us) the realization that imagination (or, if you will, writing) can create reality—and offer the paradoxical solace that seems to rest at the heart of Blanchot's writing: the

sense that even language that expresses meaninglessness can't help but contain and, therefore, convey meaning.

Even from this very brief summary it should be clear that, whatever else you may think of *Awaiting Oblivion* as a piece of fiction, it uses waiting as a *strategy*, just as have all of the other writers in this chapter. The strategy is designed to tell us something about the gap between language and its referents, or between language and meaning, and the gloominess that this gap can cause some individuals. (Think, at the simplest, of the way that language can be twisted in politics and even in human relations.) I don't believe that Blanchot has any special interest in the experience of waiting. His man and woman are waiting for "meaning" and it never comes, though they discover that even gibberish, you could say, means something. I mention Blanchot here because what we seem to be viewing in *Awaiting Oblivion* is the persistent idea of a Reality behind reality. The meaninglessness of language that so perturbs our male and female is the reality (with the small "r"). Lurking behind this gibberish is some sort of order, some sort of meaning, Blanchot is claiming. As I have been suggesting, with this Reality we are pretty much in the locale of God or a God of some sort or another—the afterlife or the beyond or the transcendent that hid behind Fontana's slash.

One of the things that holds nearly all of the people together from this chapter and their interest in transcendence and the fear of death is their lack of interest in other human beings. It's particularly striking in Sartre's case. One of the weaknesses of his very stagey plays (he was a dramatist as well as a philosopher) is that his characters don't come to life. His best non-philosophical literature is all about himself (the novel *Nausea*, which was based on his time as a schoolmaster in Le Havre, and his autobiography, *Words and Things*). I believe that you could also level this objection against Maurice Blanchot's jejune characters in *Waiting for Oblivion*. Blanchot's ideas are interesting enough, but their evocation is not something that would have thrilled Aristotle. I suppose that if that's your taste in books it's fine, but the bulk of us are more grounded in the messy minutiae of human life. The sort of religious speculation that animates Lucio Fontana, Heidegger, Weil, Sartre, and Blanchot is the Reality behind the reality. If you don't believe in the existence of this Reality, if you don't believe that its existence has any demonstrable basis, and if, like me, you are easily bored by the transcendent, then this stuff will not be for you.[22] There are other ways to deal with the fear of death than by creating Reality (with a capital "R"). And: what has all of this speculation got to do with the Sermon on the Mount, says Bazza Simpkins to me.[23]

During the 1980s, for a little while, this cigarette advertisement (Figure 7.3) was on billboards all over the place. This was especially true in the United Kingdom. The image was so widespread that there was even a very funny discussion of it in David Lodge's extremely popular 1989 campus novel, *Nice Work*. Robyn Penrose, a temporary lecturer at the University of Rummidge in English (with a specialization in feminism and the industrial novel), thought the *Silk Cut* advertisement was especially lubricious. Here she is seen arguing with Vic Wilcox, the manager of J Pringle & Sons Casting & General Engineering ("Pringle's") whom she has been assigned to "shadow" at his work as part of her university assignment. This is a description of what Robyn and Vic are arguing about:

HEAVEN CAN WAIT | 203

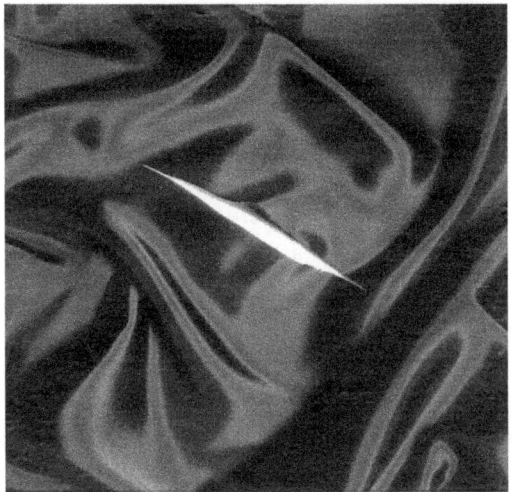

SMOKING WHEN PREGNANT
HARMS YOUR BABY
Chief Medical Officers' Warning
5mg Tar 0.5mg Nicotine

FIGURE 7.3. Silk Cut cigarettes magazine advertisement, UK. © The Advertising Archives/Bridgman Images.

Every few miles, it seemed, they passed the same huge poster on roadside hoardings [the Silk Cut advertisement that I've reproduced in Figure 7.3], a photographic depiction of a rippling expanse of purple silk in which there was a single slit, as if the material had been slashed with a razor. There were no words in the advertisement, except for the Government Health Warning about smoking. . . . The shimmering silk, with its voluptuous curves and sensuous texture, obviously symbolized the female body, and the elliptical slit, fore-grounded by a lighter color showing through, was still more obviously a vagina.

I don't blame Robyn for being irritated. It's another vagina that we have here, and that sort of a display is no way to advertise anything. But there's more going on here than just sub-pornography. The Silk Cut image has a history. Even if you look at it just with a proper sense of righteous indignation, you can see how it's picked up on Lucio Fontana's *Spatial Concept "Waiting"* from 1960. The version of the cigarette advertisement that I have here comes from 1983, a mere 23 years after Lucio Fontana. And actually, not just 23 years, for the indefatigable maestro had produced a number of other near identical versions of the slash as late as 1968, and one in blushing, rubbery red. The advertising agency could have known our painting. The staff of the London advertising agency pushing the cigarettes could have even seen Fontana's *Waiting* for themselves. The Tate Gallery purchased the picture in 1964 and you can still see it there. Lucio Fontana had, as we've just said, produced a number of well-known replicas.[24] In fact he painted this image again and again, in different colors, occasionally in different media, and often with more than one slash. Fontana's enthusiasm for the slash is reminiscent of the less lubricious Povel Wallander who painted the same landscape, just as successfully I believe, over and over again. Wallander's paintings seem to have sold too. Povel was the fictional father of the book and TV detective Kurt Wallander, created by Henning Mankell. Lucio Fontana's images of waiting apparently sold well in the 1960s. They sold so well that one of his friends, the dashing Enrico Castellani, created versions of this very same image.[25] He appears to have had the same ideas about the future of art as did the Argentinian-Italian Lucio Fontana. Enrico Castellani called the work he did using this waiting image Zeromovement Painting. It sold and sells well too. There is money to be had in vaginal waiting concepts.

No wonder that Saatchi & Saatchi, the advertising agency responsible for the Silk Cut campaign, was keen on the image.[26] And the advertising campaign worked. For a while the *Silk Cut* image was everywhere and lots of people smoked back in the days when cigarette smoking didn't give you cancer. You wouldn't get away with the *Silk Cut* image these days. Robyn is right, though she doesn't seem necessarily to have known about Lucio Fontana and Enrico Castellani. Let's go back to Robyn Penrose's argument with Vic. She explains what she means like this:

> ROBYN: "In the case of the Silk Cut poster, the picture signifies the female body metaphorically: the slit in the silk is like a vagina . . ."
>
> VIC: (flinching) "So you say."
>
> ROBYN: "All holes, hollow places, fissures and folds represent the female genitals."
>
> VIC: "Prove it."
>
> ROBYN: "Freud proved it, by his successful analysis of dreams . . . But the Marlboro ads don't use any metaphors. That's probably why you smoke them, actually."

Robyn's not right about Freud, but I think she's right about the slit. And if that's the case, then she'd be right to make the same claim about Fontana's painting. Where does that leave us? With commercial sub-pornography, I guess.

But there's more to come. Most of this chapter has been trying to explain the link between the idea of the Reality (with the capital "R"—transcendence, the afterlife, the beyond, even God) behind reality. Waiting, we've seen, is often touted as a very efficient means for getting in touch with

Reality. Just as Wilhelm Sasnal showed, that's the tradition to which Fontana's *Spatial Concept "Waiting"* belongs and, crazy and all as it may seem, that is the tradition to which the Silk Cut advertisements belong. How could it have ended up this way? Is it something in the very nature of religious waiting, something that is profoundly trite and something that easily draws its embodiment to hack work? Or is it all just one of those accidents of history? Why should the powerful idea that there exists behind reality (the banal one with a small "r") a transcendental Reality, one that points to the beyond, and one to whose access waiting offers a special approach, why should such an idea have become so trivialized? My own opinion, as you probably know well by now, is that there is no link to be found between waiting and the perception of the beyond, the afterlife, the transcendental, or even God.[27] Waiting, as it's understood by the thinkers of this chapter, is little more than a situation, a handy idea, an idealized process, a mere symbol. Symbols are anyone's business. Symbols can lead as readily to pornography as to the afterlife. In all of this, I think you'll agree, the empty chair has been forgotten.

8

"THE LITTLER WAITING ROOM"

Can You Make the Best of Dread—and of Waiting for Approaching Death?

> I hate when they make you wait in the room. 'Cause it says "Waiting Room" there's no chance of not waiting. 'Cause they call it the waiting room, they're going to use it. They've got it. It's all set up for you to wait.

THIS IS THE VERY WEALTHY comedian Jerry Seinfeld. He's complaining about waiting rooms in doctor's offices.[1] The beefs come from his 1990s TV show, *Seinfeld*. The episode was entitled *The Girlfriend*. Seinfeld is right about waiting rooms.[2] They're as boring as can be. Their décor never makes them any better, either. I'll bet if Jerry Seinfeld had looked up at the wall of his waiting room then he'd have spotted a vapid but pretty reproduction just like Pierre Bonnard's *Early Spring. Little Fauns* (Figure 8.1).

It's the French countryside in the spring in the south about five years before the First World War. Pierre Bonnard, who was around 42 when he created this canvas, hadn't quite

208 | DEATH, RELIGION, AND DREAD

FIGURE 8.1. What to watch for in the waiting room. Pierre Bonnard (1867–1947), *Early Spring. Little Fauns*, 1909. Oil on canvas. 102.5 cm × 125 cm. The State Hermitage Museum, St. Petersburg. Photograph © The State Hermitage Museum /photo by Vladimir Terebenin.

yet found a reliable voice. Bonnard, despite this canvas, is a usually pretty good painter. This image concerns hope and a waiting for the full burst of spring. Those fauns really ruin the picture, but you can see what Bonnard means. Seinfeld's doctors might have put the canvas up on their waiting room walls as an image of what their treatments will offer to the ailing patient. From their waiting room will come spring, hope, health, and a touch of the vivifying supernatural. Pierre Bonnard, in his early years at least, often had quite a line on calming clichés like this one. He could, when he wanted to, paint the perfect images, especially of children or child-like figures and animals, for reasonably intelligent waiting rooms.

> And you sit there, you know, and you've got your little magazine. You pretend you're reading it, but you're really looking at the other people. You know, you're thinking about them, things like "I wonder what he's got. As soon as she goes, I'm getting her magazine."

It's still the tedium that's bugging Jerry Seinfeld. But illness is starting to creep in. Seinfeld isn't just in the waiting room for nothing. What have the other waiters got wrong with them, he asks?

> And then, they finally call you and it's a very exciting moment. They finally call you, and you stand up and you kinda look around at the other people in the room. "Well, I guess I've been chosen. I'll see you all later."
>
> You know, so you think you're going to see the doctor, but you're not, are you? No. You're going into the next waiting room. The littler waiting room.

The waiting for your diagnosis is postponed. What's really going to happen in the littler room? Maybe it's so small because they want to carry out some sort of medical procedure on you?

> But if they are, you know, doing some sort of medical thing to you, you want to be in the smallest room that they have, I think. You don't want to be in the largest room that they have. You know what I mean?

Going under the knife? That would mean a very big room and who knows how many people watching on. The littler room is much safer. They can't do much to you in one of those.

> You ever see these operating theaters, that they have, with like, stadium seating? You don't want them doing anything to you that makes other doctors go, "I have to see this!" "Are you kidding? Are they really gonna do that to him?" "Are there seats? Can we get in?" Do they scalp tickets to these things? "I got two for the Winslow tumor, I got two."

Is it really going to be the knife?[3]

But dread isn't all that it's cracked up to be.[4] Not if you're Jerry Seinfeld. His way of dealing with a wait for something that might be very bad for your long-term well-being is to make as light of the experience as he can. There is, and not just in Seinfeld's sketches, a dose of frivolity and of fun that can be attached to the prospect of waiting to find out how ill you are. Well, there is in the way that Seinfeld has dressed it up. It's not that waiting to learn that you are suffering from something terrible, even fatal, is ever pleasant. It's not that waiting to be treated for something that could be life threatening is ever pleasant either. The surprise is that sometimes the waiting is unexpectedly better—no, I should say less worse or even littler—than you could ever have imagined. That's what I hope anyway. And if the experience isn't always fun (yes, I am serious—I am sure to experience it sooner than you), then some people turn the experience of waiting without much hope in the waiting room of life to their own advantage. That's what I'll be talking about in this chapter.

The wait for wrinkles to appear might demonstrate my point. The possibility of wrinkles on her face produced such dread for 50-year-old Tess Christian that, in an effort to avoid them, she hadn't smiled for decades. She claims it worked: "I don't have wrinkles because I have trained myself to control my facial muscles. . . . Everyone asks if I've had Botox, but I haven't, and I know that it's thanks to the fact I haven't laughed or smiled since I was a teenager. My dedication has paid off, I don't have a single line on my face." Dread, waiting in fear for something bad to happen, is said to be exacerbated by the amount of time spent waiting. By this point Mrs. Christian ought to be living in complete horror. But it seems, from her photos, that she's managed the horror. The attractively smooth finish of her complexion shows just how well Tess has turned dread and, yes, waiting in the waiting room of life, to her own advantage. [5]

Were it not for the visible success of Mrs. Christian's cure you might be tempted to say that dread is always a very bad thing. But, sitting opposite her current beloved at the dinner table, she can be sure of one thing: dread has helped her to keep her looks. Who knows, maybe it's helped keep her beloved in place in the dining room too. This disturbing version of waiting, dread I mean, seems to have served Tess Christian very well.[6] Psychologists believe they can demonstrate that most individuals will chose more pain sooner, rather than a drawn-out easier process of pain (never laughing or smiling must be painful.) Waiting for pain is almost as painful as pain itself. It wasn't the case for Mrs. Christian. Dread, which I understand loosely to be a state of waiting in fear ("anticipating with great apprehension or fear" expands the *Oxford English Dictionary*), seems to have done Tess Christian an unexpectedly good turn. What I admire about Ms. Tess Christian is that she might be aging, but she's still in the game. She's turned waiting to her own advantage.

> And so it stays just on the edge of vision,
> A small, unfocussed blur, a standing chill
> That slows each impulse down to indecision.
> Most things may never happen: this one will,
> And realization of it rages out
> In furnace-fear when we get caught without
> People or drink. Courage is no good:
> It means not scaring others. Being brave
> Let's no one off the grave.
> Death is no different whined at than withstood.
>
> <div align="right">PHILIP LARKIN, <i>Aubade</i></div>

An *Aubade* is a poem written for the appearance or even the wait for dawn. That's the time of day when Bonnard's fauns were at work. Philip Larkin is waking at dawn, without fauns, and he records his reaction. It's all about death— "Death is no different whined at than withstood."[7] Where is the waiting? It's shown when Larkin tells us that death is "just on the edge of vision," that it's a "standing chill that slows down each impulse to decision." Larkin is full of "furnace-fear" of the prospect of death. Maybe he is right to be, as his death was not a good one. He died of inoperable esophageal cancer on December 2, 1985, at the age of 63. With the *Aubade* it's as if he opts out of the game.

The poet Clive James is waiting to die right as I am writing. He's not imagining the prospect like Philip Larkin. James is matter of fact about the closeness of his death. He doesn't hide his doom for one sentence, despite Larkin's "being brave lets no one off the grave." But I need to be cautious. Clive James was open about waiting to die when I was first writing this sentence. Whether the Australian writer and broadcaster will still be alive when this sentence is finally revised is difficult to predict. (Alas, he isn't.) Despite his emphysema and leukemia, it feels as if Clive James is in with a chance. I'd punt on Clive James if I were a gambler. Why I want to bring him up here is that I have never read of any dying man who could make such a shameless joke of his condition. Clive James may be an accomplished poet, but he doesn't react to death like Philip Larkin. If ever there was an illustration showing that, sometimes, waiting without much hope is unexpectedly better than you could ever have imagined, then Clive James provides it.

After an off-and-on career as a boozer and a smoker, then 71-year-old James owned up in 2011 that he was suffering from B-cell chronic lymphocytic leukemia. At that point he'd been in treatment for 15 months at Addenbrooke's Hospital in Cambridge. He also admitted at that time to having been diagnosed with emphysema and kidney failure in 2010. But he keeps—or kept—on going. In an interview with Charlie Stayt on the BBC that was aired on the 31st of March 2015, Clive James gave a sample of his attitude to his own not so rapid decline. He characterized himself on that occasion as "near to death but thankful for life." Six months later he pulled the rug from beneath everyone's feet. In October 2015 James confessed to feeling "embarrassment" at still being alive.[8] He'd achieved his longevity because of a new and experimental drug treatment. There is—or there was, and how I dread the was—something almost saintly about the joking way that Clive James has tackled his embarrassment of a death.

Clive James was born named Vivian Leopold James in the working-class suburb of Sydney called Kogorah. The great day was the 7th of October 1939. As he grew older, he didn't like having what he saw as a woman's name and chose what he reckoned was the manly moniker of Clive instead of Vivian. James is by aspiration an Australian poet, author, critic, broadcaster, translator, and memoirist. But he might as well be a British writer for all that—he has lived in England since 1962 and perhaps it's the English who love him best. To many readers Clive James is most well-known for his autobiographical series *Unreliable Memoirs* and others to follow. For others he's most admired for his voluminous journalism that focused mainly on television (and which has been collected again and again in such books as *The Crystal Bucket* or *Glued to the Box*). But if you watch TV then you may know him best for his very funny chat shows and documentaries. Clive James really has lived as an Englishman since he left Australia aged 23 and soon after graduating from the University of Sydney (where he was a contemporary of the feminist Germaine Greer, author of *The Female Eunuch*, and of the late art critic Robert Hughes, author of *The Shock of the New*.) What is James best at? I think he'd like most to be remembered as a poet. The jury is out on that one. His greatest gift may be as a humorist. Robert McCrum explains, "Ask him what kind of a writer he is—critic, novelist, poet, memoirist, translator, or journalist—and he's likely to say, with earnest flippancy, that he's running a mixed business. 'In Australia,' he explains, 'it's the one shop in the suburb that sells a bit of everything: fishing line, frying pans and flypaper. It's quite a hard thing to run.'"[9] That just proves the point about humor. I'd also say that there aren't too many mixed businesses left in Sydney. Maybe Clive James will take them with him.

Clive James managed to turn waiting to die into a pretty good joke.[10] Perhaps it helped that he was not in pain—or so he claimed—but Clive James is a tough geezer and would probably make a joke of his pain anyway. "What I've got doesn't hurt," he explained to Robert McCrum. "I've been lucky. The treatment has been benign. I don't know if I could concentrate if I was in pain. I've never had to stop." When James was first diagnosed, apparently after a trip to Emergency, he maintains that he got serious about his life: "I am restored by my decline," he wrote, "and by the harsh awakening that it brings." This is a humorous way of putting the insight that a number of the creative figures seem to have experienced.[11] Clive James' stark insight appears to have set him working. Until now James had published five books, and we are still counting, since his death sentence.[12] Robert McCrum points out that "Many writers half his age and twice as fit would be thrilled to be so productive." In fact, Clive James made something of a late profession out of dying. He made so many final public appearances (first in London and then at the Cambridge Union) that his friend, the humorist and essayist P. J. O'Rourke, advised him to "soft-pedal this death's door stuff, Clive, because people will get impatient." No wonder that Clive James claimed, "I'm embarrassed to be still alive." Well, he wasn't one bit. He milked dying for all he can get out of it and he even wrote a column in the *Observer* entitled "Reports of My Death."

"If you are blindly optimistic and you haven't steeled yourself for the possibility of failure, you might be caught flat-footed," says Kate Sweeny, a professor of psychology at the University of California, Riverside. She was speaking to the *Wall Street Journal* "Bonds" columnist and Barnard College sociologist, Elizabeth Bernstein.[13] "But if you've worried, you've done a lot of the psychological work already, no matter the outcome," continues Sweeny who researches the psychology of waiting for a living. Maybe Clive James has done a lot of the psychological work already and maybe he shows this to us through his recent writing and his recent public talks. Is this how he copes—or coped—so extravagantly with his approaching death? Elizabeth Bernstein continues: "It turns out there is a way to 'wait well,' researchers say. People who feel anxious or pessimistic or who ruminate while awaiting news fare better than others when it finally arrives, the researchers say. (There really is hope for me.) Such people are more prepared for bad news and more excited about good news." Clive James did wait well. To judge by the frequency with which he discussed his approaching death, maybe he worried and ruminated a lot more than he admits. What would we say of Philip Larkin then? Who waits best, James or Larkin?

Let's hear a bit more from Professor Kate Sweeny and see whether she can tell us which of the poets waits best. "Waiting for uncertain news is often distressing," she explains, "at times even more distressing than facing bad news." How Dr. Sweeny and her team examined strategies for "waiting well" went like this. She tested two types of waiting that involve dread. "First," she explained, "people can wait in such a way as to ease their distress during the waiting period. Second, people could wait in such a way as to ease the pain of bad news or enhance the thrill of good news." Sweeny based her test on 230 people from the 27 Californian law schools who had taken the California bar exam and were still waiting for the results. The California bar exam is said to be the most difficult to pass in the United States. Approximately half of all candidates fail on their first attempt at this exam. What did Sweeny and her team learn about these fearful and waiting examinees? She found that "participants were quite unsuccessful at waiting well by our first definition . . . their coping strategies were ineffective for reducing distress associated with uncertainty, apparently even backfiring in some cases. . . . However, many participants were successful at waiting well according to our second definition." How did this second group do it? "Participants who suffered through a waiting period marked," Sweeny explains, "by anxiety, rumination, and pessimism responded more productively to bad news and more joyfully to good news, as copared with participants who suffered little during the wait."[14]

Philip Larkin fits perfectly into Kate Sweeny's second response to dread and waiting. The *Aubade* with its anxiety, rumination, and pessimism is perhaps the best way to respond to the possibility of bad news in Jerry Seinfeld's waiting room.[15] What of Clive James? Is he just a little too optimistic for his own good? Does he fit too well into Sweeny's first category for his own good? Was his death day, despite all of the self-protective humor, a worse one for him than for Larkin? I'd say not. Clive James, holding on like Madame Grusinskaya from the Grand Hotel or the smoothfaced Tess Christian, wouldn't let go and kept his eye resolutely on the main event, his death. If his rumination is couched more in black humor than in self-pity, then all we can say is what do you expect from a kid from Kogorah?

The aim is to turn dread and waiting to your own advantage, whether it is through eloquent complaint or working-class humor. Larkin's and James' techniques both work. Dread and waiting can be helpful in other worrying contexts. These may offer some additional support for Kate Sweeny's argument. Imagine that you were a fluffy member of a sheep herd. You graze happily on the Northern Tablelands of New South Wales in Australia near where I used to live. Dread encouraged by the threat and by the actual presence of predators such as wild dogs, dingoes, huge feral cats, and ill-tempered rustlers is probably a useful thing to feel, because there's plenty of all of them around. Dread, or deep sheep paralysis, will instill cautious waiting and assist in unharmed longevity. I mention this because a team of scientists in Australia, linked with the Australian research institution, the CSIRO in Armidale NSW, and in France, were reported to have been working on a project that aimed to breed fear and anxiety, and with it of course troublesome waiting, out of sheep and cattle. The article explains, "scientists found animals with an anxious disposition behaved in a dangerous manner when confined." A CSIRO scientist explained, "If we can identify these animals with this simple test, we can breed for more docile behavior and that will make farming practices safer in the future. . . . Less stress in farm animals will also lead to better meat-quality in beef cattle and sheep and dairy cows will be more productive." That is what was said in the report that appeared on February 23, 2015, in *The Armidale Express*.[16]

Is there value in breeding out dread and waiting?[17] Hmm, the animals will be able to wait for slaughter in peace and to become no longer subject to dread. That I suppose would be an advantage for these abattoir destined creatures. They'd be much easier to handle when they were penned and waiting for slaughter. There would be a real bonus for human carnivores. By removing the pre-mortem dread and waiting from the animals as they queue for their end in the slaughterhouse and get ready to grace the counters of places like N. Hill & Son's, they can be killed much more easily and packed for eating all the faster. And consider it, there will also be no sour taste of adrenalin released within the sheep as they face their killers. That's great for the supermarket butchers. This immunity to dread will no doubt have a variety of other unexpected advantages. Breeding out dread will also make the sheep easier to shear, something that with a hurrying shearer confronting the restless, frightened animal is often painful and bloody. The sheep will be easier to drench, to brand, to herd into uncomfortable trucks, and of course to castrate. Do you ever castrate sheep? You do cattle at least. Dread and the inability to wait well, the New England researchers seem to reason, does not help producers to serve animals up on Mrs. Tess Christian's dinner table. That the story was news at all suggests that some people believe that breeding out dread and the evolutionary advantage bestowed by waiting would be a very good idea.

Stay a little longer with this theme of dread and waiting and the dinner table. The inability of creatures to tolerate waiting in circumstances that may lead to pain, their dislike of dread and of waiting is no doubt a good and sensible thing, whatever the researchers may believe. I think Dr. Sweeny would agree. Waiting well means experiencing dread. There is in addition an evolutionary advantage bestowed on all creatures by possessing a capacity to feel dread and to wait well. The sheep of the Northern Tablelands of New South Wales, those poor innocents subject to this strange scientific experiment, will offer an easy feed for dingoes and for wild dogs if their capacity to experience dread and to practice cautious waiting is removed. Why would they protect themselves against predators if they feel no dread? It's very easy to see the danger and the cost here to be associated with the loss of dread. The sheep and cattle are liable to end up on a dingo's dinner table rather than that of Mrs. Tess Christian. If I were a sheep, or a sheep owner, I'd want to be able to stand up for myself or at least to know when to run away fast and to hide.

Dread and cautious waiting, there's no doubt about it, will enable this. This CSIRO experiment may therefore prove, if successful, to be a very costly adventure. By neutralizing dread and by maximizing an animal's tolerance of fearful waiting, there may remain slim chances for their protecting themselves. The beneficial nature of dread for creatures and for dinner tables is, when you come to think of it, pretty obvious. This is something stressed by David Barlow in his 2002 book, *Anxiety and Its Disorders*. Seen from an evolutionary point of view, dread and fearful waiting are very useful emotional states. And that just proves one of the points that Kate Sweeny makes.[18]

That's quite enough of Australia and its sheep. The date now is December 8, 1995, and we're in France. On that day a youngish French journalist, Jean-Dominique Bauby, suddenly and unexpectedly found himself subject to a medical misadventure that put him in a position that was more extreme than that of Clive James. On that day the then editor-in-chief of the French version of *Elle* magazine suddenly faced death. It was as if he'd all at once become old, but within a single day, and he was facing death. Jean-Dominique Bauby suffered a huge stroke on December 8, 1995, and sank into a 20-day coma. He died 15 months later on March 9, 1997, from pneumonia.

The wealthy and ambitious Jean-Do was just 43 years old on December 8, 1995. When he awoke later from his stroke-induced coma he was completely paralyzed and had little chance of long-term survival. Bauby was now trapped in a condition that is known as Locked in Syndrome (LIS). Jean-Dominique Bauby was mentally aware of his surroundings, as are most victims of LIS, but his physical paralysis allowed only a small amount of movement. This was of his head and eyes. You would imagine that this should have been the end for Bauby. But, like James, the imposition of "decline and . . . the harsh awakening that it brings" produced from the former editor of *Elle* magazine perhaps even more remarkable writing than James achieved in the period within life's littler waiting room. Jean-Dominique Bauby somehow succeeded to write his best-selling memoir, *The Diving Bell and the Butterfly* (its remarkable French title is *Le Scaphandre et le Papillon*) despite the seeming impenetrability of his LIS. The short classic describes his life before and after his stroke. It provides one of the best descriptions you could find of waiting and of Locked in Syndrome. *The Diving Bell and the Butterfly* is a memoir about waiting, a memoir about one of the most alarming versions that waiting can take. *The Diving Bell and the Butterfly* was also made into a very successful movie. There are not a lot of films about waiting.[19]

It's worth pausing over this alarming and novel version of waiting that is represented by Locked in Syndrome. What actually is LIS? It's understood as quadriplegia (paralysis of all four limbs) and anarthria (loss of ability to articulate). Consciousness is preserved—but are the higher faculties? For those suffering with LIS the primary mode of communication is by eye movements or blinking. What causes Locked in Syndrome? It can result from concussion, by traumatic head injury that is, or from Parkinson's Disease (which is a degenerative disorder of the central nervous system; its slowly emerging symptoms are shaking, rigidity, slowness of movement, and difficulty with walking and sometimes complete paralysis; mortality ratios are approximately twice those of people who are spared the illness). It can also be produced by ALS (amyotrophic lateral sclerosis, or Lou Gehrig's Disease—an illness in which progressive painless muscle weakness and wasting takes place that can lead to complete paralysis; this is the condition, but in a slow version, that Stephen Hawking lived with). It can also be brought on by lack of oxygen. When Chantal Bryan of Chippenham, Wiltshire, was 36 weeks pregnant she and her family were involved in a car accident on their way to a pub lunch in nearby Oxfordshire.[20] Chantal, her partner Christopher, a vicar, and their two young girls were badly bruised but unharmed. Chantal began to bleed, however, and the unborn baby boy, Jonathan, was delivered soon after in Bristol Children's Hospital by caesarian section. The impact of the accident had caused a placental abruption and Jonathan was badly deprived of oxygen. The prognosis for baby Jonathan was cerebral palsy and his version of the illness, the doctors discovered, was a bad one. He might not "run, walk, sleep, laugh, see, hear or recognize" his parents, the medical attendant suggested. Jonathan Bryan was, as a result, "locked in" and waiting for the first seven years of his life—waiting for an escape, for a means to express himself, for an awakening. Did Jonathan live in a state of locked in dread? He could communicate only by flickering his eyes, slight smiles, and uncontrolled arm gestures. Jonathan remained mentally unimpaired, however. The doctors would not believe this, but Jonathan's mother insisted that she knew otherwise. Chantal managed to teach her oxygen deprived little boy to read and to read very well. He now communicates confidently with a message board like that of Stephen Hawking and Bryan attends school. But he will not live long. He told Amy Oliver, a newspaper reporter who wrote up his story, "I'm going back to Jesus's garden soon."

Locked in Syndrome is more common than you'd expect, and I think most of you have known or known of someone trapped in this condition. I knew a man once, the father-in-law of a friend of mine, Bazza Simpkins, who had suffered a contest-ending stroke in his late 60s. This former Australian pub owner lingered on after his stroke in a rural hospital with LIS for three or more years until he died without remission, as he knew he would. I believe that death was pneumonia, just as it was for Jean-Dominique Bauby. The publican could communicate emotion during those three odd waiting years only by crying. He did this in response to good news (his children's successes), or pleasure (such as seeing his grandchildren or his wife), or to bad news (his youngest child's divorce). How much dread was there in his waiting?

One more version of waiting associated with Locked in Syndrome remains that I'd like to mention. This one, the most alarming of the versions of LIS, was produced by an illness that reached epidemic levels right around the globe between 1915 and 1926. It was called encephalitis lethargica—"sluggish headitis" as that Greek term seems to say. Oliver Sacks describes the victims of the condition like this: "They would be conscious and aware—yet not fully awake; they would sit motionless and speechless all day in their chairs, totally lacking energy, impetus, initiative, motive, appetite, affect or desire; they registered what went on about them without active attention, and with profound indifference. They neither conveyed nor felt the feeling of life; they were as insubstantial as ghosts, and as passive as zombies."[21] It's been estimated that up to five million people were affected by encephalitis lethargica. Encephalitis lethargica seems nowadays, more or less, to have disappeared. The University of Calgary neuroscientist Dr. Manuel Hulliger suggests that the illness may have been absorbed into the more general classification of Parkinson's disease. Encephalitis lethargica is sometimes referred to as post-encephalitic Parkinson's disease. It certainly shares many of the symptoms of Parkinson's proper. So maybe it's still with us. Of those affected by encephalitis lethargica, about one and a half million perished according to Manuel Hulliger. Many of those who did survive remained trapped and waiting within this version of Locked in Syndrome. They seem to have been aware of their imprisoned state within encephalitis lethargica, despite their complete passive and awkward demeanors. Did they dread their future?

But what about Jean-Dominique Bauby and his Locked in Syndrome? We seem to be losing track of him. If Bauby was trapped within LIS how did he write *The Diving Bell and the Butterfly*? And how did he feel about being locked in and waiting? I'll come to the second of these questions shortly, but first let's look at his writing: Jean-Dominique learned to write, as you might know from the movie, by blinking. He could still move his eyes. So, gradually, over the last 15 months of his short life he learned again to communicate. And when he did, like Clive James, he communicated how it felt to be waiting, irrevocably, for the end. Only one of Bauby's eyes functioned. His right eye was sewn closed to prevent excessive dry eye. With a speech therapist who'd been sent to help him recover, Bauby struck on an effective but laborious method of communication. He blinked his left eye as the therapist read a list of the letters of the alphabet to him and, in this manner, he was able to indicate whole words and eventually whole sentences and paragraphs. I have read that the entire book took Bauby, working at four hours per day, 10 months to put together. Some wait. An average word took him approximately two minutes to signal by blinking.

The Diving Bell and the Butterfly comprises approximately 200,000 blinks. It is sobering to think what Bauby might have achieved had his health not been destroyed. He was apparently commissioned to compose a new version of *The Count of Monte Cristo*, but with a woman as protagonist. I think that Clive James is right about death—we are better off with a great work like *The Diving Bell and the Butterfly* than a man's woman's *Monte Cristo*. Bauby, though awfully, was restored by his decline, by his waiting, and by its harsh awakenings.

How did Jean-Do feel? In the 1990 movie version of Oliver Sack's book *Awakenings* (1973), a beautiful film about LIS and encephalitis lethargica if ever there was one, Dr. Peter Ingham speculates on the mental state of patients who have been trapped like Jean-Dominique Bauby in LIS. When asked by Sacks' double, Dr. Malcolm Sayer, concerning the minds of individuals stuck for long periods of time inside LIS and whether such victims could be intellectually sentient and, as well, whether encephalitis lethargica could spare the patient's higher faculties, Ingham (played by Max Von Sydow, the husband of the schizophrenic Karin in *Through a Glass Darkly*) splutters, "the virus didn't spare the higher faculties." "Why?" asks Sacks' double. Ingham replies, "the alternative is unthinkable." Peter Ingham seems to have believed that being stuck permanently within LIS would destroy any normal person's mind. The real-life neurologist Oliver Sacks didn't believe him. Sacks was convinced that his patients' mental faculties were preserved. Before I offer an answer to that question, how did Jean-Do feel, maybe we should take further heed of Oliver Sacks.

Levodopa, or L-DOPA, was the wonder drug that Oliver Sacks in real life used to revive his locked-in patients. L-DOPA is said to be able to cross the protective blood-brain barrier and, once within the brain, it encourages the increased concentration of dopamine within the brain. (Remember the cats on the quayside?) This is beneficial to treatment of Parkinson's disease, one of the major causes of Locked in Syndrome. In the movie you can see, movingly, how Sayer, or should we call him Sacks, is convinced of the value of the new drug Levodopa and administers large doses to his catatonic patients. They awaken gradually in real life, en masse in the film. The success of the medicine provided the definitive answer to Dr. Ingham's incorrect guess. The patients had not lost their mind within their long period of waiting. But the revival afforded by levodopa is of limited duration and patients gradually slip back into catatonia, despite increased doses. The side effects of high doses of L-DOPA, I have read, can entail (and did for Sack's patients) disorientation, confusion, heightened emotional states (excessive libido—that Leonard Lowe displayed in real life), anxiety, vivid dreams, hallucinations, delirium, "festination" (hurrying about), freezing, tics, and oculogyric (whirling eyed) crises. Apparently, in the period of hospitalization since, the real-life patients of Oliver Sacks have had other less spectacular awakenings. That the "higher faculties" remain intact has also been shown in a variety of treatments since. There then is part of the answer to the question, how did Jean-Dominique Bauby feel. But we can't yet say anything about dread.

Reviving LIS or apparently vegetative—you could say waiting—patients is something that is being done with greater frequency. They seem to be glad, not mad for the remit. In the *New Scientist*, February 26, 2014, there was a report concerning Louis Viljoen, who in 1999 "had been in a persistent vegetative state for three years." He began to exhibit disturbed sleep at night. He was prescribed the insomnia sedative zolpidem. Helen Thomson in the same article explains, "Within minutes of being given the drug by his mother, Viljoen turned his head and said 'hello mummy.' The effect lasted a few hours. The drug now allows him to communicate for about 10 hours a day. Such a response is rare." Sacks might have seen it as further proof of his contention. Electrical stimulation of the brains of these waiting patients has also been successfully used. In the *New Scientist*, March 1, 2014, there was a report concerning a medical team led by Steven Laureys at the Liège University Hospital in Belgium who "worked with 55 people who had experienced a traumatic brain injury or lack of oxygen to the brain and were in a minimally conscious or vegetative state. They placed electrodes over their left dorsolateral prefrontal cortex—an area involved in memory, decision-making and awareness. Then they delivered 20 minutes of stimulation to some of the people and a sham treatment to the others. The next day, the two groups received the opposite therapy." Helen Thomson reports, "During brain stimulation, 13 people with minimal consciousness and two people in a vegetative state showed signs of awareness that were observed neither before the stimulation nor after the sham treatment. . . . For most of these people the changes were moderate, but some recovered the ability to communicate." Four years later Helen Thomson reported again on the Liège group.[22] By this point the team had been able to extend wakefulness to one week by applying stimulation five times per week.[23] Their latest advance is to allow family members to take the brain stimulation device home and to apply it to the vegetative patients themselves. What sort of improvements did the Liège group notice? Their latest study involved 27 people, one of whom had been minimally conscious for 33 years. After treatment every weekday for four weeks "a fifth showed improvements in awareness," Helen Thomson summarizes, "[and] a few people regained the ability to answer questions such as 'Am I touching my nose?'" It is hard to imagine that these vegetative patients felt too pleased about their pre-waking experience, if they felt anything at all (Leonard Lowe, in *Awakenings*, compared himself to a caged panther). Their wait seems to have left their higher faculties often intact. But such waiting cannot be a fructifying experience. Leonard Lowe, in real life, managed to write book reviews that were widely read in his hospital, but I don't think that he could be said to have turned the experience of waiting without much hope in the spiritual waiting room of life to his own advantage. Or if he did, we'll never know. He died in 1981 at the age of 61. He'd been given three additional L-DOPA treatment-episodes, and all were unsuccessful. The successful period of his awakening lasted only from March to April of 1969.

Oliver Sacks' work and, as we've seen, quite a lot of work since have demonstrated that the higher faculties are often preserved within the minds of these LIS or apparently vegetative patients during their long wait. The conclusion is counter-logical if ever there was one. You'd expect, as did Dr. Ingham, that being locked in for so long would erode the "higher" mental faculties and would cause an individual simply to give up at first to anger, then to depression, and then to abandon cognition itself. But it does not. This has been shown a number of times since Sacks' book. There is a corollary. You would also imagine that a victim of LIS would despair and, as well, live in a state of dread at their inability to shape their future and to avoid death. But that does not seem to be the case either. The almost sanguine ability of a man such as Jean-Dominique Bauby to manage a condition that

"THE LITTLER WAITING ROOM" | 229

ought to have made him despair and to turn his woeful position to creative gain suggests that it is not necessarily or just recent circumstance that enables in peoples' brains their capacity to wait—or in these cases should we say endure—but the pre-existing endowment of the brain of some individual's brains with such waiting-enhancing capacities or even the right brain chemicals. But who could know?

Do we have an answer now to the question, how did Jean-Do feel? It seems that the experience of intolerable waiting, in a medical setting at least, is not necessarily as unthinkable nor is it as dread laden as you might have expected. Surprisingly the longer the waiting, the better the attitude of the patient. But there is more still that can be said to our question.

"What? Happiness?" That was the reaction of a psychiatric friend to the results of a remarkable paper by Marie-Aurélie Bruno, Jan L. Bernheim, Didier Ledoux, Frédéric Pellas, Athena Demertzi, Steven Laureys (that really is the whole cast—there is even the Belgian Steven Laureys, the same individual that we've just met in an earlier paragraph). The lead author, Marie-Aurélie Bruno, is a researcher with the Coma Science Group, Cyclotron Research Centre and Neurology Department, University and University Hospital of Liège in Belgium. What a locale. The title of the paper is "A survey on self-assessed well-being in a cohort of chronic locked-in syndrome patients: happy majority, miserable minority."[24] The paper, deriving from the same Belgian hospital that we've just met, is concerned to investigate how people who are trapped in LIS really do feel about their lives. The results are not what you, me, or Dr. Ingram would have expected. They certainly were not what my psychiatric friend expected.[25]

What were Marie-Aurélie Bruno and her team actually aiming to investigate? And where does the happiness come in? Let's hear from Dr. Bruno: "Given appropriate medical care, [LIS] patients can survive for decades. We studied the self-reported quality of life in chronic LIS patients." How did they go about their research? Marie-Aurélie Bruno reports, "168 LIS members of the French Association for LIS were invited to answer a questionnaire on medical history, current status and end-of-life issues. They self-assessed their global subjective well-being with the Anamnestic Comparative Self-Assessment (ACSA) scale, whose +5 and 5 anchors were their memories of the best period in their life before LIS and their worst period ever, respectively." Dr. Bruno explains that of her respondents (91 patients, 54% of her target group responded) 47 patients "professed happiness" while 18 "professed unhappiness" (26 patients were excluded because of incomplete data). Marie-Aurélie Bruno continues: "Variables associated with unhappiness included anxiety and dissatisfaction with mobility in the community, recreational activities and recovery of speech production. A longer time in LIS was correlated with happiness." That last observation is striking and completely unexpected. Perhaps this is why Bauby was so remarkably productive during his period in hospital. Perhaps, in a similar way, it offers some explanation for Clive James' cheerfulness. Dr. Bruno's conclusions are striking. She stresses the need for extra palliative care, for therapy to minimize anxiety, and for assistance with mobility. LIS patients do adapt to their condition. And then: "Recently affected LIS patients who wish to die should be assured that there is a high chance they will regain a happy meaningful life . . . our data show that a non-negligible group of chronic LIS survivors self-report a meaningful life and their demands for euthanasia are surprisingly infrequent."

We started out in a doctor's waiting room with Jerry Seinfeld. On the wall in that waiting room there was a calming, attractive, but unchallenging painting by Pierre Bonnard. It showed a pair of fauns, playing on a pipe, and looking out across a vernal southern French landscape. I was being unfair to Pierre Bonnard by reproducing that canvas. It is far from his best, even in that period of his life. Now you can view another one of Bonnard's paintings (Figure 8.2), but this one comes not from his early middle age, but the period near the end of his life. It is a self-portrait completed by Pierre Bonnard, aged 78, and it was finished 18 months before his death. His wife, Marthe de Meligny, whom he so often painted, was dead now. They had no children. The master may have been broken down, but he was still in the game. The British portraitist, Timothy Hyman, in his 1998 study entitled, simply, *Bonnard*, believes—and who could not agree?—that Pierre Bonnard's late works are among his very best. Hyman characterizes *Self-Portrait in The Bathroom Mirror* like this: "At seventy-eight Bonnard's touch achieves the intimacy of late Titian, where pigment and flesh and atmosphere are fused. And everywhere the brush has been supplemented by the artist's own hands, smearing and fingerprinting white and yellow blobs of an unmatched tenderness."

As the artist Pierre Bonnard grew older and began to decline physically, his sense of distance from his contemporaries seems to have grown. This was not LIS of the body, but there's a sense in Bonnard in this period of an LIS of the soul. His style of painting, that some linked to the 1890s, had been

232 | DEATH, RELIGION, AND DREAD

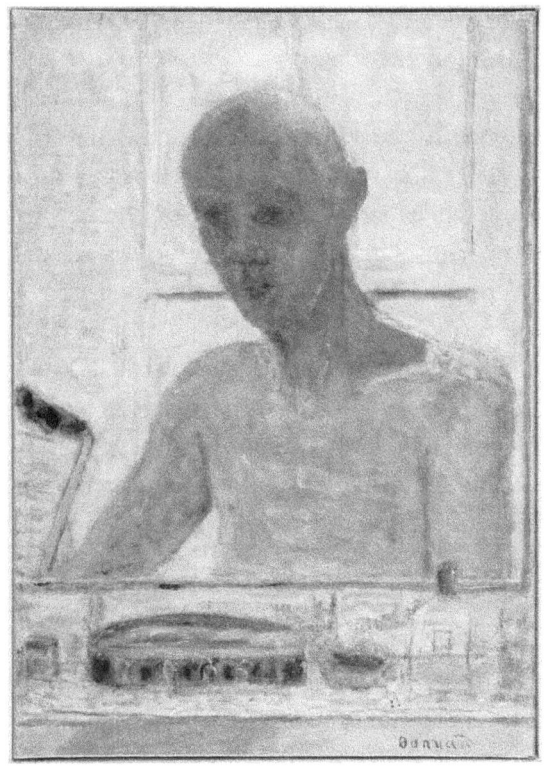

FIGURE 8.2. The master was broken down, but still in the game. Pierre Bonnard (1867–1947), *Self-Portrait in The Bathroom Mirror*, 1939–1945. Oil on canvas, 73 cm × 52 cm. AM1984-698. Photo: Jacques Faujour. Musée Nationale d'Art Moderne. © CNAC/MNAM/Dist. RMN-Grand Palais/Art Resource NY.

passed over by modernism and the avant-garde (itself on the wane), his friends were dying, his wife was dead. He was living in an occupied France during the Second World War.[26] His own health was not good. He died in 1947 and in the year of his death the Greek connoisseur and cataloguer of Picasso's art, Christian Zervos, linked the dead but still warm Bonnard to the half-century-old painting style of Impressionism, and dismissed his abilities. In Bonnard's work, he wrote, "he never brought into the mainstream any disruptive or rejuvenating ideas ... there is nothing that is sharp, nothing that stirs us, no celebration of vigor." Henri Matisse was one voice to come to Bonnard's defense ("Yes, I certify," he wrote, "that Bonnard is a great painter, for today and for the future").[27] Posterity and art buyers since have sided with Henri Matisse, not with Christian Zervos. It's been reported that on February 9, 2011, Christie's sold Bonnard's *Terrasse à Vernon* (1923) in a public sale for €8,485,287 (£7,014,200). Christian Zervos must have been purblind, for some of Bonnard's very greatest paintings come from his very last years, very close in time to when Zevros delivered his judgment.[28] As Clive James suggests, mostly of himself: "For any kind of artist, the most generous possible gift from the fates is to be granted a hand in writing the script for your own exit." So it was for the septuagenarian Bonnard. The master was broken down, but he was still in the game.

In Pierre Bonnard's *Self Portrait in the Bathroom Mirror* it feels as if we are in those very last successful days of Clive James or Jean-Dominique Bauby.[29] This trio, James, Bauby and Bonnard, are waiting to die. They're still in the game. Even LIS can't stop the game. They confront in a remarkable way the problem of how to make the best of waiting despite failing vigor, illness, dread, and approaching death, how to make the best of Jerry Seinfeld's littler waiting room.[30] They turn lingering, without much hope in the waiting room of life and being near to that empty chair, to their own advantage. They turn dread and cautious waiting to their own advantage. I don't believe that they solve the problem of this waiting for the end. You cannot. But they show how the experience can sometimes be transmuted from irremediable loss into inspiring gain. Bonnard could have uttered Clive James' words: "I am restored by my decline and by the harsh awakening that it brings." Pierre Bonnard's words were "he who sings is not always happy."[31]

EPILOGUE

ONE–TWO–THREE

A Better Description for Waiting?

PAIRING, THE FREEZE-FRAME PAUSE, THE empty chair, these were the versions of waiting that I've tried to exemplify. The experience of waiting that we encounter most in our daily lives, I suspect, is the first of this trio, pairing. As I've said, if you were to try quickly to envisage waiting and to imagine how you would paint it or photograph it or describe it, the most common representation would entail two people. In this final section I'd like to go back to pairing, the "two" of this chapter title. I'd like to show how we may understand waiting even more clearly by comparing it with emotional experiences that entail not pairs, but the single individual (the "one") or a trio of individuals (the "three"). These are boredom and jealousy.[1] I'll begin with the "one." This will be boredom, an emotion that I was once convinced was the very same thing as waiting. No, it's not.

ONE

Godon Deegan helps out. Deegan reported on August 3, 2017, in the *Irish Examiner* that the Irish government's "prison system's library service cost €230,000 to operate . . . with the expense including books on cocaine smuggling, yoga, Pilates—and boredom." The books purchased included "the best-selling *Cocaine Confidential—True Stories Behind the World's Most Notorious Narcotic* by Wensley Clarkson and *The Cocaine Diaries—A Venezuelan Prison Nightmare* by Jeff Farrell and Paul Keany." Godon Deegan, who has a posher Irish name than I do, snootily adds that "Those [among its 3,700 strong prison population] seeking inner fulfillment while serving their time can read *10 Secrets for Success and Inner Peace* while others bored with the daily routine while locked up can dip into *Boredom: A Lively History* by Peter Toohey." Thank you, Godon Deegan. Godon's point about my book is that prisoners—imagined locked up on their own with nothing to do and bored as can be—may seek solace in what he implies is a silly book describing what they suffer a lot. Although Deegan mightn't have meant it, I take it as a great compliment that some of these 3,700 prisoners seek solace in my book on boredom. Godon Deegan also makes the point pretty clearly that boredom is to be associated with the solitary individual, especially if they're locked up in jail.

The young woman seated in the pub in war-time Britain is even more helpful than Godon Deegan. The woman in Edward Le Bas' *Saloon Bar* (Figure E.1) is bored, though she's not in jail and she's not reading my book on boredom. There are several reasons why we can tell that she's bored. First of all, she has the typical bored posture (the visual phenotype,

EPILOGUE | 237

FIGURE E.1. Bored on her own. Edward Le Bas (1904–1966), *Saloon Bar*, 1940. Canvas, 34 3/4 × 43 1/4 in (88 × 110) cm. Tate Gallery. Photo Credit: © Tate, London, 2019.

could you say?) of head on hand, elbow resting on a table, and eyes staring off into the near distance (this is sometimes called the 12-foot gaze in a 10-foot room, or the Arctic stare). And, second, the young woman is on her own despite the man to the rear who seems to be trying to hit on her.[2]

What else is happening at this table? It appears as if the young woman is in the pub with two other men (indicated by the drinks and the smokes: bitter in a glass and smokes waiting for the man on our side of the table; some sort of mild beer waiting for the man on the opposite side). They've both gone off perhaps to play darts, leaving the woman temporarily alone with her sherry—is it really sherry? During this interlude the man to her rear starts flirting. You might expect the woman to be irritated, by her companions leaving her alone and by the flirting of the man to her rear. But irritation is not what the picture seems to be telling us of the woman's emotional state. There's no getting away from the head on the hand and the elbow on the table. It is the most common visual indicator of boredom that you can see.[3] There's also the muck on the table.[4] Tobacco, a newspaper (going clockwise), a used ash tray, a quarter full pint glass of bitter or lager, a sherry glass in the woman's left hand, an empty glass, a two-thirds full pint glass of mild or stout, and, finally, the vase of flowers. It's a messy, mildly disgusting collection of smelly objects on a dull brown table—brown, if you see this painting in color.[5] Brown is a vomitous color. The young woman appears to have had enough of her drink in this Knightsbridge pub. She toys with the stem of her glass with her left hand rather than showing much enthusiasm for it. Maybe she's bored with the drink too. Boredom is regularly associated with being too full up with drink or food. One way to show this (and to show disgust) is to display abandoned food or drinking or smoking utensils. The young woman is bored and maybe she's a little disgusted as well. She also looks a little tired. I've argued that the most all-embracing definition for boredom is "an emotion of mild disgust produced by temporarily unavoidable and predictable circumstances."[6] I could have added that boredom is also an experience that tends to look inward rather than outward. By inward I mean psychologically, for boredom is the most solitary of experiences. The young woman is certainly stuck in a temporarily unavoidable and predictable circumstance—look at her suitor's face. Boredom is all about your frustration and your disgust (that sherry?). Boredom is something you normally feel on your own (unlike, say, love or anger or surprise or hatred) or, if you are with other people, boredom is a feeling that cuts you off from others.[7] You could say that the emotional state of the young woman in Edward Le Bas' painting has nothing to do with waiting. The solitary and disgusting side of boredom acts as a vigorous enemy of waiting. It takes away the pairing, and what remains is a restless solitude.[8] That's the young woman in the pub. It's probably the case for those Irish inmates as well.

Some writers and some artists will focus more, in their strongest works, on solitaries. If you like to read Jean-Paul Sartre's *Nausea* (there's the theme of disgust again) or Albert Camus' *The Outsider* or even Franz Kafka's short stories, you'll know what I mean. These books are relentlessly focused on solitary individuals. You might also recall our visit to Strandgade 30 in Copenhagen. On that occasion Vilhelm Hammershøi's wife, Ida, stood bolt still in the central room of their apartment in the shadows of this inner room. She was on her own as she is so often in her husband's paintings. Hammershøi is a master of solitude. If it's mental illness that concerns you—and I began with Jenny Didier and her depression and anxiety—if it's mental health that's behind many of your worries, then your focus is likely to be with this single figure, with the "ones." Boredom is not mental illness. But if it is unrelieved, really unrelieved, then depression may follow. "Sunday," clarifies Jean-Dominique Bauby, "I dread Sunday." Jean-Dominique is trapped within Locked in Syndrome (LIS). Actually, he isn't frightened of Sundays, though maybe he should be. What he dreads is not Sundays themselves, but the awful boredom that Sundays in the hospital will bring for him. He's not bored on the other days of the week. It's just on Sundays. "If I am unlucky enough to have no visitors there will be nothing at all to break the dreary passage of the hours," Jean-Dominique explains. "No physiotherapist, no speech pathologist, no shrink. Sunday is crossing the desert. Its only oasis is a sponge bath even more perfunctory than usual." Locked in Syndrome can make a life busy, in its way, and Bauby shows exactly how as he adapts to his condition of waiting. But his Sundays are a different matter. "On such days the nursing staff is plunged into gloomy lethargy by the effects of Saturday-night drinking, coupled with regret at missing the family picnic, the trip to the fair, or the shrimp-fishing denied them by the Sunday-duty roster. The bath I am given bears more resemblance to drawings and quartering than to hydrotherapy. A triple dose of the finest eau de toilette fails to mask the reality: I stink." The disgust that Sunday brings for the completely paralyzed and speechless Jean-Dominique is insupportable. Solitary Jean-Do ends his chapter on Sundays with a disgusting insect: "A very black fly settles on my nose. I waggle my head to unseat him. He digs in. Olympic wrestling is child's play compared to this. Sunday."

You could easily associate all of these bored solitaries with waiting. It would be simple to believe that they are all waiting for something. Maybe they are, but that's not really the point of their laments. Their worlds embody the permanent extinction of engagement (a personal connection with the world around), their worlds enforce the extinction of curiosity (how can you be curious when you are completely unable to explore?), and the extinction of interest (which is impossible on Jean-Do's Sundays).[9] None of these solitaries seem to exemplify the experience of waiting—it's boredom or depression or just being on your own. Waiting is based on expectation—the waiter is holding on. The waiter stays and focuses on future arrival. Boredom might look like

EPILOGUE | **241**

waiting—and boredom, like frustration or impatience, can be a natural response to waiting. But boredom, an adaptive emotion, aims to spur you into action. It wants you to escape from the circumstance in which you are entrapped, the circumstance that denies you interest, curiosity, and engagement. Boredom wants you to move on. Its simplest correlate is escape. Waiting, on the other hand, offers its adaptive advantage from a person's staying and from their focus on something that in the future will arrive. Boredom is really an enemy of waiting. Boredom is the enemy of staying put.

TWO

And now to waiting and to pairs. This is the "two" of my chapter title.

It's the pairing in François Barraud's *Le malcontent* (Figure E.2) that makes it unmistakably about waiting. (Recall Degas' pair, the dancer and the chaperone in his *Waiting*.) The white rose at the bottom of Barraud's painting offers a clue to how waiting works for this pair. The white rose is associated with love and marriage. It lies, stem snapped, at François' feet (Francois is the creator of *Le malcontent* and the woman is his wife, Marie.) The rose is saying that the pairing between these two, the artist and his wife, is soon to be over. That's what they're waiting for (unless they are merely acting out this little tableau). But if it's the real thing that Barraud is representing, then maybe the trouble between the pair derives from François being a malcontent, an unsettled individual who is always waiting and longing for something better. (It's also possible that what François Barraud means by the title *Le malcontent* is "melancholic." Barraud

FIGURE E.2. Marriage. François Barraud (1899–1934), *Le malcontent*, 1930. The Picture Art Collection/Alamy Stock Photo.

has painted himself as a melancholic in his *François with the head of death—Melancholia*. Could it be that his depression has driven the pair apart?) We've spoken a lot about marriage and waiting. *The Malcontent* is dramatizing marriage but also the role of love in marriage. One partner, the miserable François, is waiting to get out of the marriage, while the other, the loving one, is waiting and pleading for things to come right. That's Marie.[10] Marie tries to draw François back with the music on her accordion. Her head is turned toward her husband, but she glances sadly down. François resists. He's waiting for her to stop playing and to leave him alone. François has moved almost to the end of the bench to escape Marie. Her right hand on the accordion seems to pursue him.

François Barraud's moving painting about waiting shows as clearly as anything just how waiting differs from boredom. Waiting and this painting are based on the interaction of two people and this interaction anticipates what might be the future that they face. Waiting has the future as its focus. This is just what we saw in Degas' canvas of two women on a bench entitled *Waiting*. Like so much that has to do with waiting, the focus also entails what are almost domestic subjects—love, affection, family, friendship. That is perhaps why waiting becomes the basis for the intimate interactions between people. These are at their best (as they are in *Le malcontent*) neither solitary nor social. Boredom, on the other hand, is solitary and, because of its link with disgust and a lack of engagement, its focus is the immediate not the future, and it's no respecter of the domestic. Waiting, the experience, the emotional state, may be at the very heart of intimate personal experience. In a sense that is what this book is all about. It's certainly why I wrote it.

Some artists love pairs—and I suspect that this, as we've seen with "one's," tells us quite a lot about their personality and what drives their creation. It may also suggest that they're very interested in domestic emotions. François Barraud regularly paints pairs. It points to his interest in this theme of waiting. Henri Matisse favors pairs again and again, inanimate and animate. Perhaps his most famous pair comprises himself and his wife—this is the domestic and famous *The Conversation*. David Hockney loves doubles as well and he comes back again and again to the theme of waiting. He imitates Henri Matisse in his "double" painting, *Mr. and*

Mrs. Clark and Percy (1970–1971). I have one last example of pairing and waiting. It is a photograph by a very young Mexican photographer, Manuel Álvarez Bravo (Figure E.3). One of Mexico's greatest photographers he was about twenty when he made this shot. Alvarez Bravo lived from February 4, 1902 until October 19, 2002.

You could compare Manuel Alvarez Bravo's image to Degas' *Waiting* as well. In *Figuras en el Castillo* the two young

FIGURE E.3. One of them will eventually be left behind. Manuel Álvarez Bravo (1902–2002), *Figuras en el Castillo (Figures in the Castle)*, 1920s.
© Archivo Manuel Álvarez Bravo, S.C.

women are also waiting for something in the near future. It seems to be linked to the strange pattern of light cast on the wall in front of them that comes from some sort of a damaged skylight. Is there a touch of dread, of the "empty chair" projected by that strange pattern reflected on the wall? Or perhaps the young women are just waiting to get to the top of the stairs to see what's in this castillo. Arm in arm these two friends, this pair, ascend the staircase in, is it, Mexico City in about 1920. The one on our left looks more cautious, more passive. The one on our right seems to be leading the way. Just now they appear to be pausing, trying to decide which fork in the stairs they should take. They are waiting to decide, and it looks as if the woman on our right will be the one to do it. She has raised a perplexed arm to her forehead to assist in her decision. Is she like Degas' chaperone? They're waiting to move. It's almost a metaphor for a young person's life. They wait to decide which is best turn for their future life. One of them will probably be left behind—that's something you sense in Degas' *Waiting* as well. In Manuel Álvarez Bravo's image this will be the young woman on the left. I suspect that this is just how the young Manuel Álvarez Bravo felt about his own life. What does this tell you about waiting and staying and arrival? Does it help with a clearer definition? The photograph is more about the pair than what's at the top of the staircase.

THREE

Jealousy's an emotion that seems incomprehensible to most people. They feel, I suppose, that they're better than jealousy. Most people, perhaps for that reason, don't believe that they've ever felt it. That's what they tell me. Maybe this is because they associate jealousy with sex—by that I mean erotic jealousy, the emotion that you may feel if your link with your loved one is threatened by another person. That doesn't happen to everyone. Or perhaps they'd prefer not to admit it. Or perhaps it doesn't happen badly enough to many people to make them feel badly. For this type of jealousy to occur there needs to be three people entangled, one of whom suspects that they are losing out in the erotic stakes to the two others. When this triangular emotion occurs, the victim, if that's the right word to use of them, believes that they'll forfeit a relationship upon which they have had some special claim. It's two against one, in erotic jealousy. The best places to see erotic jealousy in action are the tabloid newspapers, or in visual art, or within your own head. Among the many artists who've periodically painted erotic jealousy, there is especially Edvard Munch (1863-1944). He paints threes regularly to show the forces of sexual jealousy.[11] Munch himself is often painted into these pictures too, not as the victim but as the perpetrator. Maybe Munch thought he was tough.

Competitive jealousy is much more common than erotic jealousy. The elements are much the same: there are usually three people involved (there can be two people and a thing); one person will be the loser and they believe that they're about to forfeit a relationship or position (if it's two people and a thing) to which they have special claim. This competitive jealousy happens all the time at work—over pay, position, or even the valued link to a colleague. The loser feels pain, just as they do in the case of erotic jealousy. I don't believe that the pain is as severe. You'll have your own opinion on this. Competitive jealousy is something on which all of our working lives are based. We all of us compete for advancement. It's you against your competitor for the attention of the boss and the big reward. We seem to measure our advancement in terms of money, but also possessions, and special relationships. That's what I think. Competitive jealousy's how we get on and how we succeed and how we can lose. It's how we trump our competitors or are trumped. It would be a very rare person who could claim that they are unaffected by competitive jealousy. Competitive jealousy is, in my opinion, at the core of life in society. It's also about the here-and-now, not about the future.

Some writers and some artists will focus a little more, in their strongest works, on threes. I suspect that this tells a lot about their interests, their psychology, their personality, and their engagement with the world around them. Because competitive jealousy is the fuel for much of life in society, it makes sense that their work will reflect this. Greek tragedy settled on just three actors for its performances, after an experiment with just two. The plays of Euripides and Sophocles are some of the most socially engaged theatrical experiences in western literature. They regale in the conflict that the triangle can evoke. The Afro-Caribbean painter from England, Denzil Forrester (born in Grenada in 1956), uses threes to capture his political vision—think of his *Three Wicked Men* (1982), *Death Walk* (1983), or *From Trenchtown to Porthtowan* (2016). The last of these images shows a line of three figures, two white policemen leading a handcuffed black man from a crowded, happy-looking beach in Cornwall in summer. Denzil Forrester is an artist who demonstrates, through his use of threes, how social life can become politics and how beauty need not be exclusive of commentary. I wish we could afford to reproduce his work for you here.[12] But we can see Vanessa Bell (1879–1961), the sister of Virginia Woolf. She shows triangles in *A Conversation* (1916) (Figure E.4), *The Schoolroom* (1913), and *Nude with Poppies*, which was created for her husband's lover.[13]

Who's losing here in Vanessa Bell's *A Conversation*? The bare-headed, short-haired younger woman in black looks like she's the loser. Her right hand is extended out almost like

FIGURE E.4. Competitive jealousy. Vanessa Bell (1879–1961), *A Conversation*, 1913–1916. Oil on canvas. Samuel Courtauld Trust, The Courtauld Gallery, London, UK. Bridgeman Images.

that of a supplicant. Her long neck looks vulnerable, her eyes are wide open and have a color, she leans forward and makes herself smaller. She's the outsider. The pair on the right in brown look richer, plutocratic, with their slit colorless eyes and pointy noses, their short necks, their hands firmly in their pockets rejecting. Even so, they're probably not half as sure of themselves as they try to project. Maybe they're afraid of losing too. The *visual phenotype* for jealousy, the visual situation that you see in a painting like *A Conversation*, appears to require the following. There'll be three people and two will be paired (physically or through dress or space) and the pair will dominate. The gaze between at least two of these individuals is often direct and combative. This seems to me to work for competitive or erotic jealousy.

Does a jealous person wait? Are the pair in brown in *A Conversation* waiting? Is the woman in black waiting? Jealous individuals may look like they're waiting, often hopelessly, for their feeling of exclusion or deprivation or rejection or, in this case, their edgy feeling of domination to be vindicated. But I don't think those smitten with jealousy sense their experience as waiting. We might, you might, but they don't. They just feel terrible, pained, deprived, and, if they're the solo one, hurt. If you can pause long enough to reason when you're jealous, you might say, "I want this to stop soon." But mostly you just want the pain to stop right now. Its remedy is "having" (partners, possessions, or even food). Jealousy, built on threes, is an experience of great and present pain. There's not much waiting in this world, though you could be tricked into thinking there is. It's pain. The "having" must be now.

Here's how I defined waiting right back at the beginning. "Waiting," I suggested, "entails the emotional experience of a situation that involves staying where you are until a particular time or event or until the arrival of a particular person." The definition places the stress on the experience of waiting just as much as on the situation of waiting. Why stress the experience? There are varying ways that waiting is experienced. This may be the case because time itself, when we're waiting, can be experienced in varying ways—as slowing, as speeding up, as terrifying, as pleasant, or even as quite neutral. Waiting can be experienced in a variety of ways that aren't necessarily dependent on its situation—it's not the situation that matters but the response in the brain, you might say. I've also tried to show you that there's a pattern to the emotional response relating to waiting, to holding on. Waiting seems to assume the status of an independent actor. This may be because of its reliance on a limited number of brain chemicals, the serotonergic bonds of friendship and dopamine-based focus of the hungry. Waiting seems to operate in its own little emotional universe, just as do boredom and jealousy. That's why, in this final chapter, I've attempted to show that waiting can be even more clearly understood by looking at it alongside two other very common emotions—involving "ones" and "threes," unlike the waiting "twos." Maybe if the experience of waiting has such a consistent and visible life, and one so clearly to be contrasted with boredom and jealousy (the "two" to their "one" and "three") then waiting should be considered to have the same emotional status as boredom and jealousy. Should waiting be thought of as an emotion in its own right?

    Staying and arrival, both at the heart of the definition of waiting, also help us to understand how waiting could assume the status of an emotion in its own right. Let me try to explain. Emotions may verify their emotional status by having what is sometimes termed a "core relational theme."[14] What is a "core relational theme." Think of anger. It's easy enough to understand how you experience anger. But it also has a real-life correlate. Understanding this makes anger's emotional status easier to comprehend. The correlate relates to threat and to the need for protection. For example, someone may attempt to harm your children. Your reaction, easily an angry one, aims to protect the children, though at the time you simply react without any reasoning and without any attempt to explain the wild, burning, and aggressive emotion you're feeling. That reaction, that instinctive aim to *protect* is what could be called the relational correlate of anger. And it's a good thing. Mind you, anger can get out of hand and it can become uncontrolled. That's the case with all emotions. Who benefits from having an angry and uncontrollable disposition? But for most people anger flares up when it's most required, when protection is needed. Protection, therefore, makes anger simpler for us to comprehend. If protection is a core relational theme for anger, and if it's something that provides part of its status as a real emotion, then you could ask whether there is such a theme for waiting. This might be to ask whether waiting is a real emotion.

The blonde-haired Hall Porter Senf from Berlin's Grand Hotel helps with this question. We met him first in Germany while he was waiting anxiously for his wife to give birth to their first child. He's probably still waiting. Can we find a relational correlate within his worried waiting that will help to answer the question as to whether waiting really has its own emotional status? At the core of Senf's experience, I'd say, is future arrival, and a desire to reach that achievement by staying. Perhaps there are a whole posse of words that can describe Hall Porter Senf's experience—words like achievement and reaching, like attainment, getting, and realization may also catch the sense of the correlate and of the imminence of Baby Senf. But I believe that staying and arrival tell you most about his experience. The Hall Porter would like the birth to arrive and he's going to stay until it does happen. Do these two words catch the sense of the relational correlate for waiting? It certainly feels that way. Do these two words help to affirm the status of waiting as a free-standing emotion?

Waiting, as an experience within the brain, seems to have a limited range that's defined especially by the presence of serotonin and dopamine and by their focus on staying and arrival. Outside the brain, in daily life, it's perhaps most commonly seen when people wait for one another (or things), when they stay and focus on arrival in a variety of situations. I suspect as well that waiting, like other emotions, offers animals evolutionary advantage. It provides a leg-up in the survival stakes. (How can you stalk if you cannot wait?) Sometimes philosophers speak of the rationality of emotions. By this they mean that emotions can direct you onto the right course of action.[15] There is certainly rationality in waiting. Does all of this confer on waiting the status of an emotion? We could be cautious and opt for the status of a quasi-emotion, or at least something very close to an emotion. But I suspect such caution is misplaced and that the experience of waiting exemplifies a real emotional state. Should we redefine waiting as "an emotion that defines the experience of a situation that involves staying where you are until a particular time or event or until the arrival of a second person?"

Waiting, with its "two's" and its focus on the future and its focus on staying and on arrival, sits plonk in the middle of solitary and present-orientated emotions such as boredom, with its "one's," and social emotions such as competitive and erotic jealousy, with its "three's." Like so much that has to do with waiting, the focus often entails domestic subjects. That's perhaps why waiting becomes the basis for the intimate interactions between people (such as, so often, love, affection, and friendship) that play as much to the future as to the present. Love, affection, and friendship are not solitary or social or competitive experiences. Waiting, the experience, the emotional state, the emotion itself, may be at the very heart of intimate personal experience—and in a sense that is what this book has been all about. Of course, there are many exceptions—the last two chapters were full of them, and so will be the illustration with which this chapter will conclude. But it seems to me to be possible that waiting is especially adapted to the intimate because it so frequently plays out with another person and because it always relates to the future and to arrival. Love, affection, and friendship need another person and they need time, future time and staying, to arrive fruitfully. "The lover's identity," says Roland Barthes, "is to be the one waiting."

At the end of my first chapter I described an endearing boozer. The question that I asked, if you can remember back that far, was couched in a description that ran like this. "Time for this boozer is no arrow. It moves in a circle that is driven by expectant and frequently pleasurable passing of sober time. It moves in a strange circle, from enforced and sober time to pleasure and then to the slow extinction of anticipation as

254 | EPILOGUE

the hooch does its best. What is going on here? Is it patience or is it waiting?" To make the answer to my query easier, I'll show you this man (Figure E.5).

What do you think of László Mednyánszky's *The Absinthe Drinker*? Does it represent patience or waiting? I say waiting. Why? Patience is a subset of waiting, though maybe it's the most famous version of waiting. You can wait patiently, or you can wait impatiently. What's happening here? Mednyánszky's

FIGURE E.5. Patient or waiting? László Mednyánszky (1852–1919), *The Absinthe Drinker*, 1898. Oil on wood, 45 cm × 34.5 cm. Hungarian National Gallery, Budapest.

EPILOGUE

absinthe drinker will soon have his paw on that stem glass. That's certain. And I'll tell you why. For now, he's just sizing it up before he pounces. You could almost say that he's stalking the drink. It's as if he's freeze-framed in the moment before his righthand moves. It's all a little like Kōshirō Onchi's diver. Splash. Dopamine! Mednyánszky's drinker is not being patient at all. He's excited, if you ask me. Patience is a much over-diagnosed virtue.

There's another way that you could look at Mednyánszky's painting of the Polish drinker. The boozer is actually you and that glass of steaming absinthe is me. What I'm waiting for is to find out what you think I taste like, what you think of this book. If you don't like this book, then the absinthe is going to be a pretty sour drop. But if you like it, the drink will taste wonderful. It will be worth the wait. You just won't know what it's going to be like until you've thrown it down your gullet. I'm waiting.

ACKNOWLEDGMENTS

MY THANKS TO STEFAN VRANKA and to Oxford University Press for patiently taking on *Hold On: The Life, Science, and Art of Waiting*. I can't name the referees, but their suggestions and those of Stefan and some of the delegates helped me better to understand things. Andy Bulloch, Manuel Hulliger, Frank Stahnisch, Hank Stam, Scott Patten, and other members of the History of Neuroscience Group (HONIG) at the University of Calgary have regularly helped me. I'd also like to acknowledge Robert Baker, Reyes Bertolin, Peter Dale, Mark Golden, James Hume, Rachel Lonsdale, Heather McCallum, Hanne Sigismund Nielsen, Bazza Simpkins, Josefa Ros Velasco, and Ian Worthington. Jason McClure's work on doubles taught me much, as has Nicole Wilson's work on pain. Thanks as well to Jacob Daughterty at Bridgeman Images, to David Thompson and Louise Burley at the Tate, to Aurelia Alvarez Urbatje at the Archivo Manuel Álvarez Bravo, S.C./Asociación Manuel Álvarez Bravo, A.C., and to Iris Labeur at the Rijksmuseum, Amsterdam. No thanks, however, to all those who did not assist with images. My gratitude as always to my family from the littlest to the biggest: H. Fox, Noa, Kinley, Jes, Matt, Linds, Kate, Franny, and Phyl. The University of Calgary has assisted me with the image reproduction fees. The Research Council of Canada offered me a SSHRC research grant over a decade ago to write about mental illness in ancient Rome. Before I completed much of that work I froze—and then I wrote a book on boredom. That led to another book, *Jealousy*. This work has followed as the last of the trio. My comradely gratitude to the Research Council of Canada for providing me with the support for this work. My sincere apologies, however, for not using the grant in the way that had been intended. This is structured dithering in action. It's the life of Waiting. I hope that's a good thing.

NOTES

Prologue

1. Kay Redfield Jamison is speaking here of Robert Lowell's third marriage. His wife was Caroline Blackwood. The quotation comes from her *Robert Lowell: Setting the River on Fire: A Study of Genius, Mania, and Character*, New York, Knopf, 2017, p. 329.
2. Nate Jenkins, "Dick Cavett Talks about His Depression," *The Huffington Post*, June 20, 2008.
3. You can read more on this repetition in A. G. M. Bulloch et al., "Recurrence of Major Depressive Episodes Is Strongly Dependent on the Number of Previous Episodes," *Depression and Anxiety*, 31, 2014.
4. The article appeared in the *Daily Mail*, August 29, 2017 (Caroline Howe), and was based on Dylan Jones' biography, *David Bowie: A Life*, Doubleday Canada, 2017.
5. Bowie's aunt won't have any of it, according to Jack Malvern in *The Times*, June 15, 2018.
6. *bbc.com*, February 23, 2015 (Adam Hadhazy).
7. The quotation comes from Claudia Hammond's *Time Warped: Unlocking the Mysteries of Time Perception*, London, Canongate, 2011.

8. You can piece together this story from *The Star*, May 1, 2017 ("April the giraffe's baby finally has a name").
9. *Global News*, April 15, 2017 ("April the giraffe gives birth before online audience of over 1 million people").

Chapter 1

1. Jake Grogan, in his *Origins of a Story: 202 Inspirations Behind the World's Greatest Literature*, Cider Mill Press, 2017 (reviewed in *National Post*, November 18, 2017 [Michael Melgaard]) tells the tale of Dr. Seuss' last book.
2. Melania Trump's gift was described in the *Daily Mail*, September 30, 2017 (James Wilkinson). Michelle Obama used to enjoy reading the books to children as well. Just before Melania's gift there appeared Philip Nels, *Was the Cat in the Hat Black? The Hidden Racism of Children's Literature, and the Need for Diverse Books*, Oxford University Press, 2017.
3. *Waiting for Godot* has many very funny expressions for waiting. My two favorites, both from Pozzo, are, "the dusk . . . the strain . . . the waiting" and "wait a little longer, you'll never regret it."
4. Though frequently bad, as Walter Kempowski's *All for Nothing*, NYRB Classics, 2016 shows. It's the story of a formerly wealthy landed German family living on a small estate in Prussia in January 1945 waiting for the Russians to invade. It could also be compared to J. M. Coetzee's novel, *Waiting for the Barbarians*.
5. Friederike Gräff's *Warten: Erkundungen eines ungeliebten Zustands*, Ch. Links Verlag, 2014 is more positive about waiting than many books. Hers is a very attractive book and, failing an English translation, you'll have to make do with me. Also from Germany there is Andrea Köhler's reflective, *Die geschenkte Zeit: Über das Warten*, Taschenbuch, 2011 (a cautiously positive take on the condition—it's hard to get but worth it; there's an English version, *The Waiting Game* [2015] and there's also *Passing Time: An Essay on Waiting* [2017], which is a retitled reissue of the previous book); Coen Simon's *Warten macht gelücklich!: Eine Philosophie der Sehnsucht*, Gebundenes Buch,

2015 (translated from Dutch by Ira Wilhelm), puts the stress on nostalgia; Stefan Geyer's and Georg Christian Dörr's (eds.) *Vom Warten*, marix Verlag, 2018, arrived too late for me. Back to English: Daniel Mendelsohn's *Waiting for the Barbarians: Essays from the Classics to Pop Culture*, New York Review Books, 2012 has some positive things to say about waiting, despite the title. Joseph Farman's *Delayed Response: The Art of Waiting from the Ancient to the Instant World*, Yale University Press, 2018 has as its theme waiting and communications. But Farman helpfully explains a lot about waiting in general. Harold Schweitzer's *On Waiting*, Routledge, 2008 is a gently passionate book. It concerns philosophy and waiting. There is also the deep learning of Lothar Pikulik's *Warten, Erwartung: Eine Lebensform in End- und Übergangszeiten in Beispielen aus der Geistesgeschichte, Literatur und Kunst*, Vandenhoeck + Ruprecht Gm, 1997.

6. I found this list in, swns.com, September 27, 2012 ("Wait in line: Nearly a year of our life is spent in QUEUES"). You might also look at Marie Marquis and Pierre Filiatrault, "Cognitive and Affective Reactions When Facing an Additional Delay While Waiting in Line: A Matter of Self-Consciousness Disposition," *Social Behavior and Personality: An International Journal*, 28(4), 2000.

7. It is of particular importance for people working with computer systems. For example: Donald Gross et al., *Fundamentals of Queuing Theory*, Wiley Interscience 4, 2008, or A. Y. Kinchin, *Mathematical Methods in the Theory of Queuing*, Dover Publications, 2013. There are many other books like this. The more general area of waiting is dealt with by probability theory: Y. A. Rozanov, *Probability Theory: A Concise Course*, Dover Publications, 1977. Here is a good example of probability theory in action: "Scott Kominers, a mathematician at Harvard University, and his colleagues derived a formula for the optimal time that you should wait for a tardy bus at each stop en route before giving up and walking on. 'Many mathematicians probably ponder this on their way to work, but never get round to working it out,' he says. The team found that the solution was surprisingly simple. When both options seem reasonably attractive, the formula advises you to choose the

'lazy' option: wait at the first stop, no matter how frustrating." This comes from the *New Scientist,* January 23, 2008.
8. *Guardian*, December 27, 2017 ("Back to front: why switching queues will get you nowhere faster").
9. Claudia Hammond, *Time Warped*. Another very good book on the experience of time is Marc Wittmann's *Felt Time: The Psychology of How We Perceive Time*, MIT Press, 2016. Time is a very popular subject and there seems to be a new book on time every few months. So, Dean Buonomano, *Your Brain Is a Time Machine: The Neuroscience and Physics of Time*, W. W. Norton, 2017, Vanessa Ogle, *The Global Transformation of Time 1870–1950*, Harvard University Press, 2015, and Alan Burdick, *Why Time Flies: A Mostly Scientific Investigation,* Simon and Schuster, repr. 2018. The most recent I've noticed are Raymond Tallis' *On Time and Lamentation: Reflections on Transience*, Agenda, 2016, and Simon Garfield, *Timekeepers: How the World Became Obsessed with Time*, Canongate, 2017. There's also Lee Smolin's *Time Reborn: From the Crisis in Physics to the Future of the Universe*, Vintage, 2013 and *Time Travel*, by James Gleick, Pantheon Books, 2016.
10. Queuing and totalitarianism is a minor genre unto itself. Vladimir Sorokin's first novel, *The Queue* (1985, repr. New York Review Books, 2008), is set in the late days of the Soviet Union. Basma Abdel Aziz', *The Queue*, Melville House, 2016 seems to be set in a fictional and totalitarian Egypt.
11. Richard Thomson's book on this painting is *Edgar Degas: Waiting*, Getty Museum Studies in Art, 1993.
12. Perhaps this could be linked with the photographer Henri Cartier-Bresson's "the decisive moment" (explained in Henri Cartier-Bresson, *The Decisive Moment*, Steidl repr., 2015, originally published 1953). Cartier-Bresson was speaking much more broadly and about photography. For vigorous criticism there is Sean O'Hagan, "Cartier-Bresson's classic is back— But his Decisive Moment has passed," *Guardian*, December 23, 2014. People still show a lot of interest in the idea: James Glossop, "Behind the shot," *The Times*, December 16, 2017.
13. The Japanese conductor Seiji Ozawa, in his discussions with Haruki Murakami *(Absolutely on Music: Conversations with*

Seiji Ozawa [translated by Jay Rubin], Bond Street Books, 2016), tells us: "In Japan we talk about *ma* in Asian music—the importance of those pauses or empty space [within the music]—but it's there in Western music, too. You get a musician like Glenn Gould, and he's doing exactly the same thing. Not everybody can do it—certainly no ordinary musician."
14. The sale was reported on December 1, 2017, in *Politiken* (Torben Benner).
15. The exhibition at the Royal Academy in London in 2008 may have marked the end of the century of waiting. The catalogue *HAMMERSHØI* (Royal Academy, 2008) by Felix Krämer, Naoki Sato, and Anne-Brigitte Foinsmark proves it.
16. This strange information concerning Harold Wilson appeared in *The Times,* December 11, 2017. The commentary on Harold Wilson, waiting, and patience came from Matt Chorley (in his *The Red Box*, December 11, 2017). Chorley was relying on a report in *The Times* on the same day by David Sanderson and Kaya Burgess. They explain, "For three decades José Burguera, a Spanish psychologist, sent questionnaires to politicians, scientists, artists and sportspeople and received about 450 replies, but the results do not appear to have been published. Gabriel Heaton, a specialist in books and manuscripts at Sotheby's, which is selling the research material in an auction tomorrow [December 12, 2017], said that because the questions were 'quite flattering you are maybe more likely to respond' . . . Heaton said that the material—comprising about 450 signed questionnaires from 1970 until 2001 and estimated to fetch between £20,000 and £30,000—had 'wonderful breadth of research potential.'"

Chapter 2

1. "Jaguar corridor initiative," *panthera.org.*
2. It's worth noting that too little dopamine is linked not just with Parkinson's disease but perhaps as well to a proneness to addiction.
3. Arif A. Hamid et al., "Mesolimbic Dopamine Signals the Value of Work," *Nature Neuroscience,* published online November

23, 2015. For a quick summary of this article see *Neuroscience News*, November 24, 2015 ("The Role of Dopamine in Motivation and Learning").
4. On risk-taking and lowered dopamine see my *Boredom: A Lively History*, Yale University Press, 2011, and "Risky Decisions Linked to Brain Chemical," *New Scientist*, July 21, 2018 (Clare Wilson).
5. Adam Hadhazy points this out in his "Fear Factor: Dopamine May Fuel Dread, Too," *Scientific American*, July 14, 2008.
6. There are quite a few representations of families waiting for fishermen. It's often the wives who receive the focus (so, for example, Homer's *Waiting for the Return of the Fishermen*, Henry Moret, *Waiting for the Fishermen to Return*, or Eugene Boudin, *Fisherwives Waiting for the Boats to Return*). They are there to help with the catch, I presume, but there is always also a sense of relief that the fishermen are back safe. Friederike Gräff's *Warten* has some material on this theme.
7. *Neuroscience News*, November 24, 2015 ("The Role of Dopamine in Motivation and Learning")
8. Dopamine has been linked with intelligence a lot lately: Andy Coghlan, "Huge Dose of Brain Chemical Dopamine May Have Made Us Smart," *The New Scientist*, November 23, 2017.
9. Dopamine may offer not just an increased ability to learn but also an evolutionary advantage particularly to humans. This is reported by Ann Gibbons, "Dopamine May Have Given Humans Our Social Edge over Other Apes," *Science (AAAS)*, January 22, 2018.
10. "Neurochemistry of Prosocial Decision Making: The Role of Dopamine, Serotonin, and Oxytocin," Carolyn Declerck and Christophe Boone, *Neuroeconomics of Prosocial Behavior: The Compassionate Egoist*, Elsevier, 2016.
11. "Dopamine: New Theory Integrates Its Role in Learning, Motivation," *Michigan News: University of Michigan*, November 23, 2015, and for the original: Arif A. Hamid et al., "Mesolimbic Dopamine Signals the Value of Work," *Nature Neuroscience* 19, 2016.
12. *Kansas City Star*, June 13, 2017 (Katy Bergen with Tony Rizzo).
13. Serotonin and dopamine can work together: G. A. Horvath et al., "Improvement of Self-Injury with Dopamine and Serotonin

Replacement Therapy in a Patient with a Hemizygous PAK3 Mutation: A New Therapeutic Strategy for Neuropsychiatric Features of an Intellectual Disability Syndrome," *Journal of Child Neurology*, 33(1), 2018.
14. K. Miyazaki, K. W. Miyazaki and K. Doya, "The Role of Serotonin in the Regulation of Patience and Impulsivity," *Molecular Neurobiology* 45, 2012 and K. W. Miyazaki et al., "Optogenetic Activation of Dorsal Raphe Serotonin Neurons Enhances Patience for Future Rewards," *Current Biology*, 24(17), 2014.
15. Serotonin is also associated with fear and dread. Antidepressants can trigger such reactions in many new users. Why this happens is little understood. There is a brief report on the problem in *Science Daily*, August 24, 2016 ("How Do Antidepressants Trigger Fear and Anxiety?").
16. M. S. Fonseca, M. Murakami, Z. F. Mainen, "Activation of Dorsal Raphe Serotonergic Neurons Promotes Waiting but Is Not Reinforcing," *Current Biology*, 25(3), 2015. Fonseca team's work is discussed by Michael A. McDannald, "Serotonin: Waiting but Not Rewarding," *Current Biology*, 25(3), 2015.
17. *Neuroscience*, January 15, 2015 ("Good Things Come to Those Who Wait? More Serotonin, More Patience")
18. S. P. Ranade, Z. F. Mainen, "Transient Firing of Dorsal Raphe Neurons Encodes Diverse and Specific Sensory, Motor, and Reward Events," *Neurophysiology*, 102(5), 2009.
19. *New Scientist*, October 12, 2014 (Phil McKenna).
20. *New Scientist*, October 12, 2014 (Phil McKenna)
21. *Daily Mail*, June 22, 2017 (Rory Tingle).
22. "How snipers use technology and skill to kill from long distances," (Behind the Story) *The Times*, June 23, 2017.
23. *Guardian*, May 26, 2016 (Ben Child).
24. It is easy to dislike dopamine. Some people give the impression that they do—that's the feeling you gain from Fred H. Previc, *The Dopaminergic Mind in Human Evolution and History*, Cambridge University Press, 2009. Previc "contrasts the great achievements of the dopaminergic mind with the harmful effects of rising dopamine levels in modern societies and [wonders whether] . . . the dopaminergic mind has evolved

that has evolved in humans is still adaptive to the health of humans and to the planet in general."
25. "For patients with Parkinson's disease, dopamine agonist use is associated with incidence of impulse control disorders [ICD] in a dose-effect relationship." This was reported in Jean-Christophe Corvol et al., "Longitudinal analysis of impulse control disorders in Parkinson disease," *Neurology*, 91(3), 2018. There seems to be no evidence for this affect in non-Parkinsonian population.
26. Anne Underwood, "A little help from serotonin," *Newsweek*, December 28, 1997.
27. "How to Increase Serotonin in the Human Brain without Drugs," *Journal of Psychiatry & Neuroscience*, 32(6), 2007.
28. Some reports on new emotions: *New Scientist*, April 5, 2017: "Are Emotions a Palette Built from Primaries?" and *New Scientist*, January 13, 2010: "Five Emotions You Never Knew You Had."
29. The development of emotional regulations in the brain is something that comes very slowly and seems to be related to the interaction between the medial prefrontal cortex (mPFC) and such sources of emotion as the amygdala. The mPFC develops its abilities quite late in human beings. We seem to wait for this self-control that may express itself through waiting. A lot on this waiting can be learned from Nim Tottenham, "The Brain's Emotional Development," *Cerebrum*, July 2017. There is also J. Panksepp, & L. Biven, L. *The Archaeology of Mind: Neuroevolutionary Origins of Human Emotions*, W. W. Norton, 2012.

Chapter 3

1. The book, *Grand Hotel*, was published in English in 1930–1931 from the German original *Menschen im Hotel*, 1929. The movie was made in 1932. There was a remake in 1945 as *Weekend at the Waldorf* and a stage musical using the same name in 1989. A less successful musical entitled *At the Grand* was staged in 1958.

2. There is a useful Wikipedia entry on vervets and, yes, I have used it. There are lots of informative websites about vervets—among others: "Vervet Monkey Facts/ South African Wildlife Guide;" "Wildlife Pictures Online: Vervet Monkey Information." I've also used the material in the notes to follow.
3. You can watch the vervet monkeys show their enthusiasm for alcoholic beverages on YouTube. It's easy though upsetting to find.
4. On the vervet's social life: "Primate Info Net: Library and Information Service: National Primate Research Centre, University of Wisconsin—Madison: Vervet *Chlorocebus.*"
5. R. M. Seyfarth, D. L. Cheney, "Grooming, Alliances and Reciprocal Altruism in Vervet Monkeys," *Nature*, 308, 1984.
6. M. J. Raleigh, G. L Brammer, A. Yuwiler, et al., "Serotonergic Influences on the Social Behavior of Vervet Monkeys (*Cercopithecus aethiops sabaeus*)," *Experimental Neurology*, 68(2), 1980.
7. "Emotional States after Grooming Interactions in Japanese Macaques (*Macaca fuscata*)," *Journal of Comparative Psychology*, 129(4), 2015.
8. Lauren J. N. Brent et al., "The Neuroethology of Friendship," *Annals of the New York Academy of Science*, 1316, 2014. And also R. A. Depue, J. V. Morrone-Strupinsky, "A Neurobehavioral Model of Affiliative Bonding: Implications for Conceptualizing a Human Trait of Affiliation," *Behavioral Brain Science*, 28(3), 2005.
9. Dominik Schoebi et al., "Genetic Moderation of Sensitivity to Positive and Negative Affect in Marriage," *Emotion*, 12(2), 2012.
10. On this subject there is James Curtis' doorstop, *Spencer Tracy: A Biography*, Knopf, 2011. Katherine Whitbourne, *Daily Mail*, October 12, 2011 provides a very helpful summary of some of the contents. As always Wikipedia assists.
11. There is a detailed and helpful "Chronology" of Alice Neel's life in *Alice Neel: Painted Truths*, 2009, The Museum of Fine Arts Houston, by Jeremy Lewison and Barry Walker.
12. Reproduced in the "Chronology" by Sarah Powers in *Alice Neel*, Philadelphia Museum of Art, 2000/1 (edited by Ann Temkin). Russell Hoban's daughter, the arts journalist and

novelist Phoebe Hoban, has written a vivid biography of Alice Neel (*Alice Neel, The Art of Not Sitting Pretty*, St. Martin's Press, 2010) and there is a monograph by the former Director of Collections at the Tate Gallery, Jeremy Lewison (*Alice Neel: Painter of Modern Life*, Mercatorfonds, 2016).

13. The notes on specific paintings and themes ("Parents and children") in *Alice Neel: Painted Truths* by Jeremy Lewison and Barry Walker emphasize that "Neel's approach . . . was colored by her own experience of parenting . . . the death of Santillana, the loss of Isabetta, and Neel's nervous breakdown had an immediate effect on her work."
14. In *Alice Neel: Painted Truths*, 2009.
15. Andreas Frick et al., "Serotonin Synthesis and Reuptake in Social Anxiety Disorder," *Journal of the American Medical Association Psychiatry*, 2015.
16. *New York Times*, December 29, 2010 (Deborah Solomon).
17. Roger Grenier, "Waiting and Eternity," in *The Palace of Books*, University of Chicago Press, 2014.
18. It can certainly go wrong and waiting can be bestowed on an inanimate beloved. That's what happened to Nigel the gannet in New Zealand—"Tragic end for seabird who spent four years courting a decoy: Nigel the gannet dies without ever finding romance (and is found next to fake bird he worshipped in the love nest he'd built her); 80 concrete birds were put on Mana Island off New Zealand's Kapiti Coast; They were meant to attract birds to nest there but one got very confused; He tried to start a family with a concrete bird and eventually died by its side." The story is from the *Daily Mail*, February 1, 2018 ("Tragic end for seabird who spent four years courting a decoy").
19. Erica the robot has become so popular in Japan that she is set to become a TV news anchor—*Daily Mail*, January 30, 2018 (Phoebe Weston). For a survey of the Japanese enthusiasm for robotics: Zaven Paré, *L'âge d'or de la robotique japonaise*, Les Belles Lettres, 2016.
20. See Agnès Giard, *Un désir d'être humain: Les love doll au Japon*, Les Belles Lettres, 2016.
21. *Daily Mail*, June 20, 2016 (Sophie Williams).

22. *bbc.com*, June 18, 2014 (Tom Stafford).
23. *bbc.com*, February 23, 2015 (Adam Hadhazy).
24. Naomi Rea, "The Prada Foundation's New Show Is Devoted to Surreal Photos of People in Love with Their Sex Dolls and Artificial Babies," *news.artnet.com*, February 18, 2019, covers an art show by Elena Dorfman and Jamie Diamond entitled "Surrogate. A Love Ideal" that ran February 21 through July 22 at the Fondazione Prada's Osservatorio space in the Galleria Vittorio Emanuele II in Milan. There is a group called the "reborners" who "typically female, make, collect, and interact with disarmingly lifelike baby dolls." Naomi Rea's article is accompanied by a number of illustrations. There is a considerable "reborn" trade on line.
25. The story comes from the *Daily Mail*, April 3, 2015 (Tim MacFarland.)
26. John Gray's *The Soul of a Marionette: A Short Enquiry into Human Freedom*, Allen Lane, 2015 believes the opposite. He argues, according to Marina Gerner (*Times Literary Supplement*, July 31, 2015) "Robot nurses, teachers, sex workers and soldiers have ceased to be the stuff of speculative fiction. . . . In the long run, humans will become redundant and those who want to continue to participate in society will have to resemble machines more closely."

Chapter 4

1. Jason McClure wrote a fascinating PhD thesis with me on doubles in Roman literature. My interest in the subject and much of my knowledge of the subject of doubles derives from Jason. The thesis is *Doubling and the Theban Mythological Tradition in Roman Poetry*, dissertation, University of Calgary, 2010. Thank you, Jason.
2. The report on Richard Anthony Jones can be found in the *Kansas City Star*, June 9, 2017. The reporter was Tony Rizzo, who, along with Katy Bergen, wrote up the Mr. Ripple story for the same paper.
3. *Kansas City Star*, December 18, 2018 (Joe Robertson).

4. On February 28, 2018, it was reported in many papers (I'm relying on *abc.net.au* February 28, 2018) that Barbra Streisand had cloned her late dog, Samantha, to produce two pups to make up for the loss. Happiness comes in doubles, but Barbra Streisand couldn't wait.
5. Doubles and the Internet can be linked in the strangest of ways. The *New Scientist*, February 10, 2018, reported in its leader, "But the biggest lever remains in the hands of consumers. In 2006, in the early days of the age of social media and user-generated content, *Time* magazine's person of the year was 'YOU.' The cover featured a mirrored panel with the words: 'You control the information age. Welcome to your world.' That may seem like a naïve declaration from a different time, but it isn't. If, like many, you are itching for a techlash, then start by looking in the mirror."
6. *Daily Mail*, November 20, 2015 ("It's creepy, freaky, crazy!")
7. *Washington Post*, January 15, 2018 (Amy B. Wang).
8. *Guardian*, July 10, 2017 (Hannah J. Davies).
9. Who had one too many rhinoplasty treatments in 2017. It was feared he would lose his nose (*Daily Mail*, July 7, 2017 [Clemence Michallon]).
10. *Daily Mail*, May 26, 2017 (Siofra Brennan).
11. *Daily Mail*, June 27, 2017 (Stephanie Linning).
12. *Daily Mail*, May 26, 2017 (Siofra Brennan).
13. *National Post*, June 28, 2017.
14. In December 2018 Nigeria's then 75-year-old President, Muhhammadu Buhari, was compelled to deny with haste that he was dead and had been replaced by a Sudanese double, a clone called Jubaril. The rumors of his death and replacement were apparently caused by Buhari's being absent in hospital in the United Kingdom for five months in 2017. It appears that the rumor began in this period of presidential convalescence. According to a report in the *Guardian* (December 3, 2018) a video showing the president denying the rumor concerning Jubaril "has been posted to the president's Twitter account, which is followed by 1.76m people, where it is pinned as his top tweet."
15. Charles M. Stang of the Harvard Divinity School produced the exceptionally interesting *Our Divine Double*, Harvard

University Press, 2016. I will let the Harvard University Press blurb speak for the book: "What if you were to discover that you were not entirely you, but rather one half of a whole, that you had, in other words, a divine double? In the second and third centuries CE, this idea gripped the religious imagination of the Eastern Mediterranean."

16. Holly Maniatty (reported by Sheeka Sanahori, *USA TODAY*, May 15, 2017) produces a very specialized sort of a doubling experience that ends the wait for the hearing impaired. Ms. Maniatty, a certified American Sign Language interpreter, uses signing to provide a mirroring for the vocals of the songs at concerts by hip-hop and rap artists like Wu Tang Clan, Snoop Dogg, the Beastie Boys, Jay-Z, and Einem. Happiness and doubles really do link up here.

17. The Tate's description concludes like this: "The artist is unknown, but the work is thought to have been painted near the Cholmondeley family's estates in Cheshire. The pose is not known to have been used in any other British painting but was frequently seen in contemporary tomb sculpture."

18. The real-life family genealogy that's associated with *The Cholmondeley Ladies* is outlined by the Tate Gallery, "the painting was in the collection of Thomas Cholmondeley (pronounced 'Chumley'), the third son of Sir Hugh Cholmondeley and his wife Lady Mary Cholmondeley . . . John T. Hopkins (1991) suggests that the portrait shows two daughters of Sir Hugh and Lady Mary Cholmondeley—Lettice, first wife of Sir Richard Grosvenor, 1st Baronet (and mother of Sir Richard Grosvenor, 2nd Baronet), and Mary Calveley (died 1616), wife of George Calveley."

19. One of the referees for this book suggested that "cases of real twins separated at birth or otherwise separated family members" would provide a clear link between waiting, doubles, and happiness—and a real life one at that. This reader offers as an example, "*The Waiting* by Cathy Lagrow, a book about a woman, Minka, who is raped at 16 and who gives her baby up for adoption but who continues loving her daughter and hoping (against hope?) to meet her some day for more than 70 years. She finally meets her daughter when the daughter is 77. The book is written by Minka's granddaughter."

20. Siamese twins could add the picture. The lives of Chang and Eng, two of the most famous of all Siamese twins, do not seem to have benefited from happiness, despite their being near doubles and their periods of waiting. Their lives are detailed in Yunte Huang's *Inseparable: The Original Siamese Twins and Their Rendezvous with American History*, Norton, 2018. (There is a documentary available on YouTube and entitled "Abigail & Brittany Hensel—The Twins Who Share a Body." Abigail and Brittany are conjoined Minnesotan twins, who share a body from the neck down.)
21. The latest of the twin movies is François Ozon's *L'amant double [The Double Lover]*, the story of a young woman, Chloé, confused over which of a pair of identical twins she actually loves. Her wait does not lead to a happy ending. Ozon's movie is based on the 1987 novel by Joyce Carol Oates (then writing as Rosamond Smith) entitled *Lives of the Twins* (also known as *Kindred Passions*).
22. *Washington Post*, August 24, 2016 (Rachel Feltman).
23. *New Scientist*, May 10, 2017.
24. There are various tales of dubious doppelgängers, of perilous pairs, or dreadful doubles. John Mullan, a professor of English at University College, London and a columnist for the *Guardian*, offered his top ten in the *Guardian*, May 2, 2009. I'd add to his list the Spanish Nobel fiction prizewinner José Saramago's *The Double* (redone as a movie in 2015 by the Canadian filmmaker Denis Villeneuve as *Enemy Within*, a study in psychopathy that won the 2015 prize in Toronto for the best Canadian film). The Polish film director Krzysztof Kieślowski is the cinematic patron saint of heautoscopy. He made a very confusing though visually beautiful film called *The Double Life of Veronique* (1991).
25. That's also what the Latin scholar Jason McClure has argued. The appearance of doubles, he'd say, won't make you one bit happy. Their appearance is traditionally associated with upcoming disaster or even mental disorder. Jason McClure, *Doubling and the Theban Mythological Tradition in Roman Poetry*, dissertation, University of Calgary, 2010, taught me a lot about this matter (and many others relating to doubling).

He links the appearance of doubles with "atmospheric disturbances" (storms, plagues, and strange times). The double can also be a harbinger of death.
26. Peter Brugger et al., "Polyopic Heautoscopy: Case Report and Review of the Literature," *Cortex*, 42(5), 2006. There is also Olaf Blanke, Christine Mohr "Out-of-Body Experience, Heautoscopy, and Autoscopic Hallucination of Neurological Origin. Implications for Neurocognitive Mechanisms of Corporeal Awareness and Self-Consciousness," *Brain Research Reviews*, 50, 2005.
27. Douwe Draaisma, "Echos, Doubles, and Delusions: Capgras Syndrome in Science and Literature," *Style*, 43(3), 2009.
28. J. Postel, D. F. Allen, "The Delusional Misidentification Syndromes: Joseph Capgras (1873–1950)," *Psychopathology*, 27, 1994.
29. Chris Fiacconi et al., "Nature and Extent of Person Recognition Impairments Associated with Capgras Syndrome in Lewy Body Dementia," *Frontiers in Human Neuroscience*, September 24, 2014.
30. A recent survey of the Capgras problem is: A. Barrelle, J. P. Luauté, "Capgras Syndrome and Other Delusional Misidentification Syndromes," *Frontiers of Neurology and Neuroscience*, 42, 2018.
31. Or was it that my mother had come to suffer a type of "face blindness" or prosopagnosia? In Capgras, as Oliver Sacks elucidates, "faces, though recognized, no longer generate a sense of emotional familiarity. Since a husband or wife or child does not convey that special warm feeling of familiarity, the Capgras patient will argue, they cannot be the real thing—they must be clever impostors, counterfeits. People with prosopagnosia [on the other hand] have insight; they realize that their problems with recognition come from their own brains. People with Capgras syndrome, in contrast, remain immovable in their conviction that they are perfectly normal, and it is the other person [the double] who is profoundly, even uncannily, wrong." Sacks discusses the condition in "Face-Blind: Why Are Some of Us Terrible at Recognizing Faces," *New Yorker*, August 2010, and in his 1985 book *The Man Who Mistook His Wife for a Hat*.

32. Here is a medical report on doubles in one dementia patient's life: Stephanie Sutton et al., "Capgras' Syndrome in an Elderly Patient with Dementia," *The Primary Care Companion for CNS Disorders*, Feb. 13, 2014. There's also S. J. Tsai et al., "Capgras' Syndrome in a Patient with Vascular Dementia: A Case Report," *Kaohsiung Journal of Medical Science*, 13(10) 1997. Here are two more general articles: D. G. Harwood, W. W. Barker, R. L. Ownby, et al. "Prevalence and Correlates of Capgras Syndrome in Alzheimer's Disease," *International Journal of Geriatric Psychiatry*, 14(6), 1999; K. A. Josephs, "Capgras Syndrome and Its Relationship to Neurodegenerative Disease," *Archives of Neurology*, 64(12), 2007.
33. The 1930s exhibited a proliferation of doubles in painting and photography. Picasso loves to paint the doubled face and it seems that his inspiration for this image comes from his partner of the period, Dora Maar. Dora Maar created a number of remarkable photographs around the image of the double (which you can find reproduced in Louise Barings's *Dora Maar: Paris in the Time of Man Ray, Jean Cocteau, and Picasso*, Rizzoli, 2017). She gave up photography after Picasso.
34. *Daily Mail*, February 14, 2018 (Sara Malm and Jennifer Newton) and *Guardian*, February 14, 2018 (Daniel Hurst).
35. Figures are from *alzheimers.net*. However, I've seen other figures claiming that right now more than 44 million people worldwide wait though some version or another of the illness.
36. And there are many examples that I have not touched on. Grief can precipitate doubling, When the jazz trumpeter Chet Baker was killed in a car crash the pianist Bill Evans, his close friend and band mate, was so grief stricken that he stopped playing and for a time wore Chet Baker's clothes (striving for happiness as a double of Chet Baker)—Peter Pettinger, *Bill Evans: How My Heart Sings*, Yale University Press, 1998.

Chapter 5

1. The quintet on the Vevo recording seems to be, apart from Miles Davis, Philly Jo Jones (died at home of a heart attack in Philadelphia, aged 62) on drums, Wynton Kelly (Kelly died in

Toronto, Canada, following an epileptic seizure, on April 12, 1971, aged 40) on piano, Paul Chambers (dead aged 33; alcohol and heroin addiction contributed to the tuberculosis, it's said) on bass, and John Coltrane on saxophones. There were, in addition, three trombonists who played the chorus to *So What* late in the piece. Of their fates I cannot speak.

2. It has a book to itself: Ashley Kahn, *Kind of Blue: The Making of the Miles Davis Masterpiece*, Da Capo Press, 2007.
3. You can learn a little about Coltrane in Ashley Kahn's *A Love Supreme: The Story of John Coltrane's Signature Album*, Penguin Books, repr. 2003.
4. There are other strange and non-performance-related versions of the pause—there is, for example, the very moving story of the 30-year-old who looks like a toddler. He is a 2 ft. 7 in. Chinese man who has stopped growing since the age of two due to an unknown condition (described by Tracy You, *Daily Mail*, November 13, 2017.)
5. Valorie N. Salimpoor et al. "Anatomically distinct dopamine release during anticipation and experience of peak emotion to music," *Nature Neuroscience*, 2011.
6. Adiel Mallik, Mona Lisa Chanda, and Daniel J. Levitin, "Anhedonia to Music and Mu-opioids: Evidence from the Administration of Naltrexone," *Scientific Reports*, 7, Article number: 41952 (2017)
7. *Guardian*, February 20, 2014 (Ralph Brown).
8. Marc Wittmann, *Felt Time*, 2016.
9. Read more in the *Daily Mail*, July 21, 2016 (Emma Glanfield).
10. Adam Shatz, in the *New York Review of Books*, February 8, 2018, has a very helpful review of an album by the jazz trumpeter Wadada Leo Smith (*Solo: Reflections and Meditations on Monk*). Smith uses silence or what I am calling the pause, he believes, not as a contrastive passage to the music in which it finds itself, but as an extension of the music. Of Thelonius Monk, Shatz, partly quoting Smith, tells us: "Monk, with his exceptional sensitivity to the spaces between notes, understood silence not as 'a moment of absence,' but 'as a vital field where musical ideas exist as a result of what was played before and after.'" Smith speaks of dropping "a silence bigger than a table."

11. Adam Schatz, again, in the *New York Review of Books*, September 29, 2016, reviewing Don Cheadle's movie *Miles Ahead*, and George Grella Jr.'s *Bitches Brew*, Bloomsbury, 2016.
12. "Silent disco fever spreads through aged care centers and helps treat dementia" is a piece by Samantha Turnbull, *ABC News*, February 24, 2018.
13. Duez' work is reported by Tara Patel in the *New Scientist*, April 16, 1994. There is also her book: Danielle Duez, *La pause dans la parole de l'homme politique*, CNRS 1991.
14. Ulla Gleset Sciølberg, *Science Nordic*, September 25, 2015, and *ScienceDaily*, September 30, 2015 ("Pauses can make or break a conversation").
15. Thomas Melin, *The University of Gothenburg/The Faculty of Arts/News and Events/News*, September 7, 2015.
16. On concentration: M. Gruber, B. Gelman, C. Ranganath, "States of Curiosity Modulate Hippocampus-Dependent Learning via the Dopaminergic Circuit," *Neuron*, 84(2), 2014.
17. Quoted by Claudia Hammond in *Time Warped*.
18. R. C. Spencer, D. M. Devilbiss, C. W. Berridge, "The Cognition-Enhancing Effects of Psychostimulants Involve Direct Action in the Prefrontal Cortex," *Biological Psychiatry*, 77(11), 2015; R. C. Malenka, E. J. Nestler, S. E. Hyman, "Chapter 13: Higher Cognitive Function and Behavioral Control," in A. Sydor, R. Y. Brown, *Molecular Neuropharmacology: A Foundation for Clinical Neuroscience* (2nd ed.), McGraw-Hill Medical, 2009; I. P. Ilieva, C. J. Hook, M. J. Farah, "Prescription Stimulants' Effects on Healthy Inhibitory Control, Working Memory, and Episodic Memory: A Meta-analysis," *Journal of Cognitive Neuroscience*, 27(6), 2015.
19. C. J. Teter et al., "Illicit Use of Specific Prescription Stimulants among College Students: Prevalence, Motives, and Routes of Administration," *Pharmacotherapy*, 26(10), October 2006.
20. Much of this from: Mason Currey, "What Do Auden, Sartre, and Ayn Rand Have in Common? Amphetamines," *Slate*, April 22, 2013.
21. Mason Currey again.
22. Marc Wittmann et al., "Impaired Time Perception and Motor Timing in Stimulant—Dependent Subjects," *Drug Alcohol Dependence*, 90(2–3), October 2007.

23. *New York Times*, September 13, 1998. This is in a review of *Bill Evans: How My Heart Sings* by Peter Pettinger, Yale University Press, 1998.
24. There is a helpful write-up from the John's Hopkins Medicine publicity, February 26, 2008 ("This Is Your Brain on Jazz"). The original article is by Charles J. Limb and Allen R. Braun, "Neural Substrates of Spontaneous Musical Performance: An fMRI Study of Jazz Improvisation," *PLoS ONE*, 3(2), February 2008. There have been other articles following up, such as: Malinda J. McPherson et al., "Emotional Intent Modulates the Neural Substrates of Creativity: An fMRI Study of Emotionally Targeted Improvisation in Jazz Musicians," *Nature*, January 4, 2016.
25. In 1931, two years after the birth of her first child, Hepworth "pierced her first carving, thus introducing the 'hole' to British sculpture. The negative space—which Hepworth used to explore balance in forms—became a hallmark of her career, and is considered her most important contribution to abstract art. Works such as *Four-Square (Four Circles)* . . . highlight the artist's interest in circular space." This is from *Christie's*, November 6, 2018.

Chapter 6

1. I've adapted some of my old work in this chapter: "Celebrating the Ordinary—The Advantages of Being Dull," *Psychology Today* (blog), Posted April 30, 2016; "Why Would Anyone Build Their Own Coffin?" *Psychology Today* (blog), Posted July 18, 2017; "Play, Primates, Jealousy, Work, and Losing Deliberately," *Psychology Today* (blog), Posted May 27, 2015.
2. *The Newcastle Herald*, March 11, 2015 (Grace Millar).
3. This sort of thing is more common than you'd expect, at least in Australia. Two years later near Melbourne in Victoria "Police . . . stopped a vehicle just after midnight on Sunday, May 14, 2017, after noticing it allegedly being driven erratically from a Mornington licensed premises. The driver, a 52-year-old Maryborough woman, returned a positive preliminary breath test and later returned an evidentiary breath test result of 0.175

per cent . . . Less than two hours later, police spotted the same vehicle again being driven through Mornington and pulled it over. This time it was the husband who returned a positive preliminary breath test, before returning an evidentiary breath test result of 0.131 per cent." *The Courier*, May 15, 2017 ("Husband and wife caught drink driving two hours apart").

4. A recent, helpful, and very optimistic book on prospection is Martin Seligman, Peter Railton, Roy F. Baumeister, and Chandra Sripada, *Homo Prospectus*, Oxford University Press, 2016.
5. Walter Mischel, *The Marshmallow Test: Mastering Self-Control*, Little, Brown Spark 2014. And: Kelly McGonigal (who has an identical twin), *The Willpower Instinct: How Self-Control Works, Why It Matters, and What You Can Do to Get More of It*, Penguin Books, 2011.
6. Walter Mischel and Ebbe R. Ebbesen, "Attention in Delay of Gratification," *Journal of Personality and Social Psychology*, 16, 1970, plus Y. Shoda, W. Mischel, and P. K. Peake, "Predicting Adolescent Cognitive and Self-regulatory Competencies from Preschool Delay of Gratification: Identifying Diagnostic Conditions," *Developmental Psychology*, 26(6), 1990.
7. Some people will argue that it is serotonin that helps people with *proception* just as it helped people wait patiently for some desired outcome in Chapter 2. So it is that the efficient management of waiting in both social and even financial situations seems to be linked with serotonin. Maital Neta, Tien T. Tong, "Don't Like What You See? Give It Time: Longer Reaction Times Associated with Increased Positive Affect," *Emotion*, 16(5), August 2016.
8. *Psychological Science*, May 25, 2018.
9. Jessica McCrory Calarco, "Why Rich Kids Are So Good at the Marshmallow Test," *The Atlantic*, June 2018.
10. The challenge against Mischel is also taken up by C. Kidd, H. Palmeri, and R. N. Aslin, "Rational Snacking: Young Children's Decision-Making on the Marshmallow Task is Moderated by Beliefs about Environmental Reliability," *Cognition*, 126(1), January 2013 ("Children in the reliable condition waited significantly longer than those in the unreliable condition . . . suggesting that children's wait-times reflected reasoned beliefs about whether waiting would ultimately pay off.")

There's also N. M Garon et al., "Making Decisions about Now and Later: Development of Future-Oriented Self-Control," *Cognitive Development*, 27(3), July–September 2012.

11. John Bargh', *Before You Know It: The Unconscious Reasons We Do What We Do*, William Heinemann, 2017, may offer some indirect comments on the basis of thin slicing.
12. Partnoy's work is a logical extension of the famous work of the Nobel laureate Daniel Kahneman. You can get a real taste for this material in Kahneman's *Thinking, Fast and Slow*, Anchor, 2011 ("Malcolm Gladwell definitely created in the public arenas the impression that intuition is magical").
13. He's not alone. Carl Honore offers two books against blinking: *In Praise of Slowness: Challenging the Cult of Speed*, Knopf, 2005, and *The Slow Fix: Solve Problems, Work Smarter and Live Better in a Fast World*, Knopf, 2004. There's also Michael LeGault, *Think!: Why Crucial Decisions Can't Be Made in the Blink of an Eye*, Simon and Schuster, 2006. Most famous of all of the books is the Nobel laureate Daniel Kahneman's *Thinking, Fast and Slow*.
14. Quoted by Megan Gambino, "Why Procrastination Is Good for You," *Smithsonian.com*, July 12, 2012.
15. Andrea Köhler has a chapter on "hesitation" in her *Passing Time: An Essay on Waiting*, (2017) and, my favorite, a chapter on "laggardness."
16. You can read the story in "Art: Degas and Mrs. Manet," *New York Times*, March 22, 1992. The piece is excerpted from Otto Friedrich's book, *Olympia: Paris in the Age of Manet*, HarperCollins, 1992.
17. It's published by Feltrinelli and the cover cuts out all of Suzanne, but the bottom left of her dress.
18. Or maybe his leg hurt and that's why he has adopted this lolling pose. Over the next decade one or the other of his legs really did hurt. It's said to be the result of syphilis and rheumatism, both of which resulted in the amputation of his left foot in 1883. He died 11 days later.
19. Adam Grant's and Sheryl Sandberg's *Originals, How Non-Conformists Move the World*, Penguin Books 2016, has a chapter (4, "Fools Rush In: Timing, Strategic Procrastination, and the First-Mover Disadvantage") on hanging back and

procrastination. Creative individuals may seem to procrastinate when they are actually incubating ideas; the less creative may simply be "funding" the "original" in the hope they'll finally deliver.
20. *abc.net.au*, July 15, 2017 (Carla Howarth). There is another good piece on the coffin trade on the same site, *abc.net.au*, February 4, 2017 (Simon Royal).
21. J. E. Tanner, R. W. Byrne, "Triadic and Collaborative Play by Gorillas in Social Games with Objects," *Animal Cognition*, 13(4), July 2010.
22. *Daily Mail*, July 21, 2016 (Martha Cliff).
23. When collections are out of hand it's usual to speak of "compulsive hoarding." There are other names for this personality problem such as Hoarding Disorder, Diogenes Syndrome (B. Lavigne et al., "Diogenes Syndrome and Hoarding Disorder: Same or Different?" [In French] *Encephale* 42(5), October 2016), Syllogomania (used more in French) (G. Zuliani, "Diogenes Syndrome or Isolated Syllogomania? Four Heterogeneous Clinical Cases," *Aging Clinical and Experimental Research*, 25(4), August 2013), Disposophobia (I am not joking), or Messie Syndrome (used more in German, thank goodness). Hoarders are like collectors, but they dither in a self-destructive way.
24. Susannah Walker has written a recent memoir about her mother's compulsive hoarding, *The Life of Stuff: A Memoir about the Mess We Leave Behind*, Doubleday, 2018. Her mother's hoarding seems to have been linked to depression.
25. Paul Salkovskis and Sinead Lambe writing for the *Guardian*, January 9, 2015.

Chapter 7

1. "MicroTate 34," in *Tate Etc.*, issue 34, Summer 2015.
2. The experience of going nowhere in the void was repeated by the Bombay born, England domiciled sculptor Sir Anish Mikhail Kapoor. He produced a similar illusion to Fontana's void by creating bottomless pits—black holes about six feet wide and eight feet deep. The pit is colored black and looks

rather like a bottomless void—the repository of Reality. Sometimes the effects are unexpected as we learn from Sarah Cascone in "A Man Fell into Anish Kapoor's Installation of a Bottomless Pit at a Portugal Museum," artnet news, August 20, 2018. In this case Reality broke the man's leg.

3. Philip Shaw, "Sublime Sexuality: Lucio Fontana's *Spatial Concept 'Waiting',*" in Nigel Llewellyn and Christine Riding (eds.), *The Art of the Sublime*, Tate Research Publication, January 2013.
4. Tolstoy's short story, "God sees the Truth, but Waits" (1872), is all about the capacity of waiting with patience for divine redemption. Stephen King based his famous novella, *Rita Hayworth and the Shawshank Redemption*, on Tolstoy's story (the novella became a very popular movie.) God is waiting, in both Tolstoy's and King's stories, and God will come to those who are willing to wait.
5. You can meet their mother in the Bille August's 1992 film *The Best Intentions* that tells some of the story of the Bergman parents. The script was written by Ingmar Bergman.
6. She tells the story herself in Letter 4, "Spiritual Autobiography," in *Waiting for God*. I am using the Emma Craufurd translation, reprinted New York, 2009.
7. Migraines are linked with mystical experiences. Oliver Sacks, *Migraine*, revised ed., Vintage, 1999, has a discussion of the link in particular with relation to the Hildegard of Bingen, the medieval mystic.
8. The *Live Science* piece is by Rachael Rettner, "Brain Tumor Triggers Woman's Sudden 'Hyper-Religious' Behavior," *Live Science*, February 15, 2017.
9. According to the report from the Spanish team (details in the next note) "one review found that up to 22 percent of all brain tumors may first appear along with psychotic symptoms." Maybe the antipsychotics quelled the religious manias.
10. A. Carmona-Bayonas et al., "Hyperreligiosity in Malignant Brain Tumors: A Case Report and Accompanying Bibliographic Review," *Neurocase*, 23(1) 2017. There is work regularly published on this sort of thing—see Helen Phillips, *New Scientist*, July 22, 2002, on the effect of dopamine and perceptions of the paranormal.

11. Here is another report: Shahar Arzy and Roey Schurr, "'God has sent me to you': Right Temporal Epilepsy, Left Prefrontal Psychosis," *Epilepsy & Behavior*, 60, July 2016: "Religious experiences have long been documented in patients with epilepsy, though their exact underlying neural mechanisms are still unclear. Here, we had the rare opportunity to record a delusional religious conversion in real time in a patient with right temporal lobe epilepsy undergoing continuous video-EEG. In this patient, a messianic revelation experience occurred several hours after a complex partial seizure of temporal origin, compatible with postictal psychosis (PIP)."
12. Franz Kafka's *The Castle* (1926) is for some people the world's best waiting book. The novel is dominated by the image of the Castle from which the K, the novel's subject, is excluded. The theme of the Reality behind reality is important for Kafka's *The Castle*. It's easy to see how. The Reality (with a capital "R") is the unseen and mysterious life that exists within the castle. It is Reality, you could say, or the real thing, because it controls how all of the aspects of how people who live around the Castle will pass their lives. The Castle has often been linked with God.
13. Deidre Bair, *Samuel Beckett: A Biography*, Summit Books, 1990.
14. Deidre Bair, *Samuel Beckett*. On Oblomov see my *Boredom: A Lively History*.
15. Lars Svendsen discusses Heidegger and boredom in his *A Philosophy of Boredom*, Reaktion, 2003 (still the best of the many books on boredom). I have relied on Svendsen here.
16. Heidegger's understanding of waiting and time to a degree echoes those of the French philosopher Henri Bergson (1859–1941). The place to learn about his vision is in his *Time and Free Will: Time and Free Will: An Essay on the Immediate Data of Consciousness* (1889, in English 1910). For a modern discussion of Bergson on waiting and time, there is also Harold Schweizer's very helpful and attractive *On Waiting*, Routledge, 2008. The concept of scientific time has changed completely since when Bergson (and Heidegger) wrote. There was a good recent article in the *New Scientist*, April 27, 2018, whose mere title will explain this: "What Is Time: You're Living a Moment That Science Says Does Not Exist."

17. Robert Zaretsky, *Times Literary Supplement*, August 17, 2018: "Seventy-five years after her death, a growing number of writers and thinkers, ranging from Hannah Arendt and Iris Murdoch to Albert Camus and Amartya Sen, claim Weil's thought as an inspiration. No less significantly, if rather more disturbingly, many of her readers claim her as a saint. T. S. Eliot elegantly fudged the matter, concluding that when we read Weil, we 'expose ourselves to the personality of a woman of genius, of a kind of genius akin to that of the saints.'"
18. Of Being, Svendsen comments "after studying Heidegger's philosophy for a number of years, I have come the conclusion that the question of Being is not a genuine question."
19. As does George Steiner in his *Martin Heidegger*, University of Chicago Press, 1987 (1978).
20. In 1950, Emil Cioran's *A Short History of Decay*, Arcade Publishing, 2012, was published. Cioran's first book in French, this is a collection of short essays on the theme of the miserable nature of modern life, or at least life in the mid-twentieth century. Waiting is at the very heart of his book. Waiting for what? The answer is in his final mini-essay entitled in Latin "How long will things be the same?" Forever, concludes Cioran, so you might as well abandon waiting.
21. Compare Emmanuel Levinas, *Totality and Infinity: An Essay on Exteriority*, Springer, 1991. Levinas' waiting is a waiting for the realizing of the otherness of the other and the little ethical epiphany that this will entail, and its encouragement of the individual to ethical behavior.
22. One exception is the 1958 story by Isak Dinesen, *Babette's Feast* (you could also call it "Waiting for God in Jutland"). It comes eight years after Weil and five after Godot. In this story (and the 1987 movie) Babette's meal is, symbolically, the Eucharist and by accepting this meal (something that is very hard for many Lutherans, the acceptance of unearned gifts) the fractious little religious group in Jutland depicted in the story are enabled to ascend to heaven (after their long wait in their dreary, seaside Danish village). The refugee Babette, therefore, becomes a sort of a Christ figure and makes her sacrifice (spending all her money on the feast) for this religious group.

284 | NOTES

23. *Waiting for Harry*, not *Waiting for Godot*, is a piece of filmed ethnography concerning the burial practices of some Australian Aboriginals (available on YouTube; there is a commentary on Wikipedia). Demonstrating another aspect of the link between waiting and religion, it tells the story of Frank Gurrmanamana, who is in charge of the final "mortuary ceremonies" for his six-year-dead brother. But the ceremonies are put on hold because Harry Diama, "the senior blood-relative of the deceased man," lives elsewhere and "is pre-occupied with a pending court-case there involving his son."
24. The former financial advisor to the vastly wealthy artist Damien Hirst, Frank Dunphy auctioned "blue-chip works such as Lucio Fontana's Concetto Spaziale, Attese [Waiting] (1961) (est. £600,000–800,000)" in a Sotheby's sale in 2018. The painting was "the most expensive lot in the sale"—Henri Neuendorf, *Art News*, June 18, 2018.
25. I am thinking of Enrico Castellani's *Superficie nera*, 1961, which you can find easily on line.
26. Was Silk Cut part of a golden age for cigarette advertising, as Peter York suggests in "The Final Cut," *The New Statesman*, March 3, 2003?
27. Marya Hornbach, *Waiting: A Nonbeliever's Higher Power*, Hazelden, 2011, offers a very interesting alternative to belief.

Chapter 8

1. And also on waiting rooms: Andrea Köhler speaks of the experience in *Passing Time: An Essay on Waiting*, "At the Doctor's," 2017; Michael J. Armstrong and Kenneth J. Klassen, speak of the situation in "Is your 10:30 medical appointment really for 11:15?" *The Conversation*, January 21, 2018. Armstrong and Klassen talk about how appointments could be made to be on time and spare you the wait in the waiting room.
2. Roger Grenier towards the end of his essay "Waiting and Eternity," in *The Palace of Books*, University of Chicago Press, 2014 has a lot to say about waiting rooms: "Once it becomes an instrument of religion, waiting itself can become a religion,

since we have built temples for it, waiting rooms. Strange places of worship, not of an unknown god, but of the void." And so on. "What happens in waiting rooms deserves a sociological study. That's precisely what I did a long time ago. I was a ghost writer for an eminent plastic surgeon who wanted to write his memoirs. . . . He got it into his head that I should spend entire mornings in his waiting room, listening to what the patients were saying, and observing their behavior."

3. According to a report in *ScienceDaily*, November 13, 2012 ("Being neurotic, and conscientious, a good combo for health"), "Under certain circumstances neuroticism can be good for your health, according to a study showing that some self-described neurotics also tended to have the lowest levels of Interleukin 6 (IL-6), a biomarker for inflammation and chronic disease."

4. Dread and fear have become popular subjects lately: so Frank Furedi, *How Fear Works: Culture of Fear in the 21st Century*, Bloomsbury, 2019, and Martha C. Nussbaum, *The Monarchy of Fear: A Philosopher Looks at Our Political Crisis*, Simon and Schuster, 2019. Both books were reviewed in the *Times Literary Supplement* (February 8, 2019) by Gavin Jacobson as "Our age of anxiety: Why doom-mongering is back in fashion." A little way back there was Marilynne Robinson's "Fear," *New York Review of Books*, September 24, 2015.

5. Mrs. Christian's photos can be found in the *Daily Mail*, May 6, 2016 (Antonia Hoyle).

6. This sort of situation is more common than you'd expect. Ray Managh in the *The Irish Times*, June 13, 2018, tells a very good story about Roisin Mimnagh (50) of Marina Village, Malahide, who became too terrified to smile. That happened after she "went to dentist, Dr Anna O'Donovan, of Griffith Avenue, Dublin, to have an incisor realigned. To her horror she afterwards found that her tooth had been filed away and replaced with an amalgam or composite that was smaller and shorter and different from her original tooth." Hence her unwillingness to smile. Ms. Mimnagh sued for €60,000 and has now settled for an undisclosed sum.

7. On death there is Andrew Stark, *The Consolations of Mortality*, Yale University Press, 2017 and, among many others, Irvin

Yalom's *Staring at the Sun: Overcoming the Terror of Death*, Jossey-Bass, 2009

8. *Guardian*, October 10, 2015 (Esther Addley).
9. *The Observer*, March 15, 2015 (Robert McCrum).
10. There is a school of literary theory entitled "late studies." It seems to have begun especially with Edward Said's *On Late Style*, Pantheon 2006. Late studies focus more on the creator's feeling that they come at the end of a long literary or intellectual tradition, though sometimes it seems to confuse itself with just last works. Other contributions on this subject: Ben Hutchinson, "A Posthumous Honor," *Times Literary Supplement*, February 19, 2016 (on late awakenings), and *Lateness and Modern European Literature*, Oxford University Press 2016, and Gordon McMullan, and Sam Smiles (editors), *Late Style and Its Discontents*, Oxford University Press, 2016. Arthur Schnitzler's novel *Late Fame*, New York Review of Books Classics, 2017, doesn't really fit into this category, but it does offer a sort of a response to "late style."
11. Katie Roiphe has written a book about the last days of a number of famous writers: *The Violet Hour: Great Writers at the End*, Random House Canada, 2016.
12. Don't confuse Clive James' achievements with "late blooming." Clive James had already bloomed. Illness did not make him wilt, that's all. On the subject of late bloomers there is Malcolm Gladwell's discussion, "Late Bloomers: Why Do We Equate Genius with Precocity," in *What the Dog Saw—And Other Adventures*, Little, Brown, 2009. You might what to compare to Clive James his Australian contemporary, the novelist Gerald Murnane. Murnane has been successful all of his life, but, internationally, came into his own in his 70s (Gay Acorn, *Guardian*, September 21, 2018).
13. This little story is from Elizabeth Bernstein, "How to manage a long wait for news," *Wall Street Journal*, May 22, 2017: "In a [2016] study . . . Dr. Sweeny and colleagues at the University of California, Riverside, showed that people resort to a number of coping strategies to manage their discomfort while waiting for an outcome. Dr. Sweeny calls this 'misery management.'"

14. Kate Sweeny et al., "Two Definitions of Waiting Well," *Emotion*, 16(1), February 2016. There is also Sarit A. Golub, Daniel T. Gilbert, Timothy D. Wilson, "Anticipating One's Troubles: The Costs and Benefits of Negative Expectations." *Emotion*, 9(2), April, 2009.
15. Henning Mankell, the author of the greatly admired thriller series concerning the Swedish detective Kurt Wallander, was given the news of his impending death reasonably well in advance of his actual passing. The then 65-year-old Mankell learned about his lung cancer and his throat cancer in early January of 2014. He died 22 months later in Gothenburg in Sweden on October 5, 2015. I don't believe that Henning Mankell ever succumbed to humor in print, or to self-doubt. He certainly never succumbed to self-deprecation. His pre-mortem musing, *Quicksand: What It Means to Be A Human Being*, Harvill Secker, 2014, tells you all of that in its title. *Quicksand* is all the same a very interesting book. Much of it was published during Mankell's last 22 months as an unstoppable stream of newspaper articles.
16. Lydia Roberts, "CSIRO's world first discovery aids live-stock," *The Armidale Express*, Monday, February 23, 2015.
17. It's interesting to read that exactly the opposite is now happening in Australia. Asley Braun (*Science*, May 24, 2019) explains that researchers are endeavoring to teach native rare animals to fear feral cats.
18. The opposite is also happening with computers. Matthew Hutson reports, "Scientists Teach Computers Fear—To Make Them Better Drivers," *Science*, May 10, 2019. This may be as silly as the CSIRO report.
19. Nor books. There is now Rikke Schmidt Kjaergaard's *The Blink of an Eye: How I Died and Started Living*, Hodder and Stoughton, 2018. I wish that I had more room here and could go through her very moving book with you. Read her memoir if you can, is all that I can say. (Two recent movies with waiting in the title are Igor Drijaca's *The Waiting Room* [2015] and Lian Lunson's *Waiting for the Miracle to Come* [2017].)
20. *Daily Mail*, July 11, 2016 (Amy Oliver).
21. Oliver Sacks, *Awakenings*, Duckworth, 1973.

22. "Woken up with a Brain Zap," *New Scientist*, May 26, 2018.
23. Geraldine Martens et al., "Randomized Controlled Trial of Home-Based 4-Week tDCS in Chronic Minimally Conscious State," *Brain Stimulation*, 11(5), 2018.
24. M. Bruno, J. L. Bernheim, D. Ledoux, et al. "A Survey on Self-Assessed Well-Being in a Cohort of Chronic Locked-in Syndrome Patients: Happy Majority, Miserable Minority," *British Medical Journal Open*, 2011
25. The BBC produced a program on the reactions of a number of women who were facing death by cancer: *A Time to Live*, May 17, 2017. Many of the women claimed that their cancer had made them feel happier, even freed. There is also Kenneth Sherman, *Wait Time: A Memoir of Cancer*, Wilfrid Laurier Press, 2012.
26. I have already mentioned Adam Grant's and Sheryl Sandberg's book *Originals: How Non-Conformists Move the World*, and in particular its chapter 4, "Fools Rush In: Timing, Strategic Procrastination, and the First-Mover Disadvantage." The characters in this chapter may owe some of their originality to coming late. But this was not by design, nor would you describe it as a "strategy." Death, or the dread produced by the approach of death, is what is at issue. Here's another example. The American painter Sam Francis led a very successful artistic career. His final burst of paintings, done with his left hand and while he was suffering with prostate cancer, have been very successful.
27. *Times Literary Supplement,* February 15, 2019 (Gabriel Josipovici reviewing the Tate Modern show of Bonnard in 2019).
28. The success of the 2019 "CC Land Exhibition" of Pierre Bonnard's works at the Tate Gallery in London also makes the point. The catalogue of the show, edited by Matthew Gale as *Pierre Bonnard: The Colour of Memory* (The CC Land Exhibition), Tate, 2019, contains an essay by Helen O'Malley, "For and Against Bonnard," which reproduces the wording of some of the controversy surrounding Zervos' judgement (by Picasso, for example, and Matisse).
29. Edward Said wrote about, amongst others, the last creative activities of Beethoven, Mozart, Richard Strauss, Britten, Jean

Genet, Glenn Gould, Lampedusa, and Cavafy in his *On Late Style*, Pantheon, 2006. This was very close to the end of Said's own life. The book was published after his death. It was in a sense his "Bonnard moment."
30. In the spirit of all this is James Marriot's "Greatest Unfinished Books" *The Times*, March 15, 2019.
31. Originally from Bonnard's diary, I believe, but it is often quoted.

EPILOGUE

1. Peter Toohey, *Boredom: A Lively History*, Yale University Press, 2011 and *Jealousy*, Yale University Press, 2014.
2. I go through some of these visual elements of boredom with more detail in painting and photography in "Is It a Good Thing to Be Bored?," in *Boredom Is in Your Mind*, ed. Josefa Ros Velasco, Springer, 2020.
3. Remember Edouard Manet listening to his wife on the piano? I have a number of other illustrations of this posture in my *Boredom: A Lively History*.
4. Wijnand A. P. van Tilburg et al. have written a helpful article on food, satiety (disgust), and boredom, "Eaten Up by Boredom: Consuming Food to Escape Awareness awareness| of the Bored Self," *Frontiers in Psychology*, April 1, 2015.
5. Jason Daley, "Disgusting Things Fall into Six Gross Categories," *Smithsonian News*, June 7, 2018.
6. *Boredom: A Lively History*, 2011.
7. A point made well by Danckert and Eastwood in their *Out of My Skull: The Psychology of Boredom* (Harvard University Press, 2020) and by the contributors to Josefa Ros Velasco's Springer (2020) collection.
8. Pain links with boredom and depression insofar as it's another solitary affair and it works in present time. I have learned a lot on the subject of pain from Nicole Wilson's *Depictions of Pain in the Roman Empire*, Ph.D. dissertation, University of Calgary, 2012.
9. The clearest description of boredom—describing its relationship with curiosity, interest, and engagement—is to be found

in Eastwood and Danckert's *Out of My Skull: The Psychology of Boredom*.
10. Maybe that's how most marriages go along. But François and Marie, who often modeled for her husband, don't seem to have split in 1930. They married in 1924 and were still married when he died of tuberculosis in 1934. (I have no knowledge of when Marie died, but I have seen the date 1942.) I suspect that they acted out rather than lived this tableau, and maybe even posed for it in front of a mirror.
11. Some of these are reproduced and discussed in my *Jealousy*, Yale University Press, 2014.
12. Naomi Rea, "Peter Doig Wants to Make Denzil Forrester, a Painter of the Afro-Caribbean Experience in England, Much More Famous," *artnetnews*, May 23, 2018.
13. You could compare the Finnish painter (born 1979) Henni Alftan's painting *Holiday* (2016) with Vanessa Bell's modernist oil on canvas *Nude with Poppies*.
14. Discussions of the notion of the core relational theme can be found in Berit Brogaard, *On Romantic Love: Simple Truths about a Complex Emotion*, Oxford University Press, 2014, Jean Kazez, *The Philosophical Parent: Asking the Hard Questions about Having and Raising Children*, Oxford University Press, 2017, and Jesse Prinz, *Gut Reactions: A Perceptual Theory of Emotion*, Oxford University Press, 2006.
15. You can get a sense of this sort of argument from the title of the following: Jesse Prinz, *The Emotional Construction of Morals*, Oxford University Press, 2009.

INDEX

For the benefit of digital users, indexed terms that span two pages (e.g., 52–53) may, on occasion, appear on only one of those pages.

ADHD, 140–41
affection, 5, 66, 68–69, 243, 253
affiliation, 66–68, 69–70, 74, 83–84
affiliative behaviors, 30, 50, 66–69
affiliative interaction, 61–62, 63–64, 69–70, 71–72, 75–77, 82–83, 86
afterlife, 21–22, 181–82, 186–87, 194–95, 201, 205–6
alcohol. *See* drunk
Allen, Amy-Louise, 168–72
ALS (amyotrophic lateral sclerosis), 221–22
American Sniper, 46
amphetamines, 137–45
Amphitryo, 107–9
anartria, 221–22
android relationships, 83–84
anger, 15–16, 30, 228–29, 237–39, 250–51
Another Earth, 104–6, 182–83

anticipation, 27–28, 35–36, 122, 123–24, 125–27, 193, 253–54
antipsychotics, 190–91, 281n9
anxiety, ix, 52, 60, 62, 64–65, 80, 216–20, 225–26, 230–31, 239
arousal, 15–16, 18–19, 21–22, 39, 140–41
Awaiting Oblivion. See Maurice Blanchot
Awakenings, 224–28
Aziz, Basma Abdel, 15–16, 262n10

Babette's Feast, 283n22
babies, 60, 61–64, 66, 71–72, 82, 86, 90–91, 98–100
Bach, J.S., 25–26, 64–65, 129–31, 132–33, 136–37, 169
Badoo, 93–96
Bair, Deidre, 193–94
ballerina, 16–19, 60–61

292 | INDEX

Banim, Declan, 162–63
Barraud, François, x,
    80–81, 241–44
Barthes, Roland, 253
Bauby, Jean-Dominique (Jean-
    Do), 220–21, 223–34, 239–40
Baum, Vicki, 60–61
Beckett, Samuel
    Waiting for Godot, 4,
    131–32, 192–96
being, 197–200
Belize, Chapter 2 *passim*
Bell, Vanessa, 247–49
Bellow, Saul, 195–96
Bendigo, 148–52, 154–55, 158–59
Benzedrine ("Bennies'), 141–43
Bergman, Ingmar, xvii, 154–28,
    185–88, 194–95
    See also *Face to Face; Fanny
    and Alexander*; Jenny Didier;
    Margareta Bergman; Karin;
    Through a Glass Darkly
Bergman, Margareta, xvii, 187–88
    See also Ingmar Bergman
Bergson, Henri, 282n16
Berlin, Chapter 3 *passim*
bi-directional affiliative
    interactions, 69–70
bioidentical hormone therapy
    (BHT), 98
bipolar disorder, xii, 110
Blanchot, Maurice, 200–2
Blue Poles, 119–20, 143–44
Board of Atomic Scientists
    (BAS), 195–96
Bonnard, Pierre, 207–9,
    212, 231–34
boredom, 13–14, 54, 197–200,
    235–41, 249–50
Bowie, David, xii–xiv, 128
brain tumour, 91–92,
    106–8, 191–92

Braun, Allen, 144–45
Bravo, Manuel Álvarez, 243–45
Brent, Lauren J.N., 68–70, 74
Brogaard, Berit, 290n14
Brothers Menaechmi
    (Plautus), 101–2
Brugger, Peter, 106–7, 109–10
Bruno, Marie-Aurélie, 229–31
Bryan, Chantal, 221–22
Buell, Ryan, 12–13
Bulloch, A. G., 111–12
Byrne, Richard, 165–68

Cage, John, 133–36
Cahill, Mike, 104–5
Camus, Albert, 195–96, 239–40
Cancer Ward (Alexandr
    Solzhenitsyn), 164–65
Capgras, Joseph, 108–9
Capgras Syndrome, 107–8, 109–12
Carlson, Leland, 167, 169–70
Castellani, Enrico, 203–4
cats, 29–30, 31–37, 39, 47–49, 125,
    152–53, 217–18, 225–26
Cavett, Dick, xii
chaperone, 16–19, 210, 241–43
Cholmondeley Ladies,
    98–101, 271n17
Christian, Tess, 210–11,
    217, 218–20
cigarette, 119–27, 142–46, 202–5
Cioran, Emil, 283n20
Clarkson, Wensley, 236
coffins, 162–64
Coffin Club, 162–64
Coltrane, John, 120–21,
    124–25, 143–44
Comedy of Errors, 101–2
community, 38–39, 62–63, 75,
    162–63, 188–90, 230–31
companionship, 15–16, 19, 72,
    73, 163–64

competitive jealousy, 246–48
compulsive hoarding,
    170–71, 172–74
concentration, 122,
    139–41, 144–45
consciousness, 221–22, 226–28
Conversation (Vanessa
    Bell), 247–49
cooperative behavior, 66
core relational theme, 250–51
Corydrane, 142–43
courage, 30, 212
Curtis, James, 267n10

D.U.I., 148–49
dancing, 18–19, 133–35
Danckert, James and John
    Eastwood, 289n7
Dangling Man (Saul
    Bellow), 195–96
Darling, David, 103–4
David and Goliath, 155–56
Dawdling, 161–62
Davis, Miles, 119–47
de Hooch, Pieter, 66–69
de Meligny, Marthe, 231
death, 3, 5, 6, 23–26, 46,
    77, 162–65, 172–74,
    179–206, 207–34
decision-making, 34–35, 48–49,
    151, 155–58, 226–28
Declerck, Carolyn and Christophe
    Boone, 35–37, 39–43, 49
Deegan, Godon, 236
Degas, Edgar, 16–19, 130–32,
    145–46, 158–62
delay discounting, 151–65
delayed gratification, 151
dementia, 111–14, 116
depression, xi, 37–38, 50–51, 52,
    228–29, 239–41
Diary of Anne Frank, 195–96

Didier, Jenny, xi, 63–64,
    79, 187–88
Didion, Joan, 16, 23–25
Dinesen, Isak, 283n22
Diogenes Syndrome,
    170–71, 280n23
disability, 43–44
disgust, 199–200, 237–41
diver, 15–16, 19–22, 39,
    130–31, 145–46
Diving. See Kōshirō Onchi
Diving Bell and the Butterfly
    (Bauby, Jean-Dominique),
    220–21, 224–25
dogs, 166, 218–19
dolls, 82–84, 96
Doomsday Clock, 195–96
dopamine, 30–55 and *passim*
doppelgänger, 90–92
double, 78–79, 87–116, 243–44.
    See Jason McClure
Dr. Vlemingck, xi–xiv
dread, xii–xiii, 6–7, 15–16, 19–23,
    31 Chapter 7 and 8 *passim.*
    See fear
drunk, 27–28, 104, 143–44, 148–
    50, 152, 195–96, 254–55
Duez, Danielle, 135–36
Dull Men of Great Britain,
    167–68, 169–70
Dull Men's Club, 167–68
Dunbar, Evelyn, 9–10
Duncan, Greg, 153–54
Dunne, John Gregory,
    15–16, 23–25

Eagleman, David, 21–22
Eastwood, Clint, 46, 49
ecstatic religious experiences, 188–91
empty chair, 23–26, 181–82,
    187–88, 205–6, 233–34,
    235, 244–45

encephalitis lethargica, 223–24, 225
endocannabinoids, 35–37, 88–89
epilepsy, 106–7, 191–92, 282n11
Erdös, Paul, 142–45
Erica the robot, 268n19
erotic jealousy, 245–47, 248–49, 253
esteem, 50, 68–69
Eternity, 97–98, 268n17
Eucharist, 283n22
Evans, Bill, 143–44
Ex Machina, 84
excitement, 15–16, 33–34, 128–29, 130
exo-planets, 102–3
expectation, 23, 31, 33–38, 60–61, 240–41
expectation, reward, and learning (dopamine), 31, 35–37
experience of waiting, 10–11 and *passim*
exuberance, 53–54
eyes, 78–79, 120–21f, 146–47, 221–22, 236–37

Face to Face (Ingmar Bergman), 125–27
family (and affiliation), 50, 55, 63–65, 78–79
Fanny and Alexander, xvii, 59
See also Ingmar Bergman
Farman, Jason, 10–11, 183–84, 260–61n5
fear, xii–xiii, 15–16, 21–23, 30 and Chapter 2 *passim*, 130, 201–2 and Chapter 8 *passim*. See dread
felt time, 22–23, 128–30, 138–40, 143–44
Fiacconi, Chris, 109–10
Fonseca, Madalena, 41–42

Fontana, Lucio, 179–90 and Chapter 7 *passim*
Forrester, Denzil, 247–48
Freud, Anna, 109–10
Freud, Sigmund, 109–10
Friberg, Helene, 125–27
See also *Face to* Face; *The Magic Flute*; Ingmar Bergman
Friedrich, Otto, 160–61
friends of dolls, 82–83
friendship, definition of, 68–69
Furmark, Tomas, 80

Game, Russell, 162–63
Garbo, Greta, 60–61
Geaney, Niamh, 91–93
Geldof, Sir Bob, 132–33
Geyer, Stefan and Georg Christian Dörr, 260–61n5
giraffe, xvi–xvii
Gladwell, Malcolm, 154–58
Gomez, Carlos Enriquez, 77
Goncharov, Ivan (*Oblomov*), 160–61, 195–96
gorillas, 165–67
Gould, Glenn, 169
Gräff, Friederike, 260–61n5, 261n6
Grand Hotel, 59–61, 65, 66–68, 72–73, 85, 217
Gray, John, 269n26
Greene, Graham, 141–42
Greer, Germaine, 213–14
Grenier, Roger, 81, 97–98
grooming, 63–71, 80, 83–84
Grusinskaya, Madame, 60–61, 217. See Greta Garbo; The Grand Hotel
guilt, 50, 88–89, 109–10

Hackensacker III, John D., 101–2
Hadhazy, Adam, xiv–xv

Hall Porter Senf, 59–61, 62, 71–72, 76–77, 85, 86, 90–91, 98, 251–52
Hamid, Arif A., 34–35
Hammershøi, Vilhelm., 23, 25–26, 239–40
Hammond, Claudia, xv–xvi, 13–14, 21–22
happiness, 15–16, 87–116, 169, 183–84, 229–31
Hawking, Stephen, 103–4, 221–22
Haynes, Deborah, 46–47
heautoscopy, 106–7, 108–9, 111
Heidegger, Martin, 197–200
hell, 97–98
Hello Kitty, 168–71
Hensel, Abigail and Brittany, 272n20
Hepburn, Katharine, 72–77
Hepworth, Barbara, ix, 146–47
Here's That Rainy Day, 127
  See also smoking
Herrera, Alexander Jheferson Delgado, 115–16
Hildegard of Bingen, 188–90
Hoagland, Hudson, 139–40
Hoarding Disorder, 170–72
Hockney, David, 243–44
Hoexum, Peter, 169–70
Hoffman, Eva, 13–14
Hollywood, 72–77, 94–96, 101–2
Homer, Winslow, 33–35, 37
Honore, Carl, 279n13
Hopper, Edward, 80–81
Hornbach, Marya, 284n27
Howarth, Carla, 162
Huang, Yunte, 272n20
Hughes, Robert, 213–14
Hulliger, Manuel, 223–24
Hunt, Amelia, 139–40
hyper-Reality, 179–80
'Hyper-Religious' Behavior, 191–92

The Iceman Cometh, 195–96
identical pair, 88–91, 93–94, 106–7
identical twins, 97–103
improvisation, 140–45
inhibitions, 144–45
insomnia, xiv–xv, 142–43, 226–28
internet, 94–96, 108
interoceptive awareness, 111
isolation, 49, 87–88

jaguar. *See* Chapter 2
James, Clive, 212–16, 217, 230–31, 233–34
Japan, 5–6, 19–23, 39–41, 59, 82–83
jazz musicians, 138–41
jealousy, 54, 109–10, 235, 245–53
John Tracy Clinic, 75
Jones, Dylan, xii–xiii
Jones, Richard Anthony, 88–91, 93, 97–98, 105–6, 107–9, 111–12, 116
joy, 184–86, 187–90
Jupiter, 108

Kafka, Franz, 239–40, 282n12
Kahneman, Daniel, 152–53, 279n12
Kansas City, 37–39, 88–91, 93, 264n12, 269–70n4
Kansas City Star, 37–39, 90, 104–5
Kapoor, Anish Mikhail, 280–81n2
Karin, 184–92, 198–99, 200, 225
Kempowski, Walter, 260n4
Kent, 3–15, 188–90, 198–99
Kieślowski, Krzysztof, 272n24
Kind of Blue, 119–20, 143–44
King, Stephen, 281n4
Köhler, Andrea, 260–61n5, 279n15, 284n1
Kominers, Scott, 261–62n7
Kyle, Chris, 46–50

Lagrow, Cathy, 271n19
Larkin, Philip, 212–13, 215–16, 217
late bloomers, 286n12
Laureys, Steven, 226–29
Le Bas, Edward, 236–39
L-DOPA, 49–50, 225–28
Le malcontent (François Barraud), 241–43
learning (and dopamine), 31, 34–36, 44–45
Leenhoff, Suzanne, 159–60
Lehman Brothers, 156–57
lethargy, 239–40
leukemia, 212–13
Levetin, Daniel, 124–25
Levinas, Emmanuel, 283n21
Levodopa. *See* L-DOPA
Levy, David, 223–24
Lewison, Jeremy, 78–79
Limb, Charles, J. and Allen R. Braun, 144–45
Locked in Syndrome (LIS), 220–29
Lodge, David, 49–50
loss, 24f, 78–79, 87–88, 114, 151, 172–74, 175, 233–34
Lou Gehrig's Disease, 221–22
love, 6, 15–16, 66–14, 72, 82–84, 237–39, 241–43, 253
Lowe, Leonard, 225–28
Lowell, Robert, xii
Lowry, Malcolm, 195–96
Lundholm Fors, Kristina, 137–38
Lutherans, 283n22

ma, 23, 262–63n13
Maar, Dora, 274n35
Madame M, 108–9
The Magic Flute, 125–27, 185–86
    See also Mozart; Ingmar Bergman

Magritte, René, 112–14
Mainen, Zacharty, 42–43
Manet, Édouard, 158–61
Maniatty, Holly, 273n26
Mankell, Henning, 203–4. *See also* Kurt Wallander
Mapother, William, 104–5
Margaret Evans Pregnant. See Alice Neel
Marling, Brit, 104–5
marriage. *See* Chapter 3
Marriot, James, 289n30
marshmallows, 152–54
mathematics and mathematicians, 10–11, 13–15, 53–54, 137–39, 142–45
Matisse, Henri, 231–33, 243–44
Mayo Clinic, 171–72
McClure, Jason, 107–8, 115–16, 269n1
McCrea, Joel, 101–2
McCrum, Robert, 213–14
Mednyasnszky, Laszlo, 254–55
Mendelsohn, Daniel, 260–61n5
Mercury, 107–8
Messie Syndrome, 170–71
methylphenidate. *See* Ritalin
migraine, 188–90, 281n7
mirror, xvii, 42–43, 47, 78–79, 87–88, 90–93. *See also* reflection
Mischel, Walter, 152–54
Mitterrand, Francois, 135–37
Miyazaki, K. 39–41
Molière, Jean-Baptiste, 109
Monk, Thelonius, 275n10
Moriarty, Kevin, 88
mother, 5, 60, 62–63, 66, 78–79, 81, 98–100, 112–14, 221–22, 226–28
Mozart, 125–27
Murakami, Haruki, 262–63n13
music, 23 and Chapter 5

Musk, Elon, 105–6
mysticism, 192–95

Naltrex, 124–25, 143–45
Nausea. See Jean-Paul Sartre
Neel, Alice, 77–81, 87–88
neuromodulator, 30, 33–34, 35, 39–41, 42–43, 47, 50–52, 53, 55, 63–64, 65, 71, 81, 133–35, 140–41
new emotions, 53–54
New South Wales, 217–20
Nice Work (David Lodge), 202
Nigel the gannet, 268n18
non-reproductive sex, 69–70
Not to be Reproduced. See René Magritte
nucleus accumbens, 123–27
Nykvist, Sven, 125–27

Oates, Joyce Carol (Rosamond Smith) 272n21
Obama, Barack, 137
Oblomov (Ivan Goncharov), 160–61, 195–96
Obsessive Compulsive Disorder, 171–72
Oh, The Places You'll Go. See Dr Suess
Oliver, Amy, 221–22
Onchi, Kōshirō, 19–23
O'Neil, Eugene, 195–96
opera, 125–27
opioids, 35–37, 124–25
opioid blocker, 125
optogenetics, 41–42
Ozawa, Seiji, 262–63n13
Ozon, François, 272n21

pain (see Nicole Wilson), 43, 78, 111, 199–200, 211, 214–17, 218–20, 246, 249

pair, 15–19 and Chapter 3 and Chapter 4
Palm Beach Story. See Preston Sturges
Paris, 16, 77, 158–59, 192–93
Parkinson's disease, 31, 221–22, 223–24, 225–26
Partnoy, Frank, 156–58, 161–62, 174–75
Patel, Tara, 136
patience, 26–27, 39–41, 50, 64–65, 253–55
pause, paused, pausing, 15–25, 39, 46–47 and Chapters 5 and 6
phenotype/phenotypic/phenotypical, 54, 68–71, 236–37, 248–49
Phillips, Helen, 281n10
Picasso, Pablo, 231–33, 274n33, 288n28
Piedras Gordas Prison, 115
Pikulik, Lothar, 260–61n5
Pixee Fox, 94–96
plague, 200–1, 272–73n25
Plautus, 101–2, 106
play, 165–66
pleasure. See Chapter 3, Chapter 4, and Chapter 5
Poland, 13–14, 179
Pollock, Jackson, 119–20, 143–44
polyopic heautoscopy, 91–92, 106–7, 111
Pompidou, Georges, 136–37
Previc, Fred H., 265–66n24
Princess Centimillia (*Palm Beach Story*), 101–2
prison, 38–39, 98, 104, 115–16, 236
proception, 151–58
procrastination, 23, 157–65, 172
Psalms, 187–88
punishment, 151, 162, 164–65

quadriplegia, 221–22
Quan, Hoanan, 153–54
queue, 4, 6–15, 132–33, 183–85, 198–99, 218–19
Queue at the Fish Shop. See Evelyn Dunbar
Queuing theory, 12, 261–62n7

Rabinowitz, Alan. *See* Chapter 2
Raleigh, M.J., 63–64
Rand, Ayn, 142–43
rats, 34–35
reality. *See* Chapter 8
reborners, 269n24
Reboul-Lachaux, Jean, 108–9
reciprocity, 68–69
Redfield Jamison, Kay, xii
reduplicative hallucination, 106–7
reflection (in a mirror), 78–81, 87–88, 112
reward, 30–54, 123–24, 151
Ripple, Mr. Lawrence John, 37–39
Rita Hayworth and the Shawshank Redemption (Stephen King), 281n4
Ritalin, 140–41, 142–43, 144–45
Rizzo, Tony, and Katy Bergen. *See* Mr. Lawrence John Ripple
Robinson, Marilynne, 285n4
Rotorua, 163–64
Rowlandson, Thomas, 172
Roy, Eleanor Ainge, 163–64

Saatchi & Saatchi, 205
Sacks, Oliver, 116, 223–29, 273n31
Said, Edward, 286n10
Salimpoor, Valorie N., 123–25
Sample, Ian, 12–13
Saramago, José, 272n24
Sartre, Jean-Paul, 142–44, 199–202, 239–40

Sasnal, Wilhelm, 179–84
scarecrow, 84–85
schizophrenia, xii–xiii, 106–7, 187–88
Schmidt Kjaergaard, Rikke, 287n19
Schnitzler, Arthur, 286n10
Schoebi, Dominik, 70–71
Schulze-Makuch, Dirk, 103–4
Schweitzer, Harold, 260–61n5
Seinfeld, Jerry (*Seinfeld*), 207–9
self-affirmation, 93–94
self-handicapping, 151–52, 165–72
Self-Portrait in The Bathroom Mirror. *See* Pierre Bonnard
Seligman, Martin, 278n4
serotonin, 30, 39–45, 47–54, 63–72, 80, 82, 83–84
Dr. Seuss, 3–5, 193–94
sexbots, 82–83
Shakespeare, 101–2
sheep, 217–20
Siever, Larry, 50
Silk Cut, 202–6
Simpkins, Bazza, 130, 201–2, 223
Simon, Coen, 260–61n5
Sinatra, Frank, 127–28
situational version of waiting, 12–13 and *passim*
skeleton, 172
slash. *See* Lucio Fontana
Small Philosophy of the Row House. *See* Pieter Hoexum
smiling. *See* Tess Christian
smoking, xi, 119–27, 203–5, 213, 237–39
snap decisions, 155
sniper, 46–49
So What, 119–21, 122–23, 127, 138–39, 143–44, 145–46
sociality, 70–71
solitude, 237–39

Solzhenitsyn, Alexandr, 164–65
Somers, Suzanne, 96–97
Sorokin, Vladimir, 15–16, 262n10
Sosia (Plautus, *Amphitryo*), 107–9
Spatial Concept "Waiting." See Lucio Fontata
Spencer, Robert, 140–41
stalking, 23, 31–33, 47, 48–49, 254–55
Stark, Andrew, 285–86n7
staying and arrival, xvii, 250–51
Steiner, George, 198–99
Stockholm, 125–27
"stop-start" song, 128
strategic pausing, 123–24
Streisand, Barbra, 270n4
Sturges, Preston, 101–2
stutter, 43–44
submissiveness, 50
suicide, xi, 6, 77, 85, 143–44
Svendsen, Lars, 198–99
Sweeny, Kate, 215–17
Sydney, 213–14
Syllogomania, 170–71
Syracuse, 101–2

Tajiri, xvi–xvii
Tanner, Joanne, 165–68
task salience, 139–40
The Castle. See Franz Kafka
"The Waiting Place." *See* Dr. Seuss
Thebes, 107–8
thin slicing, 155
Thomson, Helen, 226–28
Thomson, Richard, 18
Through a Glass Darkly (Ingmar Bergman), 185–91
time, *passim*
Time Warped. See Claudia Hammond
Tolstoy, Leo, 281n4
Tracy, Louise Treadwell, 72–77

Tracy, Spencer, 72–77
traffic, xiv–xv, 7–8
transcendent/transcendental, 180–84, 186–87
tryptophan, 50–51, 52
Twins Day Festival, 100–2, 116
Twin Strangers, 92–93
twins, 78–79, 90–91, 98–103, 106
Twinsburg, Ohio, 100–1

Ullmann, Liv, 127
Ulverstone, 162
Under the Volcano, 195–96
unhappiness. *See* happiness
Uppsala, 63–64, 80

vascular dementia, 111–14
Velasco, Josefa Ros, 289n2
Ventura, Jesse, 48–49
vervet monkeys, 61–66
Viljoen, Louis, 226–28
Vladimir and Estragon. *See* Samuel Beckett (*Waiting for Godot*)
void, 179–82, 280–81n2
Von Sydow, Max, 187–88, 225

"Waiting and Eternity," 97–98
Waiting for God. See Simone Weil
Waiting for Godot. See Samuel Beckett
Waiting for Harry, 284n23
Waiting for pain, 211
waiting room, 217, 220–21, 233–34 and Chapter 8 *passim*
Walker, Susannah, 280n24
Wallander, Kurt, 203–4, 290n15
Ward, James, 169–70
watching, 119–20
Watts, Tyler, 153–54
Weil, Simone, 188–92
Whittington, Sheree, 162–63
Williams, Katie, 163–64

Wilson, Harold, 26–27
Wilson, Nicole, 289n8
winning, 166
Wittmann, Marc, 18–19, 22–23, 128–29, 143–44
Woolf, Virginia, vii
wrinkles, 210–11

Year of Magical Thinking (Joan Didion), 15–16, 23–25
Yoshimoto, Banana
  Moshi Moshi, 5
Young, Simon, 50–52

Zervos, Christian, 231–33

www.ingramcontent.com/pod-product-compliance
Ingram Content Group UK Ltd.
Pitfield, Milton Keynes, MK11 3LW, UK
UKHW021251180426
11946UKWH00004B/88